Women Workers and Gender Identities, 1835–1913

Women Workers and Gender Identities, 1835–1913 examines the experiences of women workers in the cotton and small metal industries and the discourses surrounding their labor. It demonstrates how ideas of womanhood often clashed with the harsh realities of working-class life that forced women into such "unfeminine" trades as chainmaking and brass polishing. Thus, discourses constructing women as wives and mothers, or associating women's work with purportedly feminine attributes, were often undercut and subverted.

Weaving together extensive archival material with a fresh interpretation, this book includes discussion of:

- Theoretical approaches to the study of women in history, from patriarchy to discourse analysis.
- Cooperation, conflict, and community in the cotton district, the Black Country and Birmingham.
- Women's activism alongside men in the Chartist, Ten Hours and trade union movements.
- The work of women in such settings as the forge and pen-making factories, emphasizing its necessity and the important role it played in working-class culture.
- The women's trade union movement.

Carol E. Morgan was formerly Visiting Scholar at the Center for Advanced Feminist Studies, University of Minnesota, and is now an independent scholar. She has written articles on women in the cotton industry and women in chainmaking.

Women's and Gender History
Edited by June Purvis

Child sexual abuse in Victorian England
Louise A. Jackson

Crimes of Outrage
Sex, violence and Victorian working women
Shani D'Cruze

Feminism, femininity and the politics of working women
The Women's Co-operative Guild, 1880s to the Second World War
Gillian Scott

Gender and crime in modern Europe
Edited by Margaret L. Arnot and Cornelie Usborne

Gender relations in German history
Power, agency and experience from the sixteenth to the twentieth century
Edited by Lynn Abrams and Elizabeth Harvey

Imaging home
Gender, 'race' and national identity, 1945–64
Wendy Webster

Midwives of the revolution
Female Bolsheviks and women workers in 1917
Jane McDermid and Anna Hillyar

No distinction of sex?
Women in British universities 1870–1939
Carol Dyhouse

Policing gender, class and family: Britain, 1850–1945
Linda Mahood

Prostitution
Prevention and reform in England, 1860–1914
Paula Bartley

Sylvia Pankhurst
Sexual politics and political activism
Barbara Winslow

Votes for women
Edited by June Purvis and Sandra Holton

Women's history
Britain 1850–1945
Edited by June Purvis

The Women's Suffrage Movement
A reference guide, 1866–1928
Elizabeth Crawford

Women and teacher training colleges, 1900–1960
A culture of femininity
Elizabeth Edwards

Women, work and sexual politics in eighteenth-century England
Bridget Hill

Women workers and gender identities, 1835–1913
The cotton and metal industries in England
Carol E. Morgan

Women Workers and Gender Identities, 1835–1913

The cotton and metal industries in England

Carol E. Morgan

London and New York

First published 2001 by Routledge
11 New Fetter Lane, London EC4P 4EE

Simultaneously published in the USA and Canada
by Routledge
29 West 35th Street, New York, NY 10001

Routledge is an imprint of the Taylor & Francis Group

Typeset in Garamond by Wearset, Boldon, Tyne and Wear
Printed and bound in Great Britain by TJ International Ltd, Padstow,
Cornwall

British Library Cataloguing in Publication Data
A catalogue record for this book is available from the British Library

Library of Congress Cataloging in Publication Data
Morgan, Carol E.
    Women workers and gender identities, 1835–1913 : the cotton and metal
    industries in England / Carol E. Morgan.
        p. cm. — (Women's and gender history)
    Simultaneously published in the USA and Canada.
    Includes bibliographical references and index.
        1. Women—Employment—England—History 2. Textile workers—
    England—History. 3. Metal-workers—England—History. 4. Sex
    discrimination against women—England—History. 5. Women labor
    union members—England—History. I. Title. II. Series.
    HD6136.W67 2001
    331.4′0942—dc21

                                                                        2001019760

ISBN 0–415–23929–X (hbk)
ISBN 0–415–23930–3 (pbk)

To David

And to Dad and in loving memory of Mom and Larry

Contents

Figures

Acknowledgments

I acknowledge the use of excerpts in Chapters 2 and 3 from my articles "Women, work and consciousness in the mid-nineteenth-century English cotton industry," *Social History*, January 1992, vol. 27, pp. 23–42 (Routledge) and "The domestic image and factory culture: the cotton district in mid-nineteenth-century England," *International Labor and Working-Class History*, Spring 1996, no. 49, pp. 26–46 (Cambridge University Press).

I wish to acknowledge the support of the Center for Advanced Feminist Studies at the University of Minnesota where I was a Visiting Scholar during 1998–9. I am most grateful to Martie Reineke, Roy Sandstrom, Jay Lees, Tim O'Connor, and Jeffrey Cox for their professional encouragement and personal support in the face of adversity and beyond. I am also grateful for the encouragement and support that the professional evaluation of my earlier work by Deborah Valenze, James Epstein, and James Schmiechen provided. And I wish to thank Neville Kirk, Marc Steinberg, Anna Clark, and Mary Jo Maynes for their continued professional encouragement and support. Special thanks go to Ruth and the memory of Eddie Frow, founders of the Working Class Movement Library in Salford, whose love of books and people helped send me on my way.

Mostly, it is with deep love and gratitude that I dedicate this book to my husband and comrade, David, who has always offered unwavering support through it all!

1 Introductory essay – gender in labor history

In "seeking to rescue the poor stockinger, the Luddite cropper . . . and even the deluded follower of Joanna Southcott, from the enormous condescension of posterity," E. P. Thompson sought to unveil "the making of the English working class."[1] In so doing, he made explicit that, while class was central to his analysis, it was not to be understood as a structure or even a category of analysis, but as "an historical phenomenon, unifying a number of disparate and seemingly unconnected events, both in the raw material of experience and in consciousness."[2] Through such an approach, he gave life to class, as well as to the people themselves, and thereby moved the fields of labor and social history away from a focus on institutional history to an emphasis on history from the ground up. Despite the fact that women themselves did not emerge center-stage, the importance of this study for women's history was implicit and its impact profound.

In this chapter we will examine major approaches to the study of women's history from that time, emphasizing in particular their significance for women's labor history. Central to this examination is the shift from an emphasis on patriarchy, and its inherent problems for the study of working-class women, to the emphasis on "gender as a category of analysis." Of especial interest is the "linguistic turn," its significance and limits for the study of gender identities and gender difference among the working classes. We then set forth the approach to be employed in this study which examines a variety of industrial settings where women and men were engaged in the manufacture of small metal and cotton. In considering primarily women's experiences and the gendered discourses, or understandings of gender,[3] that emerged during periods when gender difference was under negotiation, we point to the fracturing of class by gender and the significance of gender difference in working-class culture. The study further serves to enhance our understanding of class and suggests that, even as its fragmentation by gender is apparent, as gender difference was re-negotiated, a simultaneous process of class formation and extension of class interests across gender lines was often in evidence.

Working-class women and industrialization

In their influential study, entitled *Women, Work and Family*, Louise Tilly and Joan Scott turned our attention to the experiences of working-class women during the process of industrialization in Europe. In thereby placing women at the center of analysis, they began to raise new questions, emphasizing the importance of breaking down the barrier between work and family in the study of labor history. Further, they effectively challenged the standard interpretation of industrialization which suggested that it was virtually synonymous with women working in textile mills. Such an interpretation, Tilly and Scott declared, was "misleading."[4] While industrialization did mean that women increasingly assisted their families financially by earning an individual wage, as textile factories created jobs for women, such employment did not provide the only nor the predominant form of wage-earning activity of women.[5] Rather, women remained concentrated in "traditional" sectors of the economy while occupations such as domestic service actually expanded as England in particular industrialized.[6]

Furthermore, even in the cotton textile mills of the Northwest, the vast majority of "women workers" were between the ages of 16 and 21 and single.[7] Married women generally worked at paid labor only if financially necessary, with full-time work confined to the years before marriage and having children. Only in such communities as Stockport and Preston, Tilly and Scott maintained, where demand for female labor was considerable, did large numbers of married women engage in outside employment, especially if married to men in low-paying jobs.[8] Pointing out that 40 percent of working women in England in 1851 were in domestic service, although in that same year the nation celebrated its industrial progress at the Crystal Palace, the authors declared that "there was no simple or uniform evolution in women's workforce participation as a result of industrial development."[9] Thus, Tilly and Scott concluded, "The impact of industrialization on women's employment was more varied and far less dramatic then [*sic*] the standard image of the mill girl implies."[10]

Michael Anderson in his study of Preston further pointed to the importance of the family as a resource during the industrializing period. Rather than breaking down as a result of the stresses and strains of industrialization, it served as an important support system. Women's employment patterns, it appeared, revolved around family rather than the reverse.[11]

The importance of these works is twofold. First, they suggested that working-class women's experience of industrialization was significantly different from men's. As the family remained of singular importance throughout the industrial period, women's role within it continued to be of greatest significance as they moved in and out of the workforce, in general, only as family needs dictated. These works thus emphasized the purported continuity in women's lives from the pre-industrial period. Secondly, they suggested that industrialization was not necessarily liberating for women as

Thompson had suggested. Rather, as industrialization proceeded, women remained subordinate within the family and the workforce alike.

Patriarchy and its troubles

At the time of publication of these works, feminist scholars in general were attempting to theorize this apparently pervasive presence of male domination. This discussion had relevance for scholars of labor and labor history since its focus was largely on the interrelationship of the worlds of work and home, an emphasis central to the work of Tilly and Scott as well as Anderson. At its earliest stage, this debate centered on the concept of patriarchy. In an attempt to define this widely used, though rather amorphous, term, Heidi Hartmann and Ann Markusen stated, "Patriarchy is a system of social relations between men and women, governing the production and reproduction of people and their gender identities." Under this system, men maintain control over the labor of women through the structures of the family and the productive system, as well as the state.[12] Thus, "women function as the property of men,"[13] declared Joan Kelly, and "Woman's place is to do women's work – at home and in the labor force. And it is to experience sex hierarchy – in work relations and personal ones, in our public and our private lives."[14] Even as the mode of production altered, patriarchal control was evident.

For materialist feminists generally, and Marxist feminists in particular, this concept, of "sex hierarchy" or patriarchy, proved problematic. While recognizing the inadequacy of Marxism in theorizing women's oppression, they were also aware of the tension between the materialist outlook and the theory of patriarchy.[15] Viewing the mode of production as the central factor in the organization of social relations, materialist feminists recognized the necessity of analyzing the subordination of women in relation to production in different historical contexts. Yet they were constantly forced to confront the pervasive and "apparently transhistorical character of women's oppression."[16] Some attempted to face this challenge by suggesting that "patriarchal relations take their particular form from dominant relations of production" and thus are historically specific.[17] Under industrialized capitalism, for instance, according to Roisin McDonough and Rachel Harrison, women's dependence on men was re-secured by legislative measures, as well as the sexual division of labor and the male breadwinner ideology.[18]

To many, then, a dual systems theory appeared to offer the answer to the dilemma they faced, since such a theory sought to incorporate and unite within one framework feminist and Marxist understandings of sex and class oppression. In this vein, Juliet Mitchell theorized that the key structures of production, reproduction, sexuality, and the socialization of children, in combination, have served to give unity to the oppression of women over space and time.[19] While women's role in reproduction is not necessarily basic to their oppression, Mitchell argued, the form that family organization has taken in western culture, based on monogamous relations, has served to institutionalize the sexual repression of women. At the same time, women's physical weakness has served to ensure them a subordinate position in the workforce, while increased time spent in the socialization of children has served as a cornerstone of further oppression.[20] The liberation of women could only be realized, according to Mitchell, if all four of these structures were radically modified. In other words, emancipation of the working class and the establishment of a socialist-based economy would be insufficient for achieving this end. Since women are victims of existing systems of both class and male domination, their full liberation depends on the demise of both systems of oppression, Mitchell concluded.[21]

Sylvia Walby too, in her study *Patriarchy at Work*,[22] defined patriarchy as "a system of interrelated social structures through which men exploit women," but she turned her primary attention to the arena of paid labor, arguing that it is the exclusion of women from paid work on the same terms as men that serves to maintain women's subordinate position within the family. In examining the textile and engineering industries as well as clerical work – economic sectors which have varied widely in terms of their gender patterns of employment – Walby basically argued (1) that every phase of capitalist development has been accompanied by new struggles with patriarchal relations, leading to a new set of gender relations; and (2) that women have not merely acquiesced as gender relations have been redefined but, rather, have been "significant actors in resisting their exploitation." Thus, in Walby's model, three players – patriarchal structures, capitalist relations, and women workers – emerge to confront each other at each stage of capitalist development. The first two of these – patriarchal structures and capitalist relations – exist separately, but "articulate" with each other through a process of competition and compromise, while women resist the patriarchal structures which are ultimately put in place.

This analysis appeared to add considerable depth to previous attempts to explain the oppression of women under capitalism in terms of both sex and class. Not only did it serve to suggest how the two systems were interrelated while maintaining their basic autonomy. It also allowed for change and development as well as the agency of women themselves. Yet, as I have shown previously, the analysis ultimately faltered on the assumption of a simple and rigid male/female antagonism inherent in any analysis based on the theory of patriarchy, serving to illustrate a major inadequacy of the theory itself. Thus, in discussing the nineteenth-century Factory Acts and their passage, Walby argued that the Acts as passed represented a compromise between "patriarchal forces" – represented by male operatives, humanitarian employers, and landed interests – and capitalist structures, dependent on female labor. Yet such an analysis, based on the assumption of a cross-class alliance among men, left out the fact that manufacturers generally fought bitterly the passage of factory legislation, at least until 1847. Further, despite Walby's insistence on the agency of women, she failed to deal adequately with the role of working women themselves in the passage of the Acts. Rather, in attempting to give support to her assumption of a sharp male/female divide, she gave considerable space to the expression of opposition from women, while discounting the support the Acts received, particularly from women in the organized trade-union movement, declaring that such women were simply enveloped in "a patriarchal hegemony."

Clearly cracks in the theory of patriarchy itself were becoming increasingly evident. With regard to women's labor history, it was not equipped to deal with expressions of unity between men and women at the workplace or with the complexities of women's responses to industrialization over space and time. Analyses based on a theory of patriarchy appeared to reduce complex interrelationships to their simplest male/female dimension. The theory of patriarchy was already facing sharp criticism.

The conceptualization of women themselves also proved to be problematic, as did the related notion of a shared oppression. Inherent in the theory of patriarchy, and feminism itself, was an assumption of unity and solidarity among all women. Yet Gerda Lerner, early on in the discussion, pointed to the difficulties involved in conceptualizing women as a group due to their dispersal throughout the population.[23] Further, argued Ann D. Gordon, Mari Jo Buhle, and Nancy Shrom Dye, in an article aptly entitled "The problem of women's history":

> The nineteenth-century notion that women are bound together by common oppression freezes and levels their enormously diverse experience. That women have suffered oppression is not to be denied. ... But oppression ... meant different things at different times to different groups and classes of women.[24]

Lerner specifically warned against seeing women only as victims of oppression, which was inherent in analyses based on a theory of patriarchy. Such an approach, she pointed out, places them in a male-defined conceptual framework whereas, she declared:

> The true story of women is the history of their ongoing functioning in that male-defined world, *on their own terms*. The question of oppression does not elicit that story, and is therefore a tool of limited usefulness to the historian.[25]

At the same time, the sharp distinction made between women and men and their respective interests began to falter as Nancy Cott noted the need for feminist theory to deal with the fact that women were the same and yet different from men. Further, she pointed out that gender identity is not separable from other shared identities, such as those of race and class, which can serve to unite groups across gender lines.[26] As suggested above in relation to Sylvia Walby's analysis, there emerged a recognition that mutuality between men and women was often present even in the context of an existing sex hierarchy. As Jane Lewis wrote, the family could be a source of emotional support as well as dependency, while the home was a center of (exploited) labor as well as love.[27] Working-class families recognized, argued Jane Humphries, that they could benefit materially as a unit if only men were the breadwinners.[28]

As Sheila Rowbotham pointed out in discussing "the trouble with 'patriarchy,'" every historically developed social form is fluid, yet patriarchy emerged as a fixed structure based on biological difference.[29] As a result, an analysis employing such a framework could not encompass women's agency or even suggest that they had the ability to transform their situation. Joan Scott concurred, concluding that an analysis based on patriarchy ultimately "rests on physical difference" which "takes on a universal and unchanging aspect." History itself then becomes epiphenomenal, according to Scott, "providing endless variations on the unchanging theme of a fixed gender inequality."[30] Some feminists, despite such far-reaching criticism, have sought to retain the concept of patriarchy, fearing that its abandonment deprives feminist theory of a means to critique those outlooks which ignore the special nature of the oppression of women.[31] But as Rowbotham concluded, although it has been stretched "in umpteen different ways . . . there is no transience in it at all. It simply refuses to budge."[32]

Gender and language

The term "woman" itself appeared to be in the same predicament, in need of stretching while its elasticity remained unclear.[33] The feminist movement emanated from the dominant social class of the period of its origins and, as such, Juliet Mitchell declared, represented its particular interests as universal, "its women as 'woman.'"[34] But feminism and feminist scholarship were failing to take this into account, "to recognize the embeddedness of [their] own assumptions within a specific historical context," Linda Nicholson argued.[35] Instead they were taking an essentialist approach by attempting to identify a single cause of women's oppression and thereby suggesting the existence of a common understanding about women and womanhood, as well as men and manhood, across cultures and historical periods.[36] Increasingly recognized was the need for "modes of theorizing . . . attentive to differences and to cultural and historical specificity."[37]

What was necessary, Joan Scott declared, was "a refusal of the fixed and permanent quality of the binary opposition" between the sexes and its replacement with "a genuine historicization and deconstruction" of the way that opposition actually operates, "reversing and displacing its hierarchical construction, rather than accepting it as real or self-evident or in the nature of things."[38] Scott thus turned to gender as "a useful category of analysis," one that rejects biological determinism and instead refers to "the social organization of the relationship between the sexes."[39] As a socially constructed category, gender is inherently grounded in a specific historical context, as it refers to the understanding of a particular society at a particular time of what constitutes manhood and womanhood. Further, analyses based on gender do not serve to isolate women but bring both men and women and relations between them into their purview.

Scott's own definition of gender revolves around its role as "a constitutive element of social relationships based on perceived differences between the sexes" which incorporate both normative concepts and subjective identity.[40] The sexual identities that emerge, however, Leonore Davidoff and Catherine Hall indicated in their important study of "men and women of the English middle class," are neither fixed nor immutable but constantly renegotiated.[41] With such an approach, it was suggested, women become "visible as active participants,"[42] enabling them to emerge from under the umbrella of an unchanging patriarchy, allowing light to fall on their own activities and experiences.

In employing gender as a category of analysis, Scott saw the study of language as central, for through such study, she suggested, a way opened up for us "to recast our understanding of the place of gender in history."[43] Through language, meaning is constructed. Thus, it is through language, in constructing meaning through differentiation, that the meaning of sexual difference and thus social understandings of gender are revealed.[44]

In support of this viewpoint, Scott took as a point of departure Gareth Stedman Jones' important essay, "Rethinking Chartism," critiquing his purported limited use of language as a tool of analysis since it was based, she argued, simply on taking words at face value. Through such an analysis, Scott maintained, Jones' attempt to demonstrate that Chartism was simply a movement for political change faltered because he did not employ "a method of analysis that shows how language works to construct social identity, how ideas such as class become, through language, social realities."[45] He thus missed "an opportunity to examine the process by which the working class was constructed" because he treated language "simply as a vehicle for communicating ideas rather than as a system of meaning or a process of signification." Rather, Scott suggested, through language a class identity was realized that in turn "constructed (and contained) social practice, through which people established, interpreted, and acted on their place in relation to others."[46]

Further, Scott contended, Jones missed the significance of gender by failing to recognize that "meaning is multidimensional." Thus the meaning of "working class" suggested inclusions and exclusions, and here gender was clearly implicated. "Had Stedman Jones attended to the way meaning was constructed," Scott concluded, "he would have seen *how* the particular category of class developed by [the Chartists] relied on gender."[47]

In the exchange appearing in *International Labor and Working-Class History*, where Scott's article first appeared, it was generally agreed that Scott was on firm ground in pointing to the significance of language as a system of meaning for working-class history. Stated Bryan Palmer in relation to the writing of labor history, "language must be attended to seriously [as] it plays a role in ordering working-class conceptions of politics and social differentiation."[48] Christine Stansell welcomed Scott's linkage of "the analytical significance of gender and language theory."[49] No longer could historians claim that women "'just weren't there'" in the movements they were analyzing, since gender was often implicated, as in the Chartist case, in the language of those movements. "It is language," Stansell evocatively suggested, "that transports the invisible presence of the feminine into the smoky taverns and coffeehouses packed with declaiming and petitioning Chartist men."[50]

Particularly welcomed in Scott's analysis was the suggestion of new conceptualizations and frameworks to be employed in the writing of working-class women's history and labor history in general. Ava Baron noted that women tended to be marginalized in the writing of that history due to assumptions made "about women workers as women and as workers" and the conceptual categories being used. In particular, Baron pointed to the assumption that working-class women were primarily wives, mothers, and daughters, while men were first and foremost workers, rather than family members, in marginalizing women as subjects of study.[51] Sonya Rose further developed this point, suggesting that the concept of separate spheres itself needed to be "jettisoned."[52]

Women's actions and family-centered rhetoric were explained by labor historians, according to Rose, as "a simple consequence either of being born female or a presumed association with domesticity," that is, by biology or by structures existing outside the economic realm.[53] Male identity, on the other hand, was formed at work, and was thereby rooted in the sphere of economic relations. With studies centered on productive relations, it was thus the male artisan in particular, with his "property in skill," passed down to his son, who "provided the template for conceptualizing working-class formation," resulting in the privileging of "certain male subjects and their actions as worthy of study." Those that "fell outside the mould" were ignored or considered peripheral.[54] By taking such an approach based on separate spheres ideology, Rose maintained, labor historians had "carried forward nineteenth-century ideology as historical argument."[55]

What was needed, Rose and others contended, was new conceptualizations in the discipline of labor history that were not centered on productive relations. In spite of the considerable contributions in women's labor history appearing by the late 1980s, Mari Jo Buhle similarly pointed to the necessity of breaking away from a "narrative baseline" and "materialist paradigms" that were so focused and that led to the assumptions and misconceptions suggested above. The actions and practices of the people themselves, she and other scholars recognized, cannot be fully explained by economic factors alone. Indeed, economic and class relations were themselves "shaped by culture." They were thus gendered, meaning imbued with the understandings regarding sexual difference that formed a part of that culture. What was necessary for scholars of the working classes, then, was to examine the significance and operation of the meanings of sexual difference, or understandings of gender, in those cultures and thus within and outside economic and class relations.[56]

Since people interpret their experiences and express such meanings through language, it is through language that we can get at gender and its meanings in the culture. The meanings of differences and interpretations of experiences so expressed must not be treated as epiphenomenal, as Rose claimed they were in materialist analyses, but as residing in materialist relations and as shaping social identity, actions, and practices. Seeing gender in this way, as she and Scott expressed it, as "a constitutive element of social relationships," appeared to open up the possibility of transcending such dichotomies as that suggested by the ideology of separate spheres.[57] As Ava Baron suggested, we could extend our analyses to examining "the many ways in which gender has shaped the work process, the wage form, workplace conflicts, and class relations between men and women in the family, the community, the union, and the factory and office."[58] The forming of unions and conflicts over control of the labor process, for example, Baron argued, all "took place on a gendered terrain" even if only men were actually present.[59] What labor historians now needed to place on their agenda for further exploration were the differing experiences of women and men and "the significance of sexual differences and the way they operate as a social force" in order to further our understanding of "the making of the working classes."[60]

What it appears was being suggested, then, was that women's labor historians needed to make "the linguistic turn," to move away from a supposed social or structural determinism, whereby language is viewed as a simple reflection of a given reality, centered in productive relations, to consideration of language itself as determining of social practices. As critics of the concept of class, as it was purportedly employed by E. P. Thompson in particular, suggested, gender and class are not given, are not natural, but are rather constructed. Thus, what was necessary was to transcend structural analyses, to employ a post-structuralist approach whereby "the relatively stable and fixed [male] class subject is accordingly decentred and deconstructed."[61]

Gender difference in working-class culture

Already by the early 1980s in England, the importance of sexual difference and the distinct positioning of men and women in working-class culture were being explored with the publication of Barbara Taylor's important work, *Eve and the New Jerusalem*.[62] Catherine Hall has pointed to the importance of this study in relation to the work with which we started this discussion, *The Making of the English Working Class*, and the question of class identity. Its significance lay in putting forth the new insight that feminist scholars were now bringing to the study of working-class culture, "that class identity, once theorized as essentially male or gender-neutral, is always articulated with a masculine or feminine subject."[63]

More broadly, recent works have brought out the significance of cultural understandings regarding gender in relation to the general process of industrialization itself, and particularly in relation to sex segregation within the workplace. As Deborah Valenze has pointed out, industrialization, with its rationalization and standardization of the work process, served to "reconstitute understandings of women" and women's work.[64] While the mercantile economy had been built upon the industriousness of all, including women, the woman worker was now increasingly represented as an obstruction to rationalized production. The discourse of political economy further served to privilege individual autonomy and the male breadwinner as central to the growth of the market-oriented economy, while women were increasingly associated with their domestic roles. The image of the woman worker, in both literary and political discourse, had fundamentally altered, from a central figure in the family production unit to a barrier to progress.[65]

Exposing this shift in perspective regarding working-class women has made it clear that industrialization cannot be viewed simply as an objective process of historical development with inevitable consequences for women workers. Rather, a "discourse of gender" had emerged which, Joan Scott argues, "elaborated, systematized, and institutionalized a sexual division of labor."[66] Ideas "about woman's place and ... gender roles" proved to be "significant determinants," according to Deborah Simonton, of women's work.[67] Capital thus proved to be, in the words of Anne Phillips and Barbara Taylor, "far from sex-blind."[68] As women continued to take primary responsibility for the household and child-rearing, even as the economy became more market-oriented and the individual wage became general, their work was defined as low-status and cheap.[69] No matter if that work was necessary, making it possible for the family to subsist, writes Eleanor Gordon, women's "status as waged labour [was] patterned by and mediated by their subordination as a gender."[70] The sexual division of labor thereby became "a powerful system of social constraint."[71]

Outlooks and prejudices regarding purported male and female attributes further served to uphold the sexual division of labor built upon the undervaluation of women's work. In industry in general, women were thought to be better suited to light work requiring quickness and dexterity, attributes which came to be considered naturally feminine. Accordingly, from tailoring to pottery-making to work in metal, women were engaged in the labor of finishing, particularly the smaller items. Generally, a clean and quiet environment was deemed appropriate for the work of women.[72] Working in filth, Jane Long points out, was thought to make women unfit for their future roles as wives and mothers.[73]

Machines, even though often worked by women and girls, were set up, maintained, and repaired by men.[74] Skill was deemed a property of the male worker, enabling him in certain instances to exercise control over wages, conditions of labor, and the quality of the goods produced, as well as entry into the trade. As mechanization progressed, male artisans attempted to defend this status, as against that of the common laborer and the woman worker.[75] Yet often, it appears, the notion of skill was contrived, as, for instance, in the hosiery industry where men claimed skill at countering which involved matching pairs of stockings, folding and boxing them.[76] John Rule thus concluded that definitions of skilled and unskilled work "were as much rooted in social and gender distinctions as in technical aptitude."[77] And Gertjan de Groot and Marlou Schrover have declared that "skill is not a workable concept."[78]

In the changing world of work, clear boundaries were thus established by the discourse of gender, by concepts of masculinity and femininity, scholars have concluded, not by technology itself. Women were to be confined to those areas where their work would complement that of men who did the "real" work defined by strength and skill.[79] Women's secondary position in the workforce was naturalized as employers expressed their hiring preferences according to predominant ideas about manhood and womanhood, often designing new technologies with the sex of the worker in mind.[80] States Gordon:

> Women's association with the domestic sphere, their consequent marginality to the labour market, and their status in society generally as dependent and subordinate individuals were the most powerful factors determining the value of the work they did, irrespective of the objective technical requirements of the job.[81]

Yet recent scholarship has also brought out the variation in women's work. As Jane Long suggests, "changing economic and social conditions and shifting cultural interpretations of femininity were dynamically interwoven."[82] The gendered division of labor thus varied and was worked out over time in relation to a variety of factors, such as existing labor markets and the extent of unionization. The outcome was not inevitable but contingent upon the strength of the negotiating parties in the particular setting. Neither mechanization nor the prevailing discourse would necessarily be determining. In questioning the "trite scenario" of the "natural" evolution of typing as women's work, for example, Meta Zimmeck points to the complex set of circumstances leading to that end. The desire to protect male workers was a continuing consideration, suggesting that the outcome was in fact unclear despite the purported, culturally-determined "fit" between typewriting and the feminine attributes of dexterity and quickness.[83] Who was to constitute the workforce when new technologies were introduced was a matter of negotiation, argues Ulla Wikander, with no consistent pattern discernible.[84]

In nineteenth-century England, while it may be readily apparent how "generalised views of femininity were deployed in everyday life," it is equally evident that "these deployments varied, were contested, and contradicted one another."[85] The extent of "working-class accommodation to the dominant ideology of gender divisions was shaped by the material reality of working-class life" which meant that the lines between men's and women's labor "were often drawn in different places."[86] As the boundaries set around women's work thus shifted, it was not always devoid of satisfaction as women often identified with their work, even as they experienced its negative aspects.[87] Earning a wage could potentially provide women with a sense of independence, Valenze points out, for which they were severely criticized.[88] Moreover, understandings of gender, suggesting women's place was in the domestic realm, Gordon contends, do not serve to explain "patterns of women's workplace behaviour." To draw such a conclusion is to conflate "a subordinate labour market position with subordination and submission in the workplace."[89]

The order and stability apparently imposed by the dominant discourse thus often gave way to such forces as economic necessity and community culture and tradition. As Simonton states, "the image of woman as persistently subordinate to man was always mediated by a range of influences, while women's experience often belied stereotypes."[90] "The dimensions of working-class women's lives … were materially and discursively linked," argues Long, but not necessarily in an orderly, static, and consistent fashion. Contradictions and tensions, as well as pressures on purportedly established boundaries, abounded.[91]

What is necessary, then, in any study of women and work is a recognition and delineation of the use of discourse analysis, as well as its limits, in considering the experiences of the people themselves. For it is on the basis of an analysis of the interplay between discourse and experience that we are able to advance our understanding of the nature and significance of gender identities in working-class culture. As Anna Clark states in her study to be considered in Part I, the analysis of rhetoric must be combined with the study of experience.[92] The following discussion puts forward the approach to this matter employed in this work.

Discourse and experience

Discourses, in the words of Nancy Fraser, and as they are viewed in this study, are "socially situated, signifying practices," anchored in social institutions and practices, not abstracted from them.[93] They ascribe particular meanings to, for example, women's work or economic transformation, thereby participating in shaping the emerging sexual division of labor as well as the industrial order itself.[94] Any discourse is then embedded in experience, not apart from it, and thus emerges as an integral part of the unfolding historical processes. In Mikhail Bakhtin's apt phrase, it is a "living utterance," taking "meaning and shape at a particular historical moment in a socially specific environment."[95]

In the study of any particular historical period, then, discourse analysis is of especial value in dissolving the artificial separation between culture and experience, as it aids, as Fraser suggests, "in understanding social identities in their full sociocultural complexity, thus … demystifying static, single variable, essentialist views of gender identity" in particular.[96] In the spirit of post-structuralism, discourse analysis serves to expose otherwise suppressed meanings, to open up purportedly stable categories,[97] such as "the working class," to examination, thereby revealing the importance of gender difference, for instance, within that supposed unity. Decentering is then proven to be of undisputed value, as Neville Kirk, a leading critic of postmodernism, points out, in acting "as a safeguard against crude 'essentialisms' and 'reductionisms,'" alerting us to the pluralistic nature of all identity.[98]

It is equally important, however, to reject the extreme view taken by Joan Scott, that experience is actually "a linguistic event," that subjects are positioned by discourses that "produce their experiences."[99] Rather, we must foreground the dynamics of the setting in which meanings are articulated so that we are not left with a snapshot in which decentered identities themselves appear to become fixed! Such identities, rather, are themselves situated, as Bryan Palmer suggests in relation to Chartist rhetoric, in "locales of contradiction, ambiguity, and perhaps possibility, rather than one-way streets where the masculinization of class proceeded unchecked … forcing women to the periphery of class struggle and radical politics."[100] Social forces, as Kirk warns us, must not be considered as "wholly constructed in theory/language."

Critics of post-structuralists have thus questioned whether, in their attempts to break down and deconstruct such essentialisms as that of class, sufficient attention has been paid to this context, or whether old purportedly unitary categories have simply been replaced by new ones. Thus, Marc Steinberg posits that, in arguing that a populist identity transcended that of class among the Chartists, Patrick Joyce and James Vernon have simply fallen prey to a new essentialism.[101] Similarly, the understandings of manhood and womanhood accompanying the emerging industrial order can themselves begin to take on an unwarranted stability and be seen as having evolved rather than continually evolving.

Any analysis needs to convey that continuing dynamic, that any such shift in predominant understandings of gender does not inevitably lead to a neat "linguistically ordered world of philosophic truth"[102] in which experiences are viewed as constructed by discourse. In such a world, Laura Lee Downs states, "There is no room for change … nor can one trace an alternative path to subjectivity, for instance, viewing identity as the fluid outcome of a more dialectical process, arising at the confluence of both identification and differentiation."[103]

As it takes on its own particular shape, Bakhtin points out, any discourse becomes part of a larger, already ongoing, conversation, becoming "an active participant in social dialogue" where it emerges as one of a "multiplicity of social voices" and enters a network of linkages and interrelationships.[104] An apparently unitary language thus constitutes merely "the theoretical expression of the historical processes of linguistic unification and centralization," suggesting a "unity of the reigning conversational (everyday) ... language."[105] However, accompanying that process of "verbal-ideological centralization and unification, the uninterrupted processes of decentralization and disunification go forward."[106] Discourses, which are inherently contingent, continually "arise, alter, and disappear over time" as material reality places pressure on them.[107]

The apparent hegemony of those groups articulating the dominant discourses, as Fraser warns, does not, then, translate into the exercise of absolute authority. Such groups do not totally control meaning.[108] Rather, the production of meanings is an ongoing process and the task of the historian, as Kathleen Canning contends, is to explore "the ways in which subjects mediated or transformed discourses in specific historical settings."[109] The rendering of meaning is embedded in all experience and implies the agency of the subject. Established discourses are then not controlling of behavior nor do they serve to reduce the subject to "a mere bearer of systemic processes."[110]

Language is then integral to struggle. And within that struggle it is a constitutive force. Certain meanings may become dominant, as a unitary language appears to emerge, articulated by those holding some degree of power. In such a context, those constructed as "others" may appear as passive victims, silenced and marginalized by a controlling, determining discourse. As a consequence, Carole Anne Taylor warns, a theory "that tries to displace or decenter binary oppositions may still complicitly devalue the positions most readily objectified."[111] But in reality a struggle within apparently established meanings, and thus the "process of counter-hegemony,"[112] continues, as discourses, like structures, are both sustained and transformed at the same time.[113] States Steinberg, "Language operates as a constitutive force in social life precisely because of the social experiences of actors which call for meaning." Consciousness and identity, then, are in the end "determined not by language, but by people."[114] While the presence of gender hierarchy within working-class culture is clear, and expressed in language, the extent of the impact and the pressures placed upon that language or discourse need to be explored and carefully examined in order to illuminate and dissect the exact workings and significance of that hierarchy as well as its limits in the given context. This point then takes us full circle, returning us to Thompson and class, with which we briefly began this essay, and consideration of the manner in which language and experience may be effectively integrated.

As we said at that point, and as has frequently been pointed out, what interested Thompson was not class as fixed structure but class as process and thus, Steinberg elaborates, the intersection, or dialectic, of the economic and cultural, of being and consciousness.[115] Language in this approach is then central to the experience of class and working-class movements and thus integral to any study taking such movements as its subject. But there is not a single language but multiple languages and those languages play multiple roles. As Kirk states in relation to the Chartist movement, languages "operated within, took their meanings from, and shaped changing social contexts." Accordingly, "changed contexts could and often did induce shifts in the meanings of language" which then, in turn, he suggests, played a role in re-shaping the movement itself.[116] Languages, then, in and of themselves do not pattern and thoroughly circumscribe behavior. They are, rather, embedded in, they express the meanings of, and play a role in shaping experience without being determinative as their meanings continue to be struggled over in the midst of the shifting contexts to which they are linked. In the hands of the powerful, discourses may serve to constrain social action. At the same time, however, as they evolve within a particular material context, among those marginalized by the dominant discourse, they may provide "the foundations for human agency."[117]

It is the purpose of this study to illustrate, in the context of sharply contrasting industrial settings, the dynamic tension and interplay existing between "the material reality of working-class life" and predominant understandings of gender. I argue that the significance of gender difference in the distinct cultural settings considered was the product in each instance of a complex, ongoing process of collaboration, conflict, negotiation, and subversion involving working women and men, male union leaders, and in the later period the women's trade union movement. Languages constructing women's work as immoral and illegitimate, or at least in opposition to women's domestic duties, circulated in a larger context in which that labor was vital and accepted. What was to constitute women's work and whether and how it was to be regulated thus became matters for negotiation in each industrial setting and, indeed, in each community. Understandings of gender, suggestive of the role of gender difference in each setting, were thus shaped and re-negotiated within a context of contradictions and tensions which analyses privileging the role of discourse fail to capture.

This general process of negotiating gender difference is examined in relation to the cotton industry of Lancashire and Cheshire and the small metal industries centered in Birmingham and the Black Country. These industries occupied opposite ends of the spectrum in terms of degree of industrialization and the organization of capital. Yet both were centers of widespread female labor and, accordingly, were at the forefront of negotiating the terms of that labor, in different periods and under vastly different circumstances. How those negotiations unfolded, and the interplay between discourse and experience revealed in the process, comprise the subject of this work.

With the growth of factories and "Coketowns" throughout the industrial Northwest and the emergence of a large concentrated workforce in which children and women were prominent from the early nineteenth century, female labor, as is well known, gained widespread attention. Particularly by the 1840s, with the spread of powerloom weaving and the domination of girls and women in that occupation as well as the preparatory processes in spinning, women's work became a "problem." A family wage rhetoric became prominent, suggesting that men were to be the primary bread-winners while women were increasingly identified with the domestic realm. If they entered the workforce, women were considered to be secondary labor-ers. According to Robert Gray in his important study of gender and factory legislation, passage of the Ten Hours Act, applying to women only among adult laborers, represented the negotiation of "a just social contract between government and citizens," whereby men emerged as independent citizens and women "as symbolic dependants."[118] Womanhood and manhood seemed clearly defined at mid-century.

Yet Gray emphasizes that this contract or settlement was fraught with tensions and contradictions.[119] Indeed, passage of the Ten Hours Act took place against a broad backdrop of women's increasing integration into the workforce and their involvement in the Chartist movement alongside the men of their families and communities. Moreover, women as workers sup-ported passage of that Act and were at the forefront of its defense when its integrity was threatened by a system of working women in shifts. They were also an integral part of the effort to organize unions among powerloom weavers and to obtain their recognition as well as a standard list of prices. Yet they also supported the Ten Hours Act at least partially on the basis that it allowed them more time to fulfill their domestic roles, thus reinforc-ing their subordinate position in the home and their secondary position as wage earners.

The understandings of gender that emerged were thus rooted in diverse experiences and ambiguities, in both mutuality and inequity, in collabora-tion and subversion, and thus encompassed this whole range of thought and activity. Consequently, I argue, they represented an uneasy and fluid settle-ment, encompassing an understanding regarding the general division of paid and household labor as well as a history of mutual struggle by the people of the cotton district to realize some measure of control over their lives. As such these gender understandings underpinned the expressed desire among the working classes for respectability, determining that such respectability was based not only on the subordination of women, but on collectivity, all be it unequal, as well.[120]

Set in an industrial milieu in sharp contrast to that of the cotton district, the process of negotiating gender difference in some small metal trades took a different form but involved similar tensions surrounding women's paid labor. By the last quarter of the nineteenth century, when it appeared that understandings of gender had been negotiated in the cotton industry, although tensions clearly persisted, female labor, its extension, morality, and legitimacy, had come to the fore as a major issue in the small metal indus-tries. In both Birmingham and the Black Country, female labor was well-entrenched. That labor was also especially exploited. In Birmingham the labor of girls was general, while married women moved into the workforce as need dictated, enabling families to survive periods of economic hardship. In the Black Country nail and chain trades, the organization of domestic and workshop labor, in which the role of middlemen was becoming increasingly predominant, was dependent on female labor, which was marked by low wages and deplorable conditions.

In this context, traditions of male skilled labor in both regions ascribed certain meanings to female labor, particularly seeing it as illegitimate and immoral, at least in circumstances where it came into competition with that of men. Two union leaders in particular, W. J. Davis of the brass trade and Richard Juggins of the Midland Counties Trades Federation, were especially associated with such an outlook, provoking what appeared to be considerable conflict on the basis of gender in both settings. As the union leaders restricted their organizing efforts to male skilled laborers and attempted to limit, or exclude in certain instances, female labor in brass working and nail- and chainmaking, the early women's trade union movement voiced their opposition, opposing legislative restrictions and defending the principle of freedom of contract in relation to women workers.

The issues, however, proved to be larger than the simple gender antagonism suggested here. In Birmingham, the nature of the work itself was altering as mechanization progressed, accompanied by the consequent degradation of skilled labor and the introduction of female labor in new areas. In the Black Country, communities dependent on female labor opposed its restriction and possible exclusion. In this larger context, gender difference was re-negotiated. Exclusionary strategies were abandoned as the necessity of female labor was recognized. Instead, support for restrictions on that labor, as well as opposition to domestic workshops, were increasingly voiced. Additionally, organizing of female labor gained increased attention from the late 1880s, involving an implicit recognition of women's position in the workforce, particularly in chainmaking. In Birmingham, pressures on existing understandings of gender intensified as the issue of sweated labor in the brass industry came to the fore, leading to a recognition of the need for the union movement to address the needs of unskilled male as well as female labor. The strike movement of 1910–13, led by the Black Country chainmakers, was consequently marked by a unity of workers across gender lines. Yet at the same time wage agreements, realized by unions and under the Board of Trade, were built on gender difference, as women's wages were universally negotiated to be lower than men's.

In all of these settings, encompassing the cotton and metal industries, gender difference was negotiated and re-negotiated, and in each setting women came up short. Constructed as secondary laborers, women were clearly expected to take primary responsibility for the home. Their subordination at home and work was clear. Yet the process of negotiating gender difference was complex and the results perhaps somewhat more ambiguous than these comments suggest, as indicated above. For as gender was inflected by class, implicit in the above brief narratives is a process of class interests increasingly extending across gender lines. Embedded in the ideology of respectability were both collectivity and inequality. Negotiating gender difference in the metal trades was accompanied by a more inclusive view of class and class interests, extending to unskilled men as well as women.

Not only, then, do we see a process of the fracturing of class by gender but a process of reconciling womanhood and paid labor. Gender thus emerged as a site of class formation. What we seek to explore here, then, are "the interplays between sources of fragmentation and unity, competition and co-operation, individualism and mutuality, and conflict and comradeship within working-class life."[121] Through such an approach, the analysis presented here is intended to serve to "illuminate both class formation and class relations" as gender participated in diverse ways in those conflicts and processes.[122]

Part I

Negotiating gender difference in the cotton district

The significance of gender difference in working-class culture has been explored with reference to the English cotton industry by a number of scholars. Anna Clark has made the point that here, in contrast to other sectors of the economy, a culture based on "patriarchal cooperation" was in existence during the earliest stage of industrialization.[1] Women participated alongside men in the political struggles of the period, most notably in the campaign for parliamentary reform.

Yet already in 1819 at the time of the demonstration for parliamentary reform at St. Peter's Field in Manchester, Catherine Hall contends, the different experiences of men and women of political events was striking. In her clever recounting of "The tale of Samuel and Jemima" Bamford at what became known as Peterloo, she notes that, while Jemima was committed to the cause of reform and attended the demonstration:

> Her arrangements were to do with their child, her first concern, once she knew that he was safe, was to get back to her. Like the majority of female reformers at the time she positioned herself, and was positioned by others, as a wife and mother supporting the cause of working men.[2]

Generally, Hall continues, the culture positioned men as "independent subjects."[3] Through their clubs, societies, and trade unions, men felt "an identity of interest" that excluded women. Under the influence of Locke and Cobbett, Radical culture emerged as a male culture where men were agents and women were "placed ... firmly in the domestic sphere."[4]

Twenty years later during the struggle for the Charter, Clark argues, a rhetoric of domesticity for women had become predominant as working-class radicals struggled "to universalize [the] class-bound notion of gender" based on "separate, complementary spheres ideology."[5] At the workplace, as men's position in spinning was threatened by mechanization as well as the introduction of cheap female competition, male spinners struggled for a Ten Hours Bill on the basis of extending employment for themselves and enabling women to fulfill their domestic roles. Indeed factory legislation generally, Sonya Rose maintains, served to define women "by their sexuality and fitness for domesticity, by their maternal roles, and finally by their maternal bodies."[6]

Yet at the same time it is clear that the experiences of women of the cotton district transcended the rhetoric of domesticity as they increasingly moved into the factories as powerloom weavers from the 1830s and 1840s, and participated in newly organized unions as well as major strikes. Despite remaining aloof from the early agitation for factory legislation, they participated in the movement for the Charter as members of families and communities, suggesting a mutuality across gender lines in spite of the apparently growing emphasis on sharply defined gender identities. Additionally, through their experiences even from the margins, the meaning of domesticity was reshaped by women, often not in opposition to, but in cooperation with, their male counterparts, as part of the struggle for control over the dignity of their daily lives.

It is argued here, then, that even as a rhetoric of domesticity was increasingly evident from the Chartist period, women's identities, and thus understandings of gender, were shaped by a complex intertwining of forces involving that rhetoric as well as women's own outlook regarding their domestic roles, the character of their paid labor, and their participation in community-based and workplace struggles alongside their male counterparts. The concept of patriarchal cooperation, usefully introduced by Clark as a way of describing gender relations in the culture of the textile districts, must be explored more fully and expanded to encompass and reveal the full dynamics and complexity of those relations, not abandoned. Ideas of gender difference seemed increasingly resolved and settled, but negotiations continued as women both confronted subordination and simultaneously gained a degree of control, in the workplace and the home, within established constraints. Both gender and class identities were continually in the process of being reshaped and redefined.

2 Cooperation, conflict, and community

Women's work in the cotton industry changed dramatically during the earliest stage of industrialization. Displaced as spinners, they came to be widely employed in handloom weaving, while entering the factories generally in the preparatory processes and as assistants to male spinners. During this period of economic distress, they were an integral part of the movement for parliamentary reform and engaged in labor disputes. With the struggle for the Charter, however, evidence suggests that, while initially active in the movement, women's participation underwent a decline as a rhetoric of domesticity became a centerpiece of the mass platform. Yet it is suggested here that such rhetoric held an appeal for women, suggestive of the contradictions and tensions present in the process of shaping gender identities. Inherently ambiguous, it served both to maintain their presence in workplace agitation and to underpin their complicity in their own subordination.

Women's work in the cotton district

In 1764 James Hargreaves, a weaver of Stanhill near Blackburn in Lancashire, invented the spinning jenny, the first invention, states Friedrich Engels, to change fundamentally the economic and social position of English workers.[7] Until the 1780s Hargreaves' jennies were widely used in cottages, enabling women to continue their traditional occupation at home. Gradually, however, improvements on the original jenny, including an increase in the number of spindles and lengthening of the machine, led to the removal of spinning from the home and into small sheds and later factories.[8] Two additional inventions contemporaneous with Hargreaves' jenny – Richard Arkwright's roller spinning machine, or water-frame, and Samuel Crompton's spinning mule – further hastened the trend toward factory production in spinning. By the 1830s the mule, which combined and improved on the jenny and water-frame, had gradually superseded them,[9] insuring "the triumph of the factory system in the spinning of cotton."[10]

Accompanying these developments was a general trend toward the displacement of women spinners by men, apparently due to the strength required to operate the new machines. "By 1788," Ivy Pinchbeck states, "jenny spinning in the cottages was over."[11] Only a small number of women continued as spinners, employed on Arkwright's frames which, unlike the larger jenny and the mule, were found to be suitable for female labor.[12] Otherwise, women were employed in factories in those processes where the cotton threads were prepared for spinning. Here women worked alongside children, who dominated the labor force in the early water-powered mills, while the proportion of adult male operatives steadily declined. Earnings for the few women spinners, as well as carders and reelers, amounted to 4s. to 5s. 6d. for a seventy-two-hour week; while adult males, in the same amount of time, working as head carders, packers, and general laborers, earned 9s. to 11s. 9d. at Sameul Greg's mill near Styal.[13] In the steam-driven cotton mills in the 1790s, the labor of children continued to predominate, particularly in areas such as Preston. However, in Manchester, the proportions of adults and children under 18 were about even.[14]

As in the water-powered mills, women continued to be employed in the lower-paid occupations. The 1795 wage book of M'Connel and Kennedy, Manchester cotton spinners, reports that women cotton pickers who worked regularly earned from 4s. to 8s. per week, while the male mule spinners averaged from 30s. to 38s. during the same time period.[15] The highest-paying job employing women was that of stretching the yarn prior to weaving. Here, paid piece-work wages, women could average 17s. 6d. per week, but men employed in the same occupation could average up to 24s. per week[16] since they were stronger and could produce a larger quantity in the same amount of time. Women's wages continued to be only a fraction of men's during the decade 1810 to 1819. The earnings of women spinners, working roller spinning machines requiring less skill, were consistently only slightly over half the wages of the fine spinners, while reelers earned generally less than one-third of the fine spinners' weekly wages.[17]

Women's work, however, was not confined to spinning and related processes during this early stage of industrialization. The inventions of Hargreaves, Arkwright, and Crompton had made possible the production of a strong cotton yarn, enabling the manufacture of all-cotton cloth. The great demand for this material, together with rapidly increasing production of yarn at the end of the eighteenth century, led to an immeasurable increase in the demand for cotton handloom weavers. In the country districts of northeast Lancashire, where there was high unemployment especially among women domestic spinners, they provided a ready labor supply and soon came to constitute a major portion of this previously male-dominated occupation.[18] Duncan Bythell estimates that, in 1808, approximately half the total number of cotton handloom weavers may have been women and children,[19] with women averaging earnings of 10s. to 15s. per week in good times, according to Ivy Pinchbeck.[20]

The good times the cotton-weaving industry experienced around the turn of the century were, however, sporadic. During the years 1802, 1805, and 1810, the industry enjoyed peaks of activity but, due to the disruptions of the Napoleonic Wars, its expansion was uneven. In the intervening years the demand for cotton goods fell while the industry remained crowded with workers who had recently entered the trade, including large numbers of women and children. This flooding of the labor market caused wages to fall sharply during these periods, resulting in widespread distress throughout the cotton-weaving areas, a situation that was to become all too familiar to the industry in the following decades. But even though their labor had a negative effect at times of slack trade, women continued to hold a prominent place in cotton weaving after the wars and as powerloom weaving came into its own.[21]

Before the 1820s, powerloom weaving was slow to be adopted. Dr Edmund Cartwright first took out a patent on a powerloom in 1786, but he was unable to interest Manchester businessmen in his invention so he was forced to abandon his mill in Doncaster in 1793. Several other mills for powerloom weaving were established during the 1790s, but these too were unsuccessful due to technical problems. It was only during the years 1802 to 1804, when William Radcliffe, a small Lancashire manufacturer, began to experiment with the different processes involved in powerloom weaving, that the expansion of this sector of the cotton industry was made possible.[22]

Radcliffe recognized that a division of labor within the mill was needed, with a separate room used for the dressing process which involved passing the yarn through an adhesive mixture, thereby serving to strengthen it before it was placed on the loom. In 1803 and 1804, he took out patents on a dressing machine and a beam warping machine that served to dress the yarn, dry it, and wind it on to the beam in successive steps.[23] These inventions greatly facilitated the development of powerloom weaving, but the application of power to weaving was not rapidly adopted in the following years. By 1820, 14,150 powerlooms were in operation throughout the United Kingdom (12,150 in England), but only 10,000 operatives were employed in weaving mills that year, as compared to 110,000 spinning mill operatives and 240,000 handloom weavers. The major expansion of the powerloom industry came only during sporadic periods in the 1820s and early 1830s,[24] but during this early period women predominated since few men were so employed.[25]

As mechanization progressed in its earliest stage in the cotton industry, a clear gender hierarchy emerged in the spinning sector as work was increasingly sex-segregated. A fissuring of class was thus in evidence, as Anna Clark has indicated. Yet also apparent, she has emphasized, was the distinctive character of the textile industry in general with respect to gender, particularly during this period.[26] Spinners expected women to work in an auxiliary capacity, while handloom weavers as well did not share the outlook of other artisans which suggested that women should be excluded from paid labor.[27] Rather, men, women, and children worked alongside each other in handloom weaving, while the daughters and wives of weavers entered the factories to work the powerlooms. In this context, the workplace and political agitations that marked the period were characterized by a degree of unity across gender lines.

Labor disputes, politics, and domesticity

By 1799 the Association of Weavers had been founded, with fourteen federated local unions in Lancashire,[28] and turned its attention primarily to petitioning Parliament for legislation regulating wages.[29] At the time, the weavers noted in outlining their grievances, prices were continually rising while wages were constantly reduced.[30] On these grounds, 23,000 individuals signed a petition calling for parliamentary action to address their distress.[31]

Due to passage of the Combination Acts, which came into force in July 1799, further organizational efforts on the part of the weavers were limited.[32] Nevertheless, they continued to organize on a local basis and, in February 1807, presented a petition, this time containing 130,000 signatures, to Parliament, calling for the establishment of a minimum wage.[33] The House of Commons refused to consider the weavers' request while the petitioning continued for another year until, on 19 May, the Commons rejected the minimum wage Bill.[34] This action led to a strike called five days later by the weavers of Manchester who were quickly joined by their counterparts in surrounding towns. Approximately 60,000 looms were stopped during the walk-out,[35] which was marked by large public meetings and some disturbances as the strikers stopped those looms that remained at work and prevented weavers from picking up yarn or turning in finished products at the manufacturers' warehouses.[36] On the whole, it appears that the strike was "extensive, well-organized and apparently effective." By the end of June, the weavers had returned to work with "some advance in wages."[37]

In 1808, women constituted a sizable percentage of handloom weavers and undoubtedly lent their support to the strike in some capacity. Indeed, the *Times* wrote, "The women are, if possible, more turbulent and mischievous than the men. Their insolence to the soldiers and special constables is intolerable, and they seem to be confident of deriving impunity from their sex."[38]

The wage advances that the weavers gained from the strike of 1808 were, however, quickly lost, and the following year they were forced to return to petitioning Parliament for legislative regulation of the trade.[39] Only in 1818, it appears, were trade societies again widespread among the Lancashire handloom weavers. That year the spinners, who were apparently highly organized,[40] demanded a return to the wage level of 1814[41] and, when they did not receive it, led a work stoppage that extended to workers in other trades including bricklayers, joiners, and dyers. The first extensive federation of trades, the General Union of Trades or Philanthropic Society, was founded in August but, with the arrest of the Spinners' Committee of Five on charges of conspiracy in late August, the strike collapsed and the Union was forced to disband in September.[42]

By that date the handloom weavers, with the apparent support of women within their ranks, were on strike for higher wages. It was reported that several thousand men, "accompanied also by a considerable number of women," from Middleton, Oldham, Ashton-under-Lyne, and other communities in the cotton district held several processions into Manchester during the work stoppage.[43] Within two weeks many weavers, especially in Manchester, had returned to work with an increase in pay,[44] reflecting the effectiveness of the strike.

The cause of parliamentary reform during the same period further witnessed organizational efforts on the part of both men and women in the cotton district, with women often adding their own distinctive voice to the agitation. By the first of January, 1817, twenty-one clubs had been formed throughout Lancashire for the purpose of petitioning Parliament in the cause of reform,[45] leading Archibald Prentice to write:

> The whole aspect of society was unfavourable. The rich seemed banded together to deny the possession of political rights; and the poor seemed to be banding themselves together in an implacable hatred of their employers, who were regarded as their cruel oppressors.[46]

The full force of the campaign got under way late in 1818 following the strike wave of that year. By that time a trade depression had forced the wages of handloom weavers, the main supporters of the agitation, down to as little as 6s. per week for the lowest grade cloth, with the highest weekly wage only slightly exceeding 11s. While wages stayed around these levels for a twelve-hour working day, prices fell little and the weavers saw little hope for improvement in their situation.[47] Radical Political Unions were then formed in and around Manchester, with one of the first being established at Stockport on 30 October. This Union, which became a model for others, was divided into classes of twelve men each, who met once a week to read and discuss available political tracts dealing with such issues as the rights of individual freedom and the sovereignty of the people.[48]

On 18 January 1819, at a Manchester Radical meeting, a Declaration and Remonstrance were passed calling for three basic reforms: annual Parliaments, universal manhood suffrage, and the repeal of the Corn Laws.[49] During the next several months, the various Political Unions around Manchester united their efforts behind this program, held regular meetings, and staged a number of demonstrations. The cause of Parliamentary Reform steadily gained support until August, when the recognized leaders of the agitation were arrested and silenced following the Peterloo massacre.

While this campaign dominated Lancashire politics in 1818–19, involving large numbers of men throughout the area, the women did not remain aloof. As Samuel Bamford indicates in an oft-quoted passage, as early as the summer of 1818, when the movement was just beginning, women played a somewhat active role in the men's associations and, at his apparent

instigation, "voted with the men at the radical meetings."[50] Soon they began
to form their own societies. Thus *The Annual Register* noted in early 1819
that "an entirely novel and truly portentous circumstance [of the agitation]
was the formation of a *Female* Reform Society at Blackburn, near Manchester."[51] As the movement reached its peak in June of that year, this Society
issued letters, "inviting the wives and daughters of workmen in different
branches of manufacture, to form *sister* societies."[52]

On 10 July, the *Manchester Observer* printed an Address presented at a
Blackburn public meeting by "The Members of the Female Reform Society
in the Town and Neighbourhood of Blackburn." Two themes are apparent
in this brief Address which appear, from the limited evidence available to
us, to have dominated the female reform societies. First, an explicit connection is drawn between the cause of Parliamentary Reform and the economic
crisis then confronting the working people of Lancashire. Every man in
England is called upon to join reform societies to obtain annual Parliaments,
universal suffrage, and election by ballot "which alone can save us from lin-
gering misery and premature death." Secondly, a reference is made to the
importance women attached to their position as mothers and, thus, instruc-
tors of children in democratic ideas so that such suffering would be unnecessary in the future. "We have already come forward," declared the Blackburn
Society, "with the avowed determination, of instilling into the minds of our
offspring a deep rooted abhorrence of tyranny."[53]

Following this example, other female reform societies were founded in
Lancashire, most notably in Stockport and Manchester. The Female Union
Society of Stockport was patterned after the male associations, with the
Society divided into classes of twelve members each and regular dues of one
penny per week. This Female Union was apparently founded, as the *Leeds
Mercury* article of 31 July states, "for the purpose of co-operating with their
male associates."[54] Yet the Declaration and Rules of the Society set forth in
no uncertain terms its members' views of the existing divisions within
society between rich and poor, the oppressed and the oppressor, in espousing
basic democratic principles:

> We who form and constitute the STOCKPORT FEMALE UNION
> SOCIETY, having reviewed for a considerable time past the apathy, and
> frequent insult of our oppressed countrymen, by those sordid, and all-
> devouring fiends, the Borough-mongering Aristocracy, and in order to
> accelerate the political emancipation of this suffering nation, we, do
> declare, that we will assist the Male Union formed in this town, with all
> the might and energy that we possess and that we will adhere to the
> principles, etc., of the Male Union and ... assist our Male friends to
> obtain legally, the long lost Rights and Liberties of our country.[55]

The female reformers of Stockport associated themselves closely with the
local Male Reform Union and implicitly accepted the principle that the

"Rights and Liberties" for which they were agitating would apply to men only. Additionally, the identical themes brought forth by the Blackburn Female Reform Society are clearly in evidence in the statements of the Stockport Female Union. Political reform is again implicitly seen as the only means of alleviating the economic distress the region was then experiencing. With the extension of political rights and liberties, it is implied, the division between the poor and the "all-devouring fiends, the Borough-mongering Aristocracy," could not continue to exist. The entire "suffering nation" must be economically relieved through political emancipation.

Also, among the Stockport female reformers, the need for their children to understand the nature of their basic rights and their responsibility as mothers to so instruct them were explicitly recognized. One of their regulations thus reads:

> We collectively and individually pledge ourselves to instill into the minds of our children a thorough knowledge of their natural and inalienable rights, whereby they shall be able to form just and correct notions of those legalised banditti of plunderers who now rob their parents of more than half the produce of their labour.[56]

With the understanding that a democratically structured Parliament would prevent such future suffering and injustice, the younger generation, if necessary, could continue the struggle or, at least, safeguard the gains realized by their elders.

In July of 1819 a Female Reform Society was also established in Manchester and produced a document of particular interest, entitled "The Manchester Female Reformers' Address to the Wives, Mothers, Sisters, and Daughters of the Higher and Middling Classes of Society."[57] This Address, signed by Susannah Saxton, secretary of the Manchester Society, is similar to the Declaration of the Blackburn Association in its emphasis on existing divisions between rich and poor. It states:

> From very mature and deliberate consideration, we are thoroughly convinced, that under the present system, the day is near at hand, when nothing will be found in our unhappy country but luxury, idleness, dissipation, and tyranny, on the one hand, and abject poverty, slavery, wretchedness, misery and death, on the other.

A new element, however, is introduced into the Manchester reformers' Address, as is implied in the title. An explicit appeal is made to women of "the higher and middling classes of society" to join with them to assist the women of the working class in alleviating their distress:

> To avert these dreadful evils, it is your duty ... to unite with us as speedily as possible; and to exert your influence with your fathers, your

husbands, your sons, your relatives and your friends, to join the Male
Union for constitutionally demanding a Reform in their own House,
viz. The Commons House of Parliament; for we are now thoroughly
convinced, that for want of such timely Reform, the useful class of
society has been reduced to its present degraded state . . .

A direct appeal was thus made by the Manchester female reformers to sym-
pathies that united all women. The inability of the poor to provide for their
children was especially noted to bring out the emotional identification that
women of a higher economic class might share with the working women of
Lancashire. The Address even asked, in highly emotional language, "How
could you bear to see the infant at the breast, drawing from you the remnant
of your last blood, instead of the nourishment which nature requires."

With such appeals, Anna Clark points out, "radical women asserted that
domestic concerns must become political issues."[58] Consequently female
societies, according to the conservative *Newcastle Courant*, became "general in
the disturbed district."[59] In Stockport the membership of the Female
Reform Association, originally founded by thirty-six women, had increased
to eighty-four by the third meeting.[60] In late July in the *Times*, a reference
appears to a West of England Female Union Society,[61] indicating that there
was an attempt to draw together the local female reform societies into some
form of federation.

Women were well represented at the reform meeting held at St. Peter's
Field in Manchester on 16 August 1819. Bamford estimates that approxi-
mately 300 to 400 women and girls marched in the Middleton-Rochdale
column in which he participated.[62] About 200 women marched with the
Oldham committee, while the Blackburn, Stockport, and Manchester
Female Reform Societies marched under their own banners. The Royton
Female Union carried a banner stating, "Let us DIE like men and not be
SOLD like slaves."[63] In the massacre that resulted from attempts by the
authorities to break up the meeting, 113 females were counted among the
600 wounded, and 14 of these were injured by saber cuts. Among the eleven
killed were two women, Martha Partington of Eccles who was "thrown into
a cellar and killed on the spot," and Mary Hays of Manchester who was
"rode over by the cavalry."[64] And among those arrested and placed on trial
for high treason, along with Bamford and Henry Hunt, was one Elizabeth
Garrett who was placed in solitary confinement for twelve days prior to the
trial. Her testimony reflected little evidence of wrongdoing and her case was
immediately dismissed.[65]

In the following years, radical women carried on their political activities,
organizing deputations to Queen Caroline, defending her against her critics
who, according to Clark, "portrayed them and her as unwomanly amazons,
viragos, illiterates, and prostitutes."[66] In so doing, they continued to appeal,
as in the parliamentary reform agitation, to sexual difference by invoking
the particular cares of motherhood. Such an outlook, however, Clark effect-

ively argues, cannot be considered conservative since the women were simultaneously defending their own dignity and expanding the definition of womanhood by justifying their participation in political affairs.[67]

This tradition of women's activism extended, particularly in the textile communities, into the Chartist period. At that time, in the words of Dorothy Thompson, women founded female Chartist associations and "presented banners, made and presented gifts to visiting speakers, and invariably marched in the great processions and demonstrations, usually at the head."[68] Chartist women, Clark argues, thereby "fashioned a political identity for themselves as mothers, workers, and activists," developing what she calls a "militant domesticity" that defined "the responsibilities of motherhood not just as nurturing children in the home but as laboring to feed them and organizing to better their lives."[69]

Yet both Clark and Thompson are quick to point to the limits of women's activism as the movement progressed. While seeing the Chartist period as something of a watershed in the participation of women in politics, Dorothy Thompson notes a change in perceptions regarding gender by both men and women. Such leading figures as Ernest Jones and Bronterre O'Brien appeared to take an increasingly "middle-class" approach to "the woman question," according to Thompson,[70] while:

> The growth of temperance, the increasing attempt to reclaim the working population for organised Christianity, and the spread of 'provided' education for both sexes, all helped to impose a less rough, more domestic, more genteel image of female behaviour.[71]

Among the Chartists, adds Clark, a rhetoric of domesticity for women became predominant, functioning both as a means to appeal to women's support and as a way to humanize and make palatable the Chartist movement and particularly Chartist men. The latter thus put forward a concept of "chivalrous manhood" as the masculine ideal. As a corollary, a feminine ideal emerged as well, which involved constructing women as wives and mothers, confined to and protected within the private realm. Robbed of their masculinity, working men expressed a desire "to exclude women from the workplace in order to protect and support them,"[72] thereby transforming, according to Clark, "the old marital misery into happy domesticity."[73]

Such rhetoric was accompanied by a large-scale withdrawal on the part of women from organized political associations, Thompson notes, as the mass demonstration was replaced by "the politics of committee" and the tensions associated with the introduction of the New Poor Law appeared to lessen.[74] Yet she also emphasizes, in contrast to Clark and as will be discussed further below, the significance of community for Chartist women and the mutuality across gender lines that community activism implies. Further, it is suggested here, through a look at labor disputes in the spinning sector of the cotton industry as well as the early factory movement, that a purportedly clear trajectory on the part of women of the cotton district from activism to withdrawal is actually somewhat more ambiguous. The rhetoric of the mass platform, perhaps precisely because of its emphasis and insistence on the dignity of the working-class home, and even women's protection within it, may have, somewhat paradoxically, played a role in integrating women into the continuing struggles of the period, a position they maintained throughout the mid-century.

Women's work, gender relations, and the factory movement

During the period of the late 1820s and early 1830s, important changes were taking place with regard to the composition of the workforce in the cotton industry which clearly impacted upon gender identities and gender relations. As we have seen, during the earliest stage of mechanization, male spinners came to enjoy a position of status in the mills, as measured by their earning of wages double or triple those of other operatives, into the 1820s. This status was reinforced by a subcontract system whereby the male spinners recruited and supervised their own assistants, and paid them piecerates. The spinners thus came to be recognized as the pace-setters within the mill and were able to maintain this position due to their strong associations, which had been in place, despite the Combination Acts, in some form since the 1790s.[75]

During the decade of the 1820s, however, intense conflict erupted between spinners and masters, serving to threaten the spinners' position within the hierarchy of the mill. With the economic crisis of 1826, the masters attempted to cut wages and introduced short time. When met with a series of strikes in response, they began hiring female spinners on all smaller wheels.[76] Further, a "putting-up motion," which utilized power, was invented and applied to the self-acting mule, thereby enabling women to operate mules with additional spindles. Women were then increasingly employed on these mules, averaging earnings of 10s. to 15s. per week, while men commanded wages of 25s. to 30s.[77]

At the same time, powerloom weaving was expanding rather rapidly, as the number of powerlooms in England was estimated at 85,000 in 1833.[78] By that year, the dominant position that female operatives would occupy was becoming increasingly apparent. While women (females over the age of 18) accounted for approximately 52 percent of adult cotton operatives in general, in weaving they constituted 58 percent of adults. Among operatives of all ages in all occupations in the industry, women accounted for approximately 31 percent of employees, while in weaving alone the proportion of women was slightly over 38 percent.[79] However, technological difficulties in the manufacture of cloth persisted, serving to restrict the expansion of the industry generally and to limit it geographically to Cheshire and Manchester and its environs.[80] Women were thus beginning to gain a foothold in the factory in one of the central processes of cloth production, but their entry was halting and their position insecure.

These changes suggest a potentially critical shift in gender relations at this early date, considerably prior to the founding of the Chartist movement. While female labor had been widely employed in low-paid positions in the spinning sector of the cotton industry, now it was introduced in spinning itself and thus in direct competition with men, and at lower wages. Tensions clearly existed, with gender relations being described as perhaps ambiguous at best, certainly within the spinning sector of the industry. Thus, when the spinners formed the Grand General Union of Spinners, they excluded women from membership although offering them their assistance.[81]

Further, women's capacity for active participation in a major campaign of the period, that for legislation restricting hours of labor, at least for children, may have been severely limited. Women's employment in powerloom weaving represented an opportunity to improve their earning power and status in the mills. Their primary interest at the time as workers, then, may have been in preserving the advances that such employment represented, especially since it was not clear just how extensive it would be, as well as retaining the earning power of their children. Under such circumstances, participation in a campaign for improvements in conditions of work, which brought them into direct conflict with their employers, may not have been considered in their interest. Thus, a question arises, to be explored below, regarding the degree of cooperation that existed across gender lines in the working-class movement at this early date.

As early as 1802 the first Act (42 Geo. 3, c. 73) regulating child labor had been passed, limiting employment to twelve hours per day, prohibiting night work, and requiring school attendance. But this Act applied only to apprentices and became virtually inoperative with the introduction of steam-powered factories, whose workforce was supplied by wage laborers of the surrounding area.[82] Only in 1819 was an Act (59 Geo. 3, c. 66) passed regulating the labor of all children employed in cotton factories. Its provisions were minimal, prohibiting labor under the age of 9, and restricting the work of children aged between 9 and 16 to twelve hours per day, not including meals. The maximum number of hours to be worked per week was set at seventy-two, with night work prohibited.[83] Over the following decade, the only further restriction placed on child labor was shortening the hours of work on Saturday to nine.[84]

The Factories Inquiry Commission of 1833 found that even these limited provisions were ineffective. In fact, children could begin to work in the cotton factories of Lancashire and Cheshire at the age of 5, and commonly began work between 6 and 8. While twelve hours was considered to be the normal working day, overtime work was common, generally extending from one to two hours daily. At all times, children were employed the same number of hours as adults, were excluded from any form of schooling, and were often subjected to permanent physical injury as a result of strenuous and continuous employment at such an early age.[85]

Following repeal of the Combination Acts in 1824, there had been some activity on the part of factory workers, at least in the Manchester area, to force employers to put the existing regulations affecting child labor into effect.[86] But it was not until the fall of 1830, when Richard Oastler wrote his famous letter to the *Leeds Mercury*, entitled "Yorkshire Slavery," that the factory movement began in earnest. In highly emotional language, which was to characterize his addresses, Oastler declared:

> Thousands of our fellow-creatures and fellow-subjects, both male and female, the miserable inhabitants of a Yorkshire town ... are this very moment existing in a state of slavery. . . . Thousands of little children, both male and female, *but principally female*, from seven to fourteen years of age, are daily *compelled* to *labour* from six o'clock in the morning to seven in the evening ... *with only thirty minutes allowed for eating and recreation*. Poor infants! Ye are indeed sacrificed at the shrine of avarice . . .[87]

With such fervent declarations, accompanied by the exposure of the facts concerning the hours of labor and working conditions prevailing in England's factories, Oastler expected an effective Bill to be easily passed. However, a core of operatives, previously involved in trade union and political activity, recognized the necessity of organizing to achieve their objectives and began to form Short Time Committees throughout Yorkshire. At first supporting a Bill introduced by John Cam Hobhouse which did little to extend already existing legislation, the Committees soon came to support a Ten Hours Bill restricting the labor of all factory workers under 18 to ten hours per day. With this objective in view, a campaign was launched in December of 1831, which was marked by great meetings held throughout the West Riding through April of the following year.[88]

As the agitation spread to Lancashire in the spring of 1832, when Michael Sadler introduced the first Ten Hours Bill, it became increasingly clear that the operatives were not only interested in limiting the labor of children but of all employees. Adult labor was generally inseparable from child labor, so any restriction on the one would clearly affect the other. Thus, the Committees' objective of shortening the working day could be achieved through legislation that either regulated the hours of child labor or restricted the motive power of the machinery.[89] In Lancashire, the operative spinners who were under the leadership of John Doherty, and who seem to have been in almost sole control of the movement, opted for the latter course. While supporting Sadler's Bill, pressure for a Bill that would shorten the working day for all laborers was clearly the focus of the movement.[90]

At the same time, the increasing employment of women, even at this early date, accompanied by the tensions resulting from attempts to introduce female labor into mule-spinning, served to focus growing attention on women workers. Indeed, when Lord Ashley introduced the Ten Hours Bill in 1833, an amendment limiting the number of working hours for women was included.[91] Resolutions passed at meetings noted that a Ten Hours Bill "would tend to equalize and extend labour, and would call into employment many male adults, who, though willing to work are obliged by the present system to spend their time in idleness."[92] In support of maintaining and expanding the employment of men, the spinners' leader John Doherty declared that, when women displaced men, it was harmful to both and, further, was against the natural order.[93] A report of a meeting of Yorkshire handloom weavers emphatically declared that one of the major reasons for their distress was "the adaptation of machines in every improvement, to children, and youth, and women, to the exclusion of those who ought to labour – THE MEN."[94]

Defenders of factory reform also argued that an additional benefit would result from limitations on women's work since women would now be able to fulfill their domestic roles. As it was, many commentators pointed out, girls were employed at such an early age that they were deprived of the opportunity to acquire domestic skills.[95] As a result, declared James Turner, a leader of the factory movement and a cotton-yarn dresser from Manchester, women are "quite ignorant as regards their family duties" and make "poor wives." "I have known thousands of instances where they could not mend a stocking or do a little washing," he contended in his testimony before the Select Committee considering Sadler's Bill.[96] Reflecting such sentiments, an oft-quoted deputation representing Short Time Committees from the West Riding of Yorkshire, in a meeting with Sir Robert Peel, claimed that women were unfit to attend to the cares of the household and proposed as a necessary remedy "the gradual withdrawal of all females from the factories."[97]

Of particular interest here are the responses of women themselves to these calls for their withdrawal from the factories and to the insults suggesting that factory women made "poor wives" and that their proper place in the natural order was in the home. The evidence is limited and needs to be treated carefully, but at the same time it offers some insight into gender relations as well as the power of the rhetoric of domesticity during this period and the latter's relevance to women's lives.

Evidence of any involvement at this early date in the Ten Hours campaign on the part of women, particularly in Lancashire, is minimal. Only in Yorkshire was women's participation – mainly evident through their attendance at demonstrations – common. Samuel Kydd, in his contemporary narrative of the factory movement, indicated that in 1831 and 1832:

> The Yorkshire meetings had features peculiarly their own. The tears, the smiles, the songs, the vows of the women and children, the sense of indignation which now and again shot from the eyes of all when the nobler feelings of their hearts were appealed to, will, by those who

witnessed these scenes, never be forgotten. . . . Here and there, a mother clasping an infant to her breast, kissing it and exclaiming: "Factory slave thou shall never be," gave to the proceedings a dramatic interest, remarkable, intense, and exciting.[98]

Women may, then, have swelled the numbers at demonstrations and served in Yorkshire to heighten the intensity of these events, but there is no evidence to suggest that women were directly involved at the organizational level in the Short Time Committees. In Lancashire, there was actually opposition to the Ten Hours Bill expressed by women.

Of eleven women operatives employed in Lancashire and Cheshire interviewed by the Factories Inquiry Commission, only one voiced support for the proposed Bill.[99] This woman, referred to only by the initials L. S., was an overlooker, 45 years of age and married. As a supervisor, an unusual position for a woman to hold, she was undoubtedly better paid than the average worker, and probably felt that she could afford to work fewer hours, even if wages were reduced.

Of the other ten women interviewed, seven explicitly stated that they would be opposed to a reduction of hours if it was accompanied by a wage cut, and two indicated that they would be "averse" to the reform. Only one woman, employed as a powerloom weaver, believed that her health had been impaired by factory work, and indicated that the same was true of her brothers and sisters who were employed as weavers and piecers. Generally, however, the women claimed to be, with some modification, in good health. "I have never felt overworked, or been unable to sleep at night, or lost my appetite," declared a woman of 26. Even women who had lost as many as three children claimed that factory work was not injurious to themselves or their children, and indicated that it would be a hardship for them if their children could not be employed before the age of 12. On the whole, the women seemed to accept their working conditions and particularly the hours of labor. As one woman responded when asked about making up an hour of lost time due to engine breakdowns each week, "that's no great difficulty is it?" Another woman of 20 declared that she "was accustomed to long work now, and did not mind it."

When asked about their domestic skills the women responded defensively, again indicating that their situation was not one of undue hardship. One of five women from Stockport declared, "I have taken notice, in my own neighbourhood, that young women brought up in factories, against those that are brought up as servants, seem to take more care of their houses and children, and to be more industrious, than the other class." Another indicated that she was "quite confident she could do as well as her neighbours and friends, whether in factories or out of them, in household work of any description." Said Sarah Parkin, a winder of 34: "There are plenty of opportunities to learn everything if girls like." A woman from Bolton registered her offence at the line of questioning: "You think we factory women can do nothing at all."

This evidence, indicating that women employed in the early factories had no complaints regarding their employment conditions and even opposed a reduction in working hours, even when restricted to children, needs to be treated with some caution. The evidence itself, in some cases, is inconsistent, with women, upon reflection, indicating that in fact their health was weakened and they were "not quite well" as a result of factory labor. Further, these women may not have been representative of the average female mill worker in Lancashire in the 1830s. Many of them were teachers in the local Sunday school, indicating that they may have achieved some degree of favored status. They may also have been employed in relatively favorable circumstances since they referred to opportunities for reading and sewing in the mills and indicated that other mills may have been operated for longer hours. Many of them worked in the mills an inordinately long period of time which, while not uncommon, was not typical either.

While women's economic security, based on their own earning capacity, may have been questionable at any time, it was certainly so in the early 1830s. Especially in Bolton, where three women workers interviewed by the Factories Inquiry Commission were employed, women's entrance into the mills lagged far behind that of their counterparts in other areas, with the exception of Oldham, due to the halting introduction of powerloom weaving in that region. While in Manchester the number of weavers equaled approximately 60 percent of the number of mule-spinners, in Bolton weavers accounted for only 12.4 percent of that total. Of the total number of employees in the cotton mills of Bolton for which statistics exist, only 13.5 percent were employed in the weaving department while 33.8 percent of the operatives in Manchester worked in weaving. Although women constituted a comparatively high percentage of weavers in Bolton, their numbers were so small that the proportion of women in the mills as a whole was not greatly altered by their employment. Even in such low-paid, unskilled jobs as carding, where women and children traditionally predominated, women were a comparatively low percentage of the workers in Bolton.

With their employment possibilities so restricted, these women probably viewed with suspicion any further threat to their earning power. Perhaps this was especially true of women such as the three stretchers interviewed by the Commission, who had attained a certain degree of security over a long period of time in relation to their fellow employees. Earning well above the average wage for women workers in some cases, in an area where women were not widely employed, they had a certain status to defend.

Yet in Stockport, too, where the number of weavers exceeded by over three times the number of mule-spinners, and where, as a result, the percentage of women employed in the cotton mills was close to the average for the major centers of production in the cotton district, women also expressed opposition to a reduction of hours. Here, the introduction of powerloom weaving had meant a dramatic increase in the percentage of women employees. In the spinning processes alone, in the mills considered in the "Supplementary Report of the Factories Inquiry Commission," women accounted for only 20 percent of the operatives. When the number of workers employed in the weaving department is included in the figures, however, that proportion is increased to nearly 30 percent. Were not, then, the women employed in the Stockport cotton mills, and in other areas where weaving had gained prominence, sufficiently secure in their employment to support a reduction in hours of labor?

Over the previous decades, powerloom weaving had been introduced only gradually in Stockport and other areas. In fact, of the five women from that region interviewed by the Commission, at least two who were working in the weaving department in 1833 had previously been employed in the card-room. This advancement, from an auxiliary occupation to one of the major operations in the mill, undoubtedly meant an increase in wages accompanied by an improvement in working conditions. Having recently bettered their circumstances, these women, like the Bolton stretchers, were probably not anxious to alter their situations, particularly if it meant a return to their previous wage levels. For women who remained in the cardroom, employment in weaving probably appeared as an opportunity for advancement which they would not wish to jeopardize.

There were, then, a variety of reasons, stemming from their position in the workforce, for women to remain aloof from the Ten Hours movement of the early 1830s. If they were employed in unskilled, low-paid occupations, they desired to retain whatever earning power they had achieved. If they had improved their circumstances, they had probably done so only recently, often after many years of labor. Any perceived threat to their position was, then, opposed. But a further compelling reason for women's absence from the campaign was probably also present: a fear of reprisals by their employers. An agitation seeking an improvement in working conditions brought employers and employees into direct conflict. If unorganized, as workers outside the spinning department were at this time, they had little recourse if they were dismissed from their employment for testifying on behalf of shorter hours.

Fear of dismissal had already been proven to be well-founded before the Factories Inquiry Commission of 1833 convened. Between 1828 and 1831, several court cases had been brought by a society of operatives against a Mr. Moore, owner of a factory in Comstall Bridge near Stockport, charging that he was employing children for a longer period of time than was allowed under the Act of 1819. A number of his employees testified to the correctness of this charge and were generally discharged after doing so.[100] Again in 1832, six witnesses from Leeds who testified before the Select Committee were dismissed from their jobs.[101]

In order to prevent similar actions, the Royal Commission included in its instructions to its interviewers a statement that was meant to protect the operatives from such harassment:

With relation to workmen or the parents of children whom you may examine, you will endeavor to obtain for them all protection for giving evidence freely, by preventing, where practicable or expedient, their names being made public, or by requiring from their masters some public assurance or pledge that they (the witnesses) shall in no way be prejudiced by any evidence which they may give.[102]

Yet, in Stockport a factory owner by the name of Mayer, who was opposed to the Ten Hours Bill, actually selected the five women who were interviewed, at least one of whom (Mary Oldham) had always worked in his factory.[103] She and the others were probably under pressure not to say anything in support of the Bill or to indicate that they had any grievances concerning their employment.

Despite these circumstances, however, it must be noted that the women interviewed by the Commission were, in important respects, representative. They represented a range of ages, from 19 to 49; a range of wages, from 8s. to 18s. per week; and a range of years worked in the mills, from just over five to forty-two. They were also engaged in a wide variety of occupations, including weaving and related tasks, spinning, and stretching and back-frame tenting, and were from different regions of the cotton district. Yet most of them voiced similar concerns regarding the issue of shorter hours. Fundamentally, they were concerned with defending their means of making a living, through their own employment as well as their children's. And they defended themselves, both as workers and as those held responsible for the maintenance of the home.

Even so, we clearly cannot conclude on this limited evidence that there was a uniformity of opinion among women cotton operatives. Undoubtedly, there were supporters of the Ten Hours Bill among women whose views were not reported or women who were fearful of reprisals. Their views, as well as their ability to express them, were circumscribed by immediate conditions which pointed to the tenuous nature of women's position in the factory. In order to attain any degree of economic security, women expected to work hard and long for low wages. Absent from the testimony of women before the Factories Inquiry Commission is any expression of the right to a say over their working conditions or a consciousness that, through struggle with their fellow workers, they could act to improve their circumstances. At this stage of mechanization in the cotton industry, women operatives were insecure, intimidated, and unorganized.

Furthermore, through the rhetoric of the factory movement, women were increasingly constructed as wives and mothers, their paid labor seen as threatening to male workers as well as to the natural order. An image of working-class life based on sharp gender distinctions was thus clearly emerging, in this pre-Chartist period, perhaps further serving to isolate women from participation in the agitations of the period. But the question to be considered here is whether the rhetoric of the mass platform simply served to reinforce such divisions on the basis of gender. For through such rhetoric, employed by men, the domestic realm became something more than a place to mend stockings. The concept of domesticity came to take on a broader meaning as appeals to it were used to give voice to the fears of both men and women. As such, it became an integral part of the political language invoked to give meaning to working-class life.

Domesticity, community, and the mass platform

In 1833, a Factory Act was passed limiting the hours of labor for children under 13 to forty-eight per week and those of youth aged 13 to 18 to sixty-nine hours.[104] The operatives, however, continued to seek a Ten Hours Bill and a campaign was revived in early 1836. The Bill introduced in Parliament was, however, withdrawn the following year as the operatives turned their attention to the agitation against the New Poor Law, then being introduced in the North.[105] Opposition to this legislation was intense, for under its provisions the unemployed would no longer receive outdoor relief, but were to be forced into workhouses where families faced forcible separation.[106]

A prominent feature of these campaigns for a factory Bill and against the New Poor Law, as well as the Chartist movement which grew out of them, was the great mass demonstration, culminating in addresses delivered by leading figures associated with the agitation. Rev. Joseph Rayner Stephens first mounted the mass platform in this capacity in response to the people of the communities of Ashton and Stalybridge, where he lived and preached, on 19 January 1836, with the renewal of the agitation for a Ten Hours Bill.[107] In the context of this struggle, as well as that against the New Poor Law which he soon joined, Stephens developed a message filled with "sympathy with suffering, a chivalrous sense of honour, a passionate hatred of oppression and avarice, a contempt for all that was mean, vulgar, sordid . . . regulated by a deep religious spirit of love for God and for Humanity."[108] In the tradition of the prophets, this message represented "a challenging call to the ethical sense,"[109] based on the principle of mutual obligations. Since "the property of the rich is fixed upon the foundation of the poor," he argued, the rich bear ultimate responsibility for the latter's well-being.[110] The tragedy of the industrial age, according to Stephens, was the abandonment of the poor by their natural guardians. The people were thus compelled to take up their own cause.

Foremost among Stephens' concerns was the people's right to material well-being, which he placed within the context of religious teachings. Provision for the poor under Jewish law, he declared, as in the time of Moses, was not to be "a niggardly one, founded upon modern political economy [as under the New Poor Law], but a bounteous one, founded upon the law of nature."[111] In return for obedience, the first law of God promised "an ample and abundant share of all that this world produces."[112] To speak of poverty "as a thing fixed and settled on a whole community" Stephens proclaimed "the foulest blasphemy that can be spoken of the Divine Being."[113] His concern, then, was not to secure the Charter, as he disassociated himself from that cause, but "to secure to every son of the soil, to every living being of the human kind ... a full, a sufficient, and a comfortable maintenance, according to the will and commandment of God."[114]

In Stephens' words, God said to Adam and Eve:

> Here is the earth; I give it unto you; take it and be masters of it; till it and it will bear enough for you and your offspring; and lest you should have any doubt at all, be fruitful – don't be afraid – be fruitful and multiply and replenish the earth, and subdue it, for all things are yours.[115]

The poor thus had a right, according to Stephens, to economic security and, above all, the comforts of home. "My politics, if I have any," he declared, "are very simple. I am for the cottager being as happy, as secure, and as contented, under his humble roof, as the Queen is on her throne in her palace."[116] And basic to the realization of those comforts, and central to our purposes, was the right of wives to remain at home while husbands earned a sufficient wage to support a family. Stephens thus glorified the supposed Golden Age:

> when every man's sweat brought bread enough and to spare for his wife and his household, times when the wedded wife was the pride of a devoted husband, and the husband was the glory of an attached and affectionate wife ... when children were looked upon as a blessing from God ... times of the cottage – times of the church.[117]

He vehemently attacked the effects of both the New Poor Law and the factory on the families of the poor, for both separated man from wife and parent from child. He decried the fact that mothers working in factories often saw children as a burden and, according to the testimony of medical men, even begged doctors not to take any pains to keep their new-born children alive, due to the hardship brought on by another mouth to feed.[118] Accordingly, Stephens called on men to prevent their wives from going to work, a practice which he considered un-Christian, unconstitutional, and opposed to the laws of God and human nature.[119] "Most of all God's gifts, [women were] to be cherished, protected, and defended," proclaimed Stephens.[120]

Clearly Stephens viewed women, not as individuals with basic rights and autonomy, but subsumed within the family where they received purportedly necessary protection. But what is equally important is what that protection, according to Stephens, entailed. The labor of women themselves, it seemed apparent, had not led to physical comfort, nor to the fulfillment of God's command to be fruitful and multiply, but quite the opposite. Embedded in Stephens' vision of a life of comfort for the working-class family was, then, the wife in the cottage, enjoying the fruits of what the husband was able to provide. "Woman's place" in the home was thus intimately linked to the realization of the material well-being of the entire family, considered out of the realm of possibility under prevailing conditions. "To have all the comfortable means of subsistence, to be by the side of the husband" and have children, these were "the great desire[s] of a woman's heart."[121] Invariably, then, in Stephens' sermons, the right to sufficient provision was joined with the provision of woman to man as "helpmate."

As Eileen Yeo has argued, Stephens' message then "was a message about women's protection, which spoke to the deepest concerns of many working-class women at the time."[122] It spoke to maintaining independence and dignity against the intrusion of the factory and the threat of the workhouse. To Stephens, women's protection and subordination within the patriarchal family were synonymous with economic well-being and the comforts of the cottage, and evoking the image of the latter served to give dignity to a form of working-class life that was fast disappearing.[123] Gender divisions and gender hierarchy were embedded in the united interests of class.

Appeals by Stephens and others to a domestic ideal were thus imbued with meaning which transcended the notion of domesticity for women. That domesticity was equated with well-being to which the people had a right, and it was in this context that home and the right to its comforts, to be provided by women, became an integral part of the larger political discourse.[124] Stephens, although failing to support the Chartist political plank, thus employed a language which Gareth Stedman Jones has noted is necessary for the success of a movement. By offering a diagnosis of the cause of the people's distress – their purported abandonment by their "natural" guardians – and providing a platform for its expression, he offered them the possibility that their suffering could be overcome.[125] "Understandably" I would say, where Clark says "admittedly,"[126] women gave broad support to Stephens.

What is also of significance, as was briefly suggested above, is that in giving their support to Stephens, and the Charter ultimately, women did so as members of a larger community. In early 1838 an article in the *Northern Star,* on the Stalybridge Radical Association and its efforts in support of repeal of the New Poor Law, referred to "the powerful effect which the exertions of Mr. Stephens" had had on that community. Previously the people had been "abject slaves; ever ready to prostrate themselves before the footstool of capital," claimed the article. Now, in contrast, it continued in rather apocalyptic language, thanks to Stephens' "thrilling eloquence," they were "awakened from their slumber."[127] As a result, 450 men were enrolled in the Radical Association which held political discussions twice weekly. And several thousand were reported to have signed a petition for repeal of the much-despised Poor Law, a large number in comparison with other communities, and surpassed only by Oldham.[128]

Soon women too were signing petitions, with over 2,000 signatures collected in neighboring Ashton and presented at a regional meeting of anti-Poor Law associations held in Manchester. Here the delegate from that cotton town indicated that, if there had been more time to circulate the petition among the women of the community, it would have contained 10,000 signatures.[129] A year later, reports indicated that thousands, constituting "an immense body of men and women," turned out to hear Stephens' sermons and his denunciations of the government responsible for such legislation.[130]

As the Chartist movement took hold over the following years, Dorothy Thompson writes, "the strength of the women's participation was in their own communities," and Ashton-under-Lyne was in the forefront. Often their involvement began with the campaign against the New Poor Law, as occurred here, as well as the campaign to support Stephens following his arrest on the charges of inciting the people to insurrection and disturbing the peace in November and December 1838.[131] At that time, forty assemblages responded to the news with resolutions and addresses offering support,[132] as women emerged in the forefront of the defense effort throughout the country.

In support of these causes, Thompson points out, "women worked in communities which were small enough for them to be known, and to spread their ideas through their families and through their daily work." As a part of a family and a community, they felt comfortable attending meetings and demonstrations where they were not as "liable to be harassed or insulted by strangers" as might occur in a larger city.[133] "Their presence," writes Thompson, "emphasises the community base of the movement" itself,[134] and the significance of that community base also, in turn, serves to place the issue of gender difference in perspective.

Stressing the nature of women's involvement in the Chartist movement, Thompson concludes:

> The women at this stage did not see their interests as being in opposition to those of their husbands – or if they did, they did not see any solution to such conflict in political action. Chartist women seem for the most part to have worked together with their husbands, sons and brothers in a joint opposition to oppression perceived as coming from employers and administrators.[135]

The question of a solely domestic role for women was simply not "the most burning issue" for working-class women at this time.[136] What was important was the immediate issues of adequate wages to provide for their families as well as the care and education of their children. Thus, what Thompson describes as "one of the most vivid of the female *Addresses*, that of Ashton-under-Lyne ... began with a list of grievances connected with the state of their homes and the suffering of their families." Further, it went on to emphasize the importance of the camaraderie between men and women, declaring that "we are determined that no man shall ever enjoy our hands, our hearts, or share our beds, that will not stand forward as the advocate of the rights of man, and as the determined enemy of the damnable New Poor Law."[137]

It was Stephens' fiery rhetoric in defense of the rights of man, the poor, and the working classes to which the people in general, with women in the forefront, primarily responded. He spoke directly to the people's needs when he condemned a Parliament which, he believed, should protect every class of society, but instead "suffered the rich to plunder and oppress the poor, allowed capital to stalk triumphant through the land, whilst labour lay prostrate under its feet, and permitted the capitalist, vulture-like, to suck the blood of the poor."[138] Expressing his views with such clarity and zealotry, in his own neighborhood he was seen as "no ordinary character, and no common agitator," an unassuming person of exemplary character, who gave them strength and confidence in themselves. Despite threats of dismissal from the manufacturers, people continued to follow him, and when they did lose their jobs, Stephens applied part of his own salary to their support.[139]

Rev. Joseph Rayner Stephens was not viewed simply as a champion of female domesticity, as demonstrated by the terms the women's associations employed to refer to him when he faced prosecution. In Bradford, the Female Radicals referred to him as "that persecuted friend of humanity,"[140] while the Female Radical Association of Leigh declared they would "make every exertion to aid and assist that noble, bold, and energetic patriot, the Rev. J. R. Stephens."[141] In Yorkshire, a Female Radical Association viewed with contempt the prosecution of Stephens, declaring that he was arrested because he obeyed the commands of God by preaching the Word and defending the rights of the poor.[142] The Stalybridge Female Association called on women to assist their husbands and brothers to oppose the New Poor Law and support Stephens as the "champion of the Working Classes."[143]

Women saw Stephens as a "friend of humanity," a "patriot," and a "champion of the Working Classes." Apparently, then given the level of support he received from women, he did not see his appeals to the domestic ideal in opposition to his larger message in defense of the autonomy and integrity of working-class life. Rather, the issues were presented and understood as integrally related, and on that basis women responded to his appeals. While in some ways subordinated by such a message, in the context of the period and the pressures the people of the factory district were confronting, the domestic ideal held meaning for women. Further, women may have even gained a sense of empowerment as they listened to a message that spoke to their interests and concerns. Thus, while the radical movement of the 1830s failed to address the issue of women's rights, thereby limiting its vision, it nevertheless attracted their unambiguous support.[144]

Further, in contrast to the early 1830s, that support carried over into the struggle for a Ten Hours Bill and the organized effort to obtain better wages and union recognition. Women continued to agitate alongside the men of their communities, now for improvements in their working conditions, as they increasingly moved into powerloom weaving. Again, the community of Stalybridge is prominent. And again, the picture is one of ambiguity and contradiction. For as women supported shorter hours, they did so at least partially to enable them more easily to meet what were determined to be their domestic responsibilities.

3 Shaping women's identities

The mid-century period is critical to our understanding of gender difference in the working-class culture of the cotton district. During this period, with the expansion of powerloom weaving, women came to occupy and dominate a central position within the workforce. At the same time important struggles, in which women were involved, were taking place over the issues of factory legislation and union recognition. Through these campaigns, working people attempted to gain some measure of control over their immediate circumstances, at home and at work.

For women, however, an ambiguous picture emerges. As women weavers particularly struggled for control over work time and family time, especially in defending the integrity of the Ten Hours Act, the constraints placed upon them were increasingly evident. As men were constructed as political actors, women were seen as dependent, in need of the protection of the state. Women appeared to collaborate in such an outlook, seeing themselves as responsible for the welfare of home and family. Yet women were not defined by the discourse of the family wage and respectability that emerged. Rather, their diverse experiences, dating from the mid-century period on, suggest that their identities were shaped by the range of those experiences as well as their multiple roles.

Women and weaving

Following passage of the Factory Act of 1833, the employment of children under the age of 13 in the cotton factories of the United Kingdom declined significantly, leveling off at only 8 percent in 1862 in Lancashire and Cheshire.[1] Accompanying this decline in the employment of children was an increase in the employment of young persons and particularly girls and women between the ages of 16 and 21. In that age group, the factory inspector Leonard Horner estimated that they constituted 64.5 percent of the employees as early as 1838.[2] However, it also appears that a considerable increase in the percentage of women alone employed in cotton manufacturing occurred between 1836 and 1845, while the proportion of women (over age 20) living in Lancashire and Cheshire who were employed in the cotton industry increased over the decade of the 1840s from 9.68 percent to 13.65 percent.[3] By 1871, the proportion of women employed in the cotton industry in Lancashire and Cheshire reached nearly 35 percent of the total employees. Among adults, women accounted for nearly 57 percent of employees.[4]

The continued expansion of powerloom weaving largely accounts for this increase in the proportion of girls and women employed in the cotton industry. In the early 1840s, technological advancements were introduced involving improvements in warping and sizing, delivery of the warp, and stretching of the cloth as produced which allowed the application of power to such cloths as calicoes, prints, and figured fabrics as well as quilts.[5] As a consequence, powerloom weaving began to expand geographically, especially into northeast Lancashire, where Blackburn became the center of production of plain calicoes for the India market. While the combined firm, with both weaving and spinning, continued to dominate the industry during this period, in new construction separate weaving mills predominated.[6] Thus the number of powerlooms reached 206,145 in Lancashire and Cheshire by 1850 and increased to 339,349 a decade later.[7]

Throughout the 1850s girls and women steadily made up approximately 59 percent of operatives over 13 employed in mills limited to cloth production.[8] Further, an increasing proportion of women and girls in the cotton industry came to be employed in such firms, with that percentage increasing in Lancashire and Cheshire from nearly 14 percent to over 26 percent during the 1850s.[9] Within the weaving area of northeast Lancashire, women's employment came to be most heavily concentrated in certain communities, particularly Preston, Chorley, and Accrington. Here the surrounding agricultural areas provided the main source of labor while in Stockport, Ashton, and Stalybridge the employment of Irish girls and women increased.[10]

With a return of prosperity following the economic crisis of the late 1840s, weavers' wages in general attained an average of approximately 11s. per week, with three-loom weavers earning over 15s. These wages compared favorably to those prevailing in other occupations where women and girls also predominated, such as drawing and tenting, where wages approximated 8s. to 9s. per week.[11] Perhaps most significantly, since weaving was not a sex-segregated occupation and the operatives were paid by the piece, women weavers earned the same piece-rates as men, although the latter often earned higher weekly wages by operating more looms.[12]

Ten Hours and gender difference

With this growth in the employment of girls and women came a renewed interest in further shorter hours legislation, now with·a shift in emphasis from children to women and young persons. In 1840, in testimony before the Select Committee appointed to review the operation of existing legislation, Leonard Horner took note of this alteration in employment patterns and, for that reason, recommended that the working hours of all operatives under 21 be restricted to twelve.[13] The following year, several short time committees were reorganized and a delegation from the West Riding of Yorkshire was sent to London to meet with a number of government ministers.[14] At a meeting with Sir Robert Peel, the delegation proposed a Bill to limit the working hours of those between the ages of 13 and 21 to ten per day. Such protection for this age group was urgent, the delegation noted, due to the increase of girls and women employed at that age.[15]

From this time until the passage of the Ten Hours Bill in 1847, "the question of shorter hours centered round the women."[16] Noting that "there are great difficulties in the way of legislative interference with the labour of men," Leonard Horner drew the conclusion that:

> The case, however, is very different as respects women; for not only are they much less free agents, but they are physically incapable of bearing a continuance of work for the same length of time as men, and a deterioration of their health is attended with far more injurious consequences to society. The substitution of female for male labour, which has increased to so great an extent of late years, is attended with the worst consequences to the social condition of the working classes, by the women being withdrawn from domestic duties . . .[17]

Noting that restrictions on female labor "would operate as a premium upon male labour," Horner went on to recommend that female employment be limited to twelve hours per day.[18]

This demand was especially popular during the commercial distress of 1841–2 when a major strike wave was provoked throughout the cotton district in reaction to a number of mill owners in Ashton and Stalybridge giving notice of upcoming wage reductions in August 1842.[19] With the revival of trade the following year, the widespread employment of women again became a major issue as mills began to work over twelve hours per day, often employing women from 5.30 a.m. to 8.00 p.m.[20] Referring to this situation, Leonard Horner stated:

> A theorist may say that these people are old enough to take care of themselves; but practically there can be no such thing as freedom of labour, when, from the redundancy of population, there is such a competition for employment.[21]

In accordance with Horner's views, support for restricting the working hours of women, even though adults, began to grow in Parliament. In February of 1844, a Bill was introduced which included women among those whose labor was to be restricted to twelve hours. Lord Ashley then introduced a Ten Hours Amendment which gained widespread support in the manufacturing districts, where numerous mass meetings were held.[22] As previously, throughout the agitation the plight of the woman factory operative gained considerable attention.

The inability of women to defend themselves against the evils of the factory, and the usual lament concerning women's employment outside the home were constant themes of these meetings. The problem of mothers nursing their infants while working in factories, unable to provide the necessary nourishment, was particularly noted.[23] In the course of his defense following his arrest during the upheaval of 1842, the Chartist and handloom weaver Richard Pilling related "the evil workings of the accursed system" where husbands carried their infants to the mills to be nursed and brought breakfast to their wives.[24] While the Ten Hours Amendment was defeated, the campaign culminated with passage of the Act of 1844 which brought women under the purview of factory legislation for the first time, prohibiting them, along with young persons, from working more than twelve hours per day.[25]

Following this limited success, a revival of the Ten Hours campaign was not long in coming, and again the hardship suffered by women working in the factories was a central theme. From its earliest number the *Ten Hours' Advocate*, organ of the Lancashire Central Short Time Committee, was filled with commonly voiced regrets concerning the necessity of women's employment. In a letter to the editor, an "Observer" decried the fact that "so many wives of mechanics and artisans may be seen going to a cotton mill half an hour before their husbands leave home in a morning, and returning two hours after them at night."[26] An article reprinted from the *Halifax Guardian* lamented "that nearly 2,000 married women are taken from their proper sphere in the family, and confined all day in the mill."[27] A further article reprinted from the *Standard* voiced the familiar desire for the day "when the husband will be enabled to provide for his wife and family, without sending the former to endure the drudgery of a cotton mill."[28] And along with Rev. Joseph Rayner Stephens, Richard Oastler too added his voice to the agitation, declaring, in the paternalist tradition which he and Stephens personified, "We want to see woman in her right place, on her own hearthstone, making it ready and comfortable for her industrious husband, when he returns to his meals and to his bed at night."[29]

As with the Chartist agitation before it, the notion of gender difference was central to the factory movement, as Robert Gray has argued. Popular radicalism, he contends, "attempted to empower the adult male worker as citizen, resisting the impositions of arbitrary power in the workplace and the wider polity," while women emerged as dependent beneficiaries of reforms. Yet he also recognizes that, while a notion of separate spheres was fundamental to the debate over factory legislation, "the reality was a network of interdependencies, in which the contributions of all household members were crucial."[30] Exclusionary rhetoric, then, suggesting that women's place was in the domestic realm, was associated with speeches from the platform rather than formal programs. The desire for a prohibition on women's employment remained an aspiration rather than a strategy. Men were to be the principal breadwinners, not necessarily the sole wage earners. Yet the significance of such a language of patriarchal protection, Gray concludes, should not be minimized for it expressed "a pervasive set of assumptions about free labour, masculinity and independent and dependant statuses."[31] The factory agitation was then "one important expression of a class-conscious working-class radicalism" that contained within it a clear notion of gender hierarchy.[32]

While concurring generally with this conclusion, I would suggest, nevertheless, that it remains necessary to explore further the tensions pointed to by Gray. For while it is important to emphasize the meanings inherent in the language of patriarchal protection, it is equally important to examine fully the position of women as supposed dependent beneficiaries of such protection as well as the tensions within that formulation. As gender and class were constructed simultaneously, women were part of that process, not simply "undifferentiated victims of allied economic and ideological forces," as Jane Humphries has pointed out.[33] As we have seen, women had been marginalized in the context of the factory movement of the early 1830s. Since that time, however, two significant developments potentially affecting women's position had taken place. Many women had become more fully integrated into the workforce, employed in a central area of cloth production, powerloom weaving, and earning equal piece-rates working alongside their male counterparts, whose entry into the factories in that capacity was generally more recent. Further, in the context of the mass platform employed by the factory, anti-Poor Law, and Chartist movements of the mid- to late 1830s and early 1840s, despite the rhetoric of domesticity employed, or perhaps even to some degree because of it, women had emerged as actors in their respective communities, struggling alongside men for the dignity of working-class life. The fracturing of class by gender even within this context was apparent, as evidenced by the preceding discussion. However, the extension of class interests across gender lines and the active role of women themselves in shaping their identities, even from the margins and within established constraints, must be considered as well.

In the context of the factory movement, even as laments were expressed regarding the necessity of women's paid labor, the actual exclusion of women from the workforce was not seriously put forward as a strategy, as Gray points out. Beyond that, it must also be added that the rhetoric was no longer solely focused on the purported need for women to be protected in the domestic realm. That both women and men would contribute wages to the household was now frequently assumed. Accordingly, during the power-loom weavers' strike of 1842, support for Ten Hours legislation was accompanied, not by the demand for an end to the employment of girls and women, but by the demand for an end to their employment at lower wages.[34] Thus, when Richard Pilling led a deputation to Orrell's and Bradshaw's mills in Stockport to request the employment of men, the issue was the apparent policy of employing only women, rather than their withdrawal and replacement by men. Thus, Pilling reported, "One female requested most earnestly that her husband might be allowed to go and work alongside of her, but she was refused."[35]

A survey conducted by Leonard Horner in the cotton district following passage of the Ten Hours Act of 1847 provides us with further insight into the interplay between home and work in the lives of women themselves.[36] While a majority of female operatives supported reduced hours of labor, to be discussed further below, some married women expressed a desire to return to twelve hours, indicating the importance of their role as wage earners to their families. Three married women employed at roving frames at one mill, for example, indicated a preference for twelve hours "to get more money." A throstle-frame tenter declared she "would rather work 12 hours for more wages," and her sentiments were echoed by several others in the same occupation at several mills. In addressing the issue of hours of work, men and women also pointed to the importance of their joint earnings. A male weaver, whose wife was also a weaver in the same factory and earned more money working broad looms, indicated his preference for twelve hours in order to make higher wages and added that his wife "is of the same mind as himself." A minder, married with one child, indicated he "would prefer working 12 hours, having a family to provide for." He then added that his "wife works in the factory and gets 7s. a-week, but pays 3s. out of that for nursing her child; thinks the higher wages would do better for them." Other operatives, voicing their support for ten hours of labor, indicated they did so in agreement with their husband or wife, also employed, suggesting a mutual expectation that they both would contribute to the family earnings. Only in two instances in the larger mills visited by Horner did male spin-ners indicate they needed higher wages because they had wives to support.

Rather than protection for women, the Ten Hours campaign was increas-ingly about improving conditions of work and gaining some control over those conditions. As such, it was based on a mutuality of interests among the operatives that transcended gender lines. In this effort, then, support from women themselves was increasingly visible.

Women, the Ten Hours Act, and its defense

The first indication that women were beginning to lend visible support to the campaign came from Preston where Robert Gardner, a manufacturer employ-ing over 650 operatives in a firm comprised of both a weaving and a spinning mill, voluntarily reduced working hours from twelve to eleven in April of 1844. One year later the workers of this firm held a festival marking this event and expressing their support, especially noting that neither wages nor production had decreased as a result of shorter hours. The female operatives were especially vocal in expressing their satisfaction with the new system, mentioning that they now had more time for domestic chores.[37]

Further evidence indicates that male leaders of the campaign began to encourage greater female participation through meetings involving women workers and publication of the *Ten Hours' Advocate* during 1846–7. At a meeting of powerloom weavers in Manchester in September of 1845, at which "a considerable number of boys and young women" were present,[38] Edward Darwen moved:

> That this meeting of powerloom weavers has long felt the necessity of a reduction in the hours of labour in factories, more especially as a large number of persons employed therein are females, who are, by the excessive toil to which they are subjected, deprived of all means of acquiring that education, both moral and domestic, which is so indispensable to their station in life, to enable them to perform those duties for which nature and circumstances have designed them.[39]

Implicit in this resolution was the notion that women belonged at home while men labored to support them, but it was clearly only a reduction in hours that was being sought. This resolution was then followed by a second, indicating that the weavers in general, both men and women, intended to play a more active part in promoting the Ten Hours Bill in the next session of Parliament, by sending petitions to the House of Commons, and memorializing the Queen. In the latter personage they expressed "the greatest confidence, that she [would] use her royal influence on behalf of those of her sex who are employed in factories."[40]

Powerloom weavers, including women, increasingly came forward on their own behalf, contributing money on a weekly basis to the campaign. Meetings of cardroom hands, where women were in the majority, were held and funds were raised.[41] At one such meeting the operatives protested at the action of a number of masters who asked their employees about their opinion of the Ten Hours Bill and recorded the information obtained.[42] The *Advocate* indicated that in Padiham, "All the factory workers in this district, both male and female, seem to look upon this question as one of the greatest blessings government can give to them."[43] The question of whether or not women could sign petitions was raised in the *Advocate*,[44] indicating an interest among women in participating in this aspect of the campaign.

It is difficult to judge, on the basis of scant evidence, to what extent these reports reflected a new awareness and involvement among women between the passage of the Act of 1844 and the Ten Hours Act of 1847. While there are indications that greater support for factory legislation was emerging among women, reports continued to circulate concerning a lack of interest among female operatives. The Secretary to the Lancashire Short Time Committee, writing to the *Advocate* in December of 1846, noted the lack of response among cardroom hands and powerloom weavers, mostly women, to fund appeals.[45] In a letter to the editor of the same journal, "Elizabeth," an operative employed at Wadsworth Mill near Todmorden, expressed her regrets concerning "the apathy that is manifested by my sex generally."[46] But the fact that a female operative even wrote a letter to the editor, voicing her concerns regarding women's position in the movement, is of considerable significance, particularly since "Elizabeth" was not content merely to note the apparent "apathy" among women, but also attempted to account for it and consider ways of overcoming it.

To "Elizabeth," the shorter hours campaign was an "important struggle for the liberty of our sex, and the protection of our children." Yet, to many female operatives, shorter hours represented only a means of reducing wages. Such an objection, "Elizabeth" noted, resulted from a misunderstanding of the laws of wages which could be answered if women read the *Advocate*. This solution was, however, unattainable, "Elizabeth" pointed out, since "unhappily for our sex, a large majority of them cannot read." Not only was illiteracy a barrier to women's involvement, but the atmosphere of mill work and the long hours of labor rendered women "unfit for any attempt at mental improvement." As a result, "Elizabeth" concluded, women's views were often "narrow and contracted," making it impossible for them to come forward as the major force in the shorter hours agitation. Even so, "Elizabeth" contended, women could be "a powerful auxiliary" in the campaign. She went on to prove her contention by collecting £8 from the workers in her mill for the Short Time Committee.[47]

In 1847, women were not yet the "powerful auxiliary" that "Elizabeth" desired, but neither was her point of view unique among women workers. Certainly the definite opposition to shorter hours legislation expressed by women a decade earlier appears to have declined. After the Act of 1844 had been in operation for approximately one year, Leonard Horner reported that, "No instances have come to my knowledge of adult women having expressed any regret at their *rights* being thus far interfered with."[48] Thus, it appears that the Ten Hours Act of 1847, which restricted the labor of women and young persons to ten per day and fifty-eight per week as of 1 May 1848,[49] came into effect amid growing support from those most imminently affected by it.

This support for the Act, and willingness to struggle for its proper enforcement, became clear as soon as it was put into effect. In Bury, the cardroom hands at Richard Kay's mills, including a large proportion of women, went on strike following the employer's attempt to reduce wages by 2s. per week due to the reduction in working hours to ten per day.[50] Before the Act had been in effect for a month, the *Manchester Guardian* reported that, "The operatives in Blackburn manifest decided dissatisfaction with the mode in which some mill owners seem disposed to carry the act into effect."[51] Specifically, the operatives objected to the replacement of women by adult males, who were then separated from the women and young persons in order to facilitate operation of the mills longer than ten hours per day. At James Pemberton's mill, when a proposal to work in this manner was put forward, the men first turned out alone in response. However, they were followed by the rest of the employees the next day. A public meeting attended by approximately 15,000 operatives was then held in support of the strike, and a petition addressed to the House of Commons was drawn up expressing "the deep disappointment we experience from the working of the Ten-Hours' Factory Bills." The operatives then went on to request an extension of the Act to cover adult males.[52]

Such disputes were generally settled with the adoption of the ten-hour day.[53] But perhaps most significant was the support that women apparently gave in these instances to the struggle for the ten-hour day as the uniform standard for all employees. Although the shorter work day had already been achieved for themselves and persons under 18, women now appeared to be willing to fight for its extension to men, even if it meant going on strike. Such action reflects a deeper commitment among women to the cause of shorter hours than had been apparent at any time previously.

The survey conducted by Leonard Horner, referred to above, indicates that, indeed, a majority of women had come to prefer ten hours of labor, even if it meant a reduction in wages. Operatives were asked to respond to the following question:

> Suppose there were three mills near together, in each of which the work was the same and all equally convenient to you, one of them working 10 hours a-day, where you would get 10s. a week, another working 11 hours where you would get 11s., and the other working 12 hours where you would get 12s., which of the three would you like to work in?[54]

Of 1,153 operatives over the age of 17 who were employed in the larger mills in Horner's district, 713 or 61.84 percent preferred ten hours; 147 or 12.75 percent preferred eleven hours; while 293 or 25.41 percent preferred twelve hours. Among men, the proportion preferring ten hours was 67.74 percent. Among women, the proportion was considerably lower at 54.18 percent, but it too constituted majority sentiment.[55] Single women, who generally gave over their wages to their parents and who did not believe they benefitted from additional leisure time, often voiced a desire to return to twelve hours. But the primary difference in views between men and women can largely be attributed to the continued employment of women in such low-paying occupations as throstle-spinning, reeling, and frame-tenting, where women expressed their opposition to shorter hours due to the accompanying wage cuts.

Of three women employed on roving-frames, Leonard Horner reported, "All say they would prefer working 12 hours to get higher wages; that the time in the evening is of no value to them; that they have to pay the same house-rent" and needed an adequate income to cover such expenses. A married woman, aged 40 and employed as a reeler, indicated that she, "Much dislikes the restriction to 10 hours, as her wages have been so much reduced." She went on to say that she "knows that the reelers are very generally opposed to the restriction, and would gladly work 12 hours." Others also indicated that they were aware of strong sentiment among women against the restriction to ten hours. A married cardroom worker, who was reported to be "most anxious for a return to the 12 hours restriction, as the alteration to 10 hours has had so serious an effect upon her wages," believed "this to be the decided opinion of the great majority of females employed in factories." At least she knew "it to be the opinion of scores with whom she has conversed."

In those factories where the owner, manager, and/or overlooker expressed opposition to the Ten Hours Act, the opinions of the operatives were at times in agreement with their superiors. However, it was also common for operatives to support the Act when their employers did not. Most important for our purposes, it appears that it was just as common for women as it was for men to take a position in opposition to that of their employers. Having gained a relatively solid position in one of the two central operations in the industry, and experienced an increase in wages, the increase in security that women realized as powerloom weavers meant that intimidation was apparently less of a factor than in the early 1830s. This conclusion is further borne out by the fact that, where divisions of opinion regarding the Ten Hours Act occurred in a single factory, they were not along gender lines but, rather, along occupational lines. While weavers and spinners often defended the Act, lower-paid workers frequently did not. Among weavers, the support for ten hours among men and women was identical, at 67.5 percent.

Those workers who supported the reduction in hours did so primarily because they felt that their health had improved and they appreciated the increased time they were able to spend with their families. Both men and women expressed such views. Particularly among women weavers, a growing sense of solidarity with their fellow workers is also apparent. Asked about the working of the Ten Hours Act, they often responded not only with their own opinion but added their impression of the opinions of others as well. In addition, they noted not only the benefit that they themselves derived from shorter hours, but also indicated that it was a question of rights – that no one should be expected to work any longer. The following responses may be considered typical:

> thinks it quite long enough to work, and believes that others think as she does. Ten hours is long enough for anyone to work, be the wages what they may, that no person ought to be employed during more than 10 hours daily.

> thinks that the great majority of her fellow-workers are completely satisfied with the restriction to 10 hours, and will never work during longer hours unless they are compelled.

Perhaps of greatest interest, however, is the determination expressed among the women weavers that all operatives should work the same regular hours, a view consistent with that voiced in connection with the strike at Pemberton's. At the time this survey was taken, this issue became increasingly significant in areas where mill owners were instituting a system of working women and young persons in shifts or relays, to be discussed further below. Many women interviewed referred to this system in their responses, expressing a desire for identical working hours among all employees. For example, two women weavers declared:

> I think 10 hours long enough, if we could all do regular and work the same time, but it is disagreeable looking to go out and leave the men working at the looms.

> I have more ease and can do more for my children when I get home. I want fellies to do 10 too.

Many women, and men as well, concluded that eleven hours would be a reasonable solution, agreeable to the employers, enabling all operatives to work the same hours. One woman weaver indicated that she would "prefer 11 hours, unless the men were not allowed to work more than 10." Another stated that she would "prefer 11 hours if all worked alike though for herself 10 hours is long enough."

The trend that emerges most forcefully in these comments is that of individual interest being superseded by the interests of the operatives as a whole. In some instances, individuals even expressed a willingness to sacrifice increased wages because it was the right of workers in general to have some leisure time. The case of four women weavers is particularly striking for the confidence they expressed in the workers' ability to realize their objectives. They indicated that, although they suffered a loss in wages, they "would strongly object to a return to 12 hours of labor, as they fully anticipate eventually to receive 12 hours' wages for 10 hours' work."

The depth of women's support for the Ten Hours Act was most apparent in those areas where the relay system was introduced. Under this system, mill owners evaded the intent of the Act by working women and young persons in shifts or relays, which allowed the machinery to be operated for up to twelve or fourteen hours, with men working the full time. Such action was made possible by the fact that the Act of 1844, which was still in effect, provided for the work of protected operatives to begin simultaneously, but did not specify that hours be consecutive. Thus it was argued that it was perfectly legal to employ women and young persons for several hours in the morning, release them for one to three hours later in the day, and then require them to work until perhaps 7.30 p.m., as long as their working hours did not exceed ten.[56] By April 1849, this relay system had been widely adopted, especially in the areas of Ashton, Stalybridge, Stockport, and Oldham.[57] In all, Leonard Horner estimated that 114 mill owners were using shifts, which enabled them to run their mills on overtime.[58]

Women expressed intense opposition to the relay system, as indicated in a letter to the *Ashton Chronicle* by a correspondent who, upon seeing a number of operatives leaving work at midday at Leech's mill in Stalybridge during January 1849, enquired of a woman worker if a strike had occurred. Responding that "it is something a good deal worse than that," the woman declared:

> They have begun a new trick this morning. They are working us in gangs now; our master is doing all he can to plague us out of our lives and get us to curse the Ten Hours Bill. We are working *shifts* . . . we are kept at it, backwards and forwards, here and there, from half-past five until eight o'clock. We can make no use of this time, but make it away as we can. There are some who are a good way from home that walk up and down anywhere, or go with a friend to their house. Others harbour with neighbours or shelter in beer houses. We are forced to skulk about and put the time in the best we know how, some one fashion and some another.[59]

Seeing that the purpose of the relay system was to "get us to curse the Ten Hours Bill," women began to take concerted action against it. In February, 600 weavers employed at the mills of Sir William Feilden and Son objected to the intention of the owners to employ men eleven or twelve hours per day, potentially allowing the introduction of the relay system.[60] The matter was apparently settled in mid-March when the men agreed to work one half-hour after the women left work and during the half-hour break for tea.[61]

This action was soon followed by another at the mill of John Leech of Stalybridge. Here, on 30 March, the women in his employ began stopping their looms after ten hours, although they had not been working during that entire period due to the system of shifts. This action prompted Leech himself to order the engines to be stopped, thus initiating a lockout.[62] The *Morning Post* then reported:

> During the whole of this week the town of Stalybridge has been kept in a state of agitation owing to the determination of females and young persons employed at various mills not to continue upon the plan lately adopted by several masters of working by "shifts" or relays.[63]

The following week, the weavers' department at Cheetham's mill was also stopped, but Leech's operatives returned. However, at the latter mill some weavers continued to stop work at 5.30 and refused to mind the looms of weavers out on shift. Reported the *Ashton Chronicle*, "No means have as yet been adopted calculated to force the relay system into operation again. Overlookers, bookkeepers, etc., have done all they could to effect this, but the sternness of the women has still prevailed."[64]

Over the following week, while attempts made at Leech's to institute the relay system continued to meet opposition, the unity of the weavers gradually began to break down.[65] Finally, Leech's discharged three women "charged with being the ringleaders of the resistance to the relay-system."[66] Deputations of men and women then met with two other manufacturers, Hindley and Cheetham. The former agreed to close his factory after ten hours, while the latter insisted on operation of the relay system.[67] Reported the *Ashton Chronicle*, "By cursing, swearing, lying and intimidation of every sort the relay-system seems now to be got on the swing again."[68] Thus, "the sternness of the women" was not sufficient to put an end to the relay system immediately.

Court action, however, eventually led to its prohibition although its success was slow in coming. Only after a series of unsuccessful prosecutions, in which women frequently testified, despite jeopardizing their jobs,[69] was a new Act (13 & 14 Vict. c. 54) passed declaring the relay system to be illegal and setting the working day for young persons and women between the hours of 6.00 a.m. and 6.00 p.m. or 7.00 a.m. and 7.00 p.m. in winter. One-and-a-half hours were to be allowed for meals, meaning that the actual working day had been extended from ten to ten-and-a-half hours. Children between the ages of 8 and 13, however, remained under the Act of 1844, which allowed their employment between 5.30 a.m. and 8.30 p.m. Not until the Act of 1853 (16 & 17 Vict. c. 104) was the employment of children before and after that of young persons and women prohibited. With this legislation, restriction on the moving power, which the men of Lancashire had championed since the early 1830s, was implicitly conceded with the notable support of women.[70]

Furthermore, over the next quarter-century, such liberal employers as Cheetham's and Leech's "consolidated their wealth and power and mellowed many of their attitudes and policies towards labour," emerging "at the forefront of the new paternalism."[71] According to Patrick Joyce, in those areas where the large combined firms predominated, as in the southeast, the factories became the center of social life, with employers organizing trips to the countryside, dinners, teas, and sports days as well as providing libraries and reading rooms for their employees.[72] As evidenced by the events of 1849, such measures must be viewed as a defensive response on the part of employers, as Richard Price has argued. Workers' responses to employer intransigence necessitated the striking of a new balance, if conflicts were to be peacefully resolved and a stable, reliable workforce was to be maintained.[73] The paternalism of the 1850s must, therefore, be viewed against the background of the militant struggles waged by the women of Ashton and Stalybridge in 1849. It is, however, the implications of this struggle for gender relations, family, and gender meanings that are of most significance here.

Control over time and its uses

The struggle for shorter hours had become less of a campaign for protection of women in the home and more expressive of the desire among both women and men for control over their time – family time and work time – as demonstrated above. "Thinks she has been long enough away from her children when she has been away 10 hours"[74] was a typical comment of married women with children, implying the necessity of their labor while expressing appreciation for the additional time with their families made possible by the Ten Hours Act. Significantly, male workers voiced similar sentiments. Thus, four male spinners, unwillingly working eleven-and-a-half hours since their labor was not covered under the Act, indicated "they find their health improved, and they have more enjoyment with their families" when working shorter hours.[75] Expanding on this theme, a male weaver with four children expressed his willingness to sacrifice in the interest of his family, a sentiment that was frequently repeated. He indicated that he "would rather work 10 hours though getting less; finds his health better, and thinks it best for his family; finds that he can do with a meal-a-day less; one's brain is not so muddled as it is when working so long as 12."[76] Further expressions of concern for his family and future generations came from a male weaver whose son was a piecer. He stated, "I speak not for myself, but for the young ones whose health will be a great deal better, I believe, for the Ten Hours Bill."[77]

Loss of control over the mutual enjoyment of leisure time by husbands and wives was particularly resented by cotton workers when the relay system was imposed. As the operatives from Over Darwen declared, it "totally deprives them of those domestic comforts which it was the object of the Ten Hours Act to afford them."[78] George Cowell, later noted for his dramatic rhetoric in connection with the Preston strike of 1853–4, maintained that it was in the interests of all operatives to eliminate the relay system "so that male and female workers should enjoy their leisure together, at their own firesides, in walking abroad, reading their Bible, or in deriving delight from perusing the works of the greatest minds that had ever lived."[79]

Although generally expressed somewhat less eloquently, a common interest expressed by the operatives at this time was the desire to make effective use of the additional time the Ten Hours Act allowed. Many workers, both male and female, interviewed by Leonard Horner and the sub-inspectors for the survey referred to above, indicated their support for the Ten Hours Act due to the opportunity it afforded them to attend evening school and to engage in reading.[80] "The 10 hours give one time for sewing and reading," remarked a winder.[81] A male weaver reported that "there is a great desire for instruction and increase of reading in the neighbourhood."[82] A single woman, aged 23, working as a throstle-piecer, said she "employs her time in the evening in sewing, and reading the Scriptures; knows many who have learned more sewing and reading since the Ten Hours Bill began, than ever they did in their whole lives before."[83]

In a survey conducted for the *Morning Chronicle* in the textile district during the fall of 1849, Angus Reach further noted the considerable attendance of both girls and young men at evening school.[84] Girls in particular, one master reported, often returned to the factory school after completing their lessons, to use the library. Further, women often attended adult classes, bringing their children if necessary.[85] Undoubtedly, the Sunday schools were the most important institutions in providing educational opportunities for young people and adults, and here men and women attended equally. Some observers, including Reach, even indicated that women were more eager to attend than men and that girls often remained in schools longer than boys.[86]

For women, however, there was an added dimension, as evidenced by their frequent coupling of time for reading and time for sewing. Positioned as wives and mothers, constraints were placed upon them as they were expected to use their additional time to fulfill their domestic obligations. In some ways, then, shortening the hours of labor may be viewed as reinforcing women's domestic role. Yet that role must not be seen merely in terms of subordination. For as women, along with their male counterparts, sought to gain increased control over their conditions of work, they also viewed the home as an arena in which their autonomy and authority were expressed.

Domesticity, respectability, and activism

During this period, despite women's increased employment and participation in the agitations for shorter hours and union recognition, appeals to the notion of domesticity were pervasive. As June Purvis has demonstrated, the Mechanics' Institutes often made deliberate attempts to exclude women, admitting them only to the lectures and library, or limiting the female curriculum to reading, writing, arithmetic, general knowledge, and, of course, sewing.[87] Reflecting the emphasis placed on domestic training, Charles Dickens, at the annual meeting of the Institutional Association of Lancashire and Cheshire, praised the women of Preston for demonstrating in their examination papers "such an admirable knowledge of the science of household management and household economy."[88] As Clare Evans has demonstrated, this emphasis was particularly evident during the cotton famine brought on by the American Civil War, when married women, rather than being considered unemployed workers, were viewed simply as women, and therefore encouraged to attend sewing schools.[89]

Further, it is apparent that, rather than enjoying the domestic comforts as a result of shorter hours, women were generally engaged in providing them. As Angus Reach reported, with the earlier closing of the mills, Saturday had become "the great weekly epoch of cleansing and setting things to rights in the houses of the Manchester workpeople."[90] At that time, he waxed eloquently, exhibiting his own prejudices, "you will marvel and rejoice at the universality of the purification which is going forward."[91]

Women thus used much of the time newly afforded them to attend to their domestic chores, and it is probably safe to assume that they did not marvel and rejoice as they did so. Yet it is also clear that to a considerable extent they sought "their social definition through their domestic and mothering roles."[92] Women were grateful for the additional time to do their chores and took pride in their accomplishment. "'I have time now to clean my house, and I do it, too, every evening,' [was] the phrase I have heard repeated a hundred times by the tenters and female weavers," Reach reported.[93] Similarly, a woman piecer proudly declared, in response to the factory inspectors conducting their survey, "Has done more with her needle since the 10 hours began than she had done all her life before."[94] Further, a married woman weaver stated, "We can now do something for ourselves at night, and it is better for us."[95]

Women also appreciated the independence they gained as a result of shorter working hours. Particularly representative was the oft-repeated comment of a married woman weaver who indicated to the factory inspectors that, as a result of the Ten Hours Act, she "has not to pay neighbours for working for her . . . for she finds time to do [it] herself."[96] And a woman working at a throstle-frame further declared, "if the money is a trifle less," she has the "privilege" of doing "what is necessary for herself and family at home."[97]

The increase in time now available to women, it appears, did indeed serve to reinforce the sense of fulfillment they may have gained from their domestic role. The pride that women took in their household labor echoed into the next century in the oral evidence, collected by Elizabeth Roberts, from women in Preston, Barrow, and Lancaster. For example, a Mrs. Mitchell related memories of her home in the 1920s as follows:

> There was no carpet or anything on the stairs. They were wooden, and the table tops were wood with polished legs, but it was who could have the whitest table top. The stairs were scrubbed every day, they shone snow-white, the wood spotless. . . .
> [Asked,] Did you ever whitewash the yard?
> [She responded,] Oh, everybody whitewashed. My yard was beautiful.[98]

Women clearly "derived a sense of self-worth" from their accomplishments and the authority they exercised in the domestic realm.[99] The possibility of devoting themselves fully to home and family thus could not help but appear attractive to many.[100] In her study of working-class housewives, based on allowing her subjects to "speak for themselves," Joanna Bourke has concluded that "many women thought that housewifery was a good – even the *best* – option." Even an intensification of labor in that realm was considered acceptable by women "because it was seen as a better and less risky way of increasing their power over their own lives and the lives of their families." An improvement in living standards accompanied by a decline in domestic abuse was generally the result.[101] Accordingly, Roberts concludes that women "rarely had any ambition to go on earning wages all their lives and regarded it as a matter of social progress and of status to be able to give up wage-earning work."[102] Due to the burdens of the double shift, women were most likely to realize that sense of the central importance of their contribution through their domestic labor. Family wage rhetoric, suggesting that men should be the breadwinners, thus had a complex history.

The issue of the family wage began to be raised in the early 1850s in conjunction with a number of strikes in the weaving district. In the midst of the Preston labor crisis of 1853–4, Margaret Fletcher, speaking to a large gathering of strikers, declared that the natural order of things was now reversed, with women going to work (especially common in Preston) while men took care of the household. A man must have a fair day's wage for a fair day's work, she maintained, providing sufficient wages to support himself and his family in comfort, thereby enabling the wife to remain at home to attend to household tasks and educate the children. It was "a disgrace to an Englishman to allow his wife to go out to work," she declared.[103] Following upon Fletcher's comments, the meeting passed a resolution declaring "That the married portion of the females in this town do not intend to go to work any more until their husbands are fully and fairly remunerated," and the chairman indicated that when the 10 percent wage increase was realized, there would be an agitation raised on behalf of married women working in factories.[104]

In Blackburn and Burnley, men were more likely to labor alongside women in powerloom weaving, due to a lack of alternative employment and a greater willingness, compared to their counterparts from south Lancashire, to abandon handloom weaving.[105] Here too, in 1859–61, during strikes in Padiham, near Burnley, as well as in Blackburn, support was voiced for the family wage. On one occasion, the Blackburn weavers resolved that "no man should allow his wife to work in the mill when she had two children to take care of."[106] During a major strike in 1878, centered in the northern weaving district, the operatives at Clayton-le-Moors reported that, of 400 looms, 60 were worked by married women. A speaker at a meeting of strikers then called on men to keep their wives at home, serving to prevent overproduction.[107] During this strike generally, Sonya Rose has argued, "trade union leaders used family-wage rhetoric . . . to inspire solidarity." Their language, she further maintains, "placed male workers in the center of the struggle" while, for women, "it was their family status that defined them."[108]

The notion of "woman's place" residing in the domestic realm, states Neville Kirk, was "widely articulated, and quickly assumed the status of natural common sense, not only in the male-dominated areas . . . but also in sectors, such as cotton textiles, in which paid women workers were present in large numbers."[109] The concept of the family wage, increasingly articulated by male trade union leaders, appears to have become the cornerstone of such an outlook. And its effectiveness is apparent in the general silencing of the voice of the woman worker over the same period, as she was less and less involved in politics and trade union affairs, even in the cotton district.

Yet it is suggested here that the history of the concept is complex and those complexities are of some significance in considering constructions of gender and the significance of gender difference in working-class culture. As has been brought out here, the origins of the concept lay in the mutual struggle for control over work time and family time, as well as in the understanding, often shared by women and men, that women were secondary laborers who were mainly responsible for the care of home and family. The ideal of the family wage thus underlay a working-class desire for respectability grounded in collectivity as well as inequality, a point made by Jane Humphries some years ago.[110] It also circulated in a context marked by a wide "gap between the prevailing ideology and the reality of women's economic roles."[111] While the rhetoric of the family wage was then pervasive, its significance as a strategy, as with the domestic ideal expressed by the Chartists at an earlier date, is questionable. Whether men were really expected to be not only the primary but the sole breadwinner is certainly brought into question[112] when we consider the limits within which the family wage at times was proposed, as with the Blackburn weavers who proposed it for women who "had two children to take care of." And in Preston, Michael Savage points out, with the continued expansion of weaving, men initially "seemed content to allow women into the weaving sector."[113] Certainly at the mid-century period, stated intentions to the contrary, nowhere was the demand for the withdrawal of married women from the cotton factories seriously pursued. Indeed, in a recent article, Anna Clark has effectively argued that the idea of a breadwinner wage only came to be recognized as a right with the unemployment insurance Act of 1908.[114] A life of "industry, thrift and sobriety" based on a division of labor within the family was key to working-class respectability and may have served as "a practical safeguard against recurrent threats of insecurity, poverty and unemployment,"[115] but so did the largely unquestioned work of wives at least at some point in their marriage into the twentieth century.

Even as the ideal of the family wage was put forward, a strong tradition of mutuality was also in evidence among male and female weavers in struggles at the workplace for improved wages, a standard list, and union recognition. In all the major strikes involving powerloom weavers at mid-century the participation of women is evident, suggesting their thorough integration into the workforce despite a family wage rhetoric. As early as 1840, women weavers employed in Bradshaws' firm in Stockport, which hired only female labor, played a militant role in a strike brought on by a reduction in wages. This strike was to last eight weeks and involve 6,000 workers.[116] During the labor upheaval of 1842, 7,000 to 8,000 Manchester powerloom weavers remained on strike for seven weeks. From the beginning of this strike, Mick Jenkins contends, women "displayed the same tenacity and courage as the men" as they participated alongside them "in all the mass actions that took place."[117]

The following year witnessed a rash of strikes among powerloom weavers for advances in wages, particularly in the Ashton area, where women and girls predominated.[118] The Preston lockout of 1853–4 was instigated by the discharging of two women, "occupied as beamers or warpers," who were considered "ringleaders" in collecting subscriptions for operatives already on strike in Stockport.[119] As this dispute sharpened to become the most intense conflict of the decade, a familiar sight was "the appearance of female delegates, who travelled about and spoke at the public meetings with all the energy, and perhaps more than the loquacity of the male coadjutors."[120]

In the major strikes that occurred in 1858–61 throughout the outlying northern weaving districts to bring wages up to the Blackburn Standard List, women's support is apparent.[121] At meetings held in Burnley and Accrington in support of the strike in Padiham, the weavers' representatives stressed the importance of women's involvement in the strike itself as well as support activities.[122] In Colne, the employers honored women by including them on a list of the "most intelligent" operatives engaged in that turnout – for the purpose of blacklisting.[123] By 1860, Andrew Bullen has estimated that the North-East Lancashire Powerloom Weavers Association and Blackburn Association together enrolled approximately 70 percent of the weavers in north Lancashire.[124] Undoubtedly women constituted a large percentage of the membership as their support proved vital both to the weavers' ability to wage the strikes of the 1840s and 1850s and to the survival of their associations.

Negotiating gender difference: The mid-century legacy

Described here has been a complex process of negotiating gender difference in the English cotton district. The emergence of a family wage rhetoric was a significant aspect of that process, but one which was embedded in an industrial setting in which female labor, as well as struggle alongside their male counterparts, was thoroughly integrated. It was thus a process that contained within it both sameness and difference, contradiction and ambiguity, which an analysis privileging language cannot fully capture. Its legacy is then located in the unity and conflict, as well as a measure of control alongside their subordination, that marked the turn-of-the-century period for working-class women.

Often not seeing their position in the workforce as lasting, from the 1890s, difficulties in organizing among women were a subject of comment among union leaders. In Bolton, the president of the Weavers' Association indicated that women "held aloof" from union affairs and suggested that mothers were often barriers to their daughters' involvement. As a result, women weavers were receiving 10 to 15 percent below list prices at some mills, he claimed. Women's service on committees was limited in many areas, often stemming from their limited time of employment, as in Bolton where few married women were employed in cotton. In situations where women and men often worked alongside one another in weaving, it was claimed that the women were willing to rely upon the men with regard to union affairs.[125]

Labor market structures often served to reinforce male domination, as Michael Savage has demonstrated. In Preston, the male overlooker controlled the hiring and firing of weavers, often hiring girls and women through contact with their fathers and husbands. Women were then discouraged from union membership and did not generally participate in labor politics. Further, although the work of weaving was "highly skilled," it was not considered so, while the overlooker's job of preparing the looms, although relying primarily on strength, was deemed skilled labor. By such means, male domination was maintained at work and apparently reinforced in the home.[126] Moreover, as weaving expanded in Preston with a heavy reliance on female labor, that labor was increasingly challenged by men as other employment opportunities, particularly in spinning and engineering, declined.[127] In this context, the secretary of the Weavers' Union denounced employers who employed "women in the sheds, leaving the husband to see to the house or walk the street."[128]

There were clearly constraints placed on women and their expectations, particularly in the circumstances described above. In this, women were often complicit, learning the lesson, Roberts states, that, whatever else they did in life, they had the ultimate responsibility for home and family. Girls in particular grew up accepting the importance of respectability and aware of what was required of them to attain it.[129] They were, then, home-centered but, in being so, inequality, collectivity, and control were intertwined. In the northern weaving areas, wives who had been or still were weavers often took the initiative, in conjunction with their husbands, in exercising fertility control, enabling smaller families to live better lives.[130] In organizing the household, training their daughters, controlling the budget, dealing with shopkeepers, battling with household dirt, and other innumerable activities, they made it possible for the family to attain that respectability sought by all. In this arena, women exercised a measure of control unattainable elsewhere.

At the same time, they continued to work in the mills as "the standard of comfort [was often] reckoned on the double wage."[131] Women expressed pride in their work and skill and opposed the introduction of a marriage bar that would prevent the labor of married women.[132] They joined unions, supported strikes, and in the aftermath of the strike wave of 1911 they appeared to take a growing interest in trade unionism. Male unionists often responded to their grievances, including driving overlookers and the problem of steaming. When women cotton workers became heavily involved in the women's suffrage movement, they often gained support from their male counterparts. In oral interviews, women did not point to the exploitation of working-class men whom they generally saw as engaged in the same battles as themselves.[133]

Yet tension was evident as well. The secretary of the Rochdale Weavers expressed his bitterness at women, indicating they "are only tempted to be unionists by what they can get, benefits, etc."[134] Under the leadership of Sarah Dickenson of the Manchester and Salford Women's Trades and Labour Council, women weavers of those communities refused to join the male-led Weavers' Amalgamation. "What the gentlemen are suffering from," stated the 1908 Report of the Manchester and Salford Powerloom Weavers, "is an inflated idea of the importance of being men."[135]

As women shaped their identities from mid-century within the constraints placed upon them, those identities proved to be multi-layered. They were clearly rooted in their domestic roles, their subordination, and their own complicity in that subordination. But their identities were also shaped by the control they exercised and the collectivity they experienced. An analysis privileging language and the articulation of a supposed separate spheres ideology fails to capture the multi-dimensionality, within the framework of a pervasive emphasis on gender difference, of working-class women's lives.

Further, the analysis presented here brings into sharp relief the extension of class interests, despite inequities across gender lines. Despite the fracturing of class by gender, expressions of united class interests were in evidence as well, as class formation proceeded apace.

Part II

Female labor and gender difference in the small metal industries

Although the textile factories of the north of England gained the greatest attention during the industrializing era, particularly for their employment of female labor, it has now been widely recognized that industrialization was a much broader phenomenon. The importance of female labor beyond these centers of production has also gained increasing notice. As Maxine Berg and Pat Hudson have demonstrated, the work of women and young people was at the core of the production process in a wide range of industries from the late eighteenth century.[1] While women needed an income, manufacturers needed labor that was plentiful and cheap,[2] leading to what Berg has called the "special use of a female labor force." Women particularly were able to provide manufacturers with the flexibility they needed to increase the intensity of labor within a low-wage setting, and their work thus came to be vital to the process of industrialization.

Such work in areas outside the northern factories, it is significant to note, was not simply a by-employment, marked by unchanging technologies and primitive industrial organization. Rather, it was often precisely in those regions where production was expanding, even if carried on in the workshop or the household, that women and young people were increasingly employed. The subdivision of tasks via mechanization, Honeyman and Goodman have noted, often generated additional homework in which women could be readily employed.[3] Factories as well, such as the silk throwing mill, established in Essex by Courtauld in the 1790s, relied "on the use of plentiful female labour" recruited among the poorest section of the female population.[4] "New work disciplines, new forms of subcontracting and putting-out networks, new factory organization, and even new technologies," claim Berg and Hudson, "were tried out initially on women and children."[5] Female labor thus played a critical role in the expansion of industrial capitalist production not only in the factories, as we saw in the previous section, but also in the new urban and rural trades. It accounted for significant gains in productivity as well as providing families with a subsistence living. So important was this trend in various regional settings, these authors argue, that it may be considered a basis for "rehabilitating" the Industrial Revolution itself from attacks suggesting that, in the aggregate, changes in growth and productivity from the late eighteenth century were not all that revolutionary.[6]

Despite the significance of female labor beyond the northern textile factories, however, it appears that ideas regarding the proper work for women, serving to restrict that labor, were increasingly taking hold throughout the nineteenth century. While in the cotton factories, as we have seen, work was not entirely sex-segregated, as women and men labored alongside one another in weaving, in other areas a clear trend toward gender segregation was in evidence. In this section we begin by examining evidence suggesting that ideas about gender and work were increasingly solidifying in relation to a variety of industries considered by other scholars. We then suggest, however, that, as in cotton, despite an apparently increasingly settled discourse, understandings of gender and gender relations continued to be re-negotiated in numerous instances among the English working classes.

This section then examines this process in relation to the small metal industries in two settings, Birmingham and the Black Country, where female labor was traditionally both widespread and acceptable. During the last quarter of the nineteenth century, reflecting general trends, the question of the appropriate character of that work, its legitimacy and morality, basically meaning its femininity, however, was raised in sharp terms. Male artisans contested the presence of women workers in certain settings on both economic and moral grounds. Exclusionary strategies were proposed either to prohibit or limit the labor of women in particular instances. Yet despite the apparent power of male union leaders and the discourse they employed, their aims in this regard could not be fully realized.

By the early nineteenth century, twenty nailmaking districts, each making a different kind of nail or spike, were in existence in the West Midlands.[7] Women were often employed at making smaller common nails such as the hob and tack, but overall there was no simple division between men's and women's work. By the mid-nineteenth century, the proportion of women in the workforce had increased to one-half, where it remained to the end of the century.[8] Similarly in chainmaking, among "the steady and industrious families" employed in that trade, women came to constitute one-third of the workforce in the Dudley Wood district in the 1870s.[9]

At this time the employment of female labor in such heavy work and under deplorable conditions, to be described below, came to represent a clear challenge to the feminine ideal. Reported Sub-Inspector Brewer in 1875, "The women are said to take the place of fathers as well as of husbands, whilst the men are idle and drunken."[10] Their very presence upset the gender order and became a major issue.

In Birmingham, female labor appeared to be less controversial. Here, in the metal trades, girls and women came to be widely employed on machines for stamping and piercing. In brass shops, they labored in the lacquering department; while in the manufacture of tinplate ware they worked in japanning which involved the dipping of items into a protective substance.[11]

Hundreds of girls and women were also employed, mainly at home, sewing hooks and eyes on cards. In the button industry they worked in small shops where they were employed in a variety of processes, including cutting and polishing and working at a lathe.

By the mid-nineteenth century, girls and women of this metropolis were introduced into such new industries as the making of metal bedsteads and steel pens.[12] In penmaking, they worked the hand and steam presses used for cutting out and piercing the pens, as well as the stamp-hammer which was operated by foot.[13] Declared *Tinsley's Magazine* in 1889, women's "quickness of eye and hand [is] eminently fitted for the various processes of forming the pens, while their strength is fully capable of managing the easily-worked presses."[14]

As this quote suggests, much of this labor, unlike nail- and chainmaking, was deemed suitable female labor, requiring close attention and dexterity rather than strength and, purportedly, skill. Only limited training was involved and competition with men was non-existent. Gendered status distinctions were also incorporated in labor agreements such as that of the Brassworkers. Here the union leadership attempted to maintain the status of the skilled craftsmen by putting in place a process of conciliation and arbitration with employers which encompassed only the labor of male artisans.

In this instance, there were alterations in the nature of work itself and its organization that served to challenge and destabilize the gender order. Increased mechanization was accompanied by a growth in the employment of women and girls, in some instances extending it into areas considered "men's work." Labor agreements were threatened by the expansion of sweated labor employed by undercutters who remained, in the brass industry, outside the employers' association. The need to confront the crisis brought on by these trends meant that a re-working of gender understandings, of "men's work" and "women's work," as well as gender relations, was at least potentially placed on the agenda. In the Black Country, opposition to attempts to exclude female labor in circumstances considered unsuitable had similar implications.

Male artisanal discourses, which attempted to confine female labor to those areas considered appropriate, I argue, proved to be embedded in a rich context of complex and sometimes shifting interrelationships. The gender order they served to uphold, in either the Black Country or Birmingham, thus could not be fully sustained by strategies of exclusion or traditional restrictions. Not only do we see, as a result, understandings of what constituted "women's work" and womanhood itself contested, but we see them actually begin to lose their moorings in the larger contexts of community and economic necessity, as well as the prevailing interests of capital itself.

4 Gender at work

Throughout Europe from the late eighteenth century, in addition to spinning, widely discussed elsewhere, women were broadly employed in glovemaking, buttonmaking, metalworking, pottery, and linen manufacture. They engaged in work which later generations determined to be "distinctly non-female." Daughters and wives thus worked alongside apprentices learning such trades as engraving in England and the book trade in France. Women also produced small items for personal grooming, such as brushes and combs, items for cleaning, such as soap and brooms, as well as needles, pins, and thimbles for sewing, all of which were unregulated and did not challenge men's craft status. In towns, as brewers, butchers, and bakers of bread and, in Germany, pretzels, they provided needed household goods for the growing urban population. In lacemaking in certain instances they controlled the industry, as in Ireland.[15]

Essex provides a striking example of an area that re-industrialized, following the demise of the cloth trade, on the basis of female labor, as Judy Lown and Pamela Sharpe have detailed. Industries that catered to the domestic market for fashion goods proved to be of particular significance. For instance, Essex became the center for the manufacture of plain silk crepe, carried out by women and girls whose employment at Courtauld's, beginning at age 17, often extended from ten to thirty years by the mid-nineteenth century.[16] Commercial lace embroidery also came to be centered in the county. Shoe-binding in a family setting and tailoring within a subcontracting system became significant areas of employment for women, while in straw-plaiting they were able to earn high wages, at least during the French wars.[17] For the most part, however, "cheap and adaptable labour . . . was the most important commodity north Essex could offer."[18]

"There was nothing inherently female or male" about such labor, as Honeyman and Goodman point out. Yet gender and work came to be identified at "the intersection of the economic and gender systems."[19] And that gender system generally in western Europe had determined that customary rights and skilled labor were the preserve of the male artisan. Guilds based in towns restricted the kinds of work in which women could be engaged. The labor in which they were employed, noted above, was then generally carried on in rural areas where there was less hostility, or outside the guild structure established in towns. In both instances, although vital, it was generally determined to be of low value.[20]

In those areas of non-mechanized work, where women had already been widely employed, their fortunes often took a somewhat different path as they came to be associated with traditional forms of labor, as well as poverty. When mechanization and standardization were introduced, Deborah Valenze points out, women were viewed as inhibiting those processes, as well as the development of new markets.[21] The western tradition of associating masculinity with science and technology held sway, and women were often replaced altogether. Accordingly, in the dairy industry women's traditional knowledge and attention to the minute detail of the making of butter and cheese, such as the temperature and time required, were now devalued.[22] Standardized machinery, operated by men, was allowed to take over their production in both England and Sweden, at a later date. Milk lost its mystery, and its intimate association with the female body, as it was subjected to chemical research; science thereby replaced myth, and men replaced the time-honored dairymaid.[23]

The industrializing era, the above trends suggest, was then an era marked by considerable ambiguity and contradiction for women workers as their fortunes and opportunities were "both waxing and waning."[24] By the mid-nineteenth century, however, scholars have generally agreed that definite trends were in evidence, with Horrell and Humphries concluding that, "in aggregate the trend in the relative contributions of women and children was probably negative."[25] By this period, skilled men had largely "achieved control over the use of technical innovations" while "the greater division of labour served to intensify the gender segregation of the workforce."[26] In the hosiery industry considered by Harriet Bradley, for instance, while women had not traditionally been viewed as incompetent and unskilled, they came to be seen as inferior workers, lacking strength, knowledge, and experience. Men thus gained the responsibility of overseeing the new machines introduced at mid-century, while women were employed in finishing work and on sewing machines, which were deemed appropriate for the employment of female labor.[27] Similar trends were in evidence outside England during periods of technological change. In the Danish textile industry, for instance, Marianne Rostgard demonstrates, the same occupations were originally followed by both men and women at different mills. However, disputes broke out as male woolen workers attempted to appeal to their tradition of craft status and restrict women laborers. In the end, a gendered division of labor and corresponding pay scale were negotiated. Ideas regarding women's work rather than mechanization itself were increasingly shown to be determining the gender of work.[28] As Horrell and Humphries conclude:

> economic variables, wages and incomes, and household characteristics are not sufficient to capture the changes occurring. Instead, changing institutional and ideological factors played a role and operated to affect adversely women's employment opportunities.[29]

At the same time, women themselves, while proud of their accomplishments and mastery at the workplace, failed to develop their own "discourse of skill," allowing their labor to be devalued.[30]

As of the late 1840s in England, Keith McClelland argues, with women's paid labor concentrated in domestic service, textiles, and clothing, the gender gap in terms of skill and earnings had widened considerably, particularly as men's employment expanded in such industries as engineering, metalworking, shipbuilding, and mining. And in that environment, notions of what constituted manhood and womanhood took firm hold.[31] Masculinity came to be increasingly identified with machinery and technology, work that was heavy and required strength and ability as well as training and scientific knowledge. Women's work, in contrast, was defined as feminine, being light and clean, and semi-skilled, requiring dexterity and careful attention rather than knowledge. Lack of training and low expectations were hallmarks of "women's work." Where conditions of employment deemed inappropriate for women were present, such as filthy surroundings and exceedingly heavy work, their labor became controversial.[32] And working alongside men was thought to signify the absence of patriarchal domination generally as well as a lack of appropriate control over female, thus particularly impassioned, sexuality.[33]

An increasingly rigid sexual division of labor thus came to be upheld on moral as well as economic grounds as the workplace became a "site for the formation of gender, gender identity, gender inequality and gender subordination."[34] Where a conflict appeared between work and femininity, attempts were made to reconcile the two, as in the case of Courtauld's silk mills, described by Judy Lown. Here employment of women, Lown states, "created moral panic among many members of the local aristocracy" as purportedly "high wages" were said to lead to "idle and extravagant habits."[35] A paternalistic regimen was then instituted, intending to shape both "workplace and household patterns of authority and status" as well as maintain women's dependence. Women workers' lives were accordingly circumscribed by low wages, limited promotion opportunities, and low status.[36] They were dismissed for "immoral" behavior, not limited to prostitution but including living with a man outside marriage and wearing the wrong type of dress. The Courtaulds thus made systematic "attempts to shape masculinity and femininity in their own image." Ideal workers were defined as "virtuous asexual respectable working-class" women and "upright and sober ... family" men. They were constructed "almost as a different species," Lown somewhat humorously contends, "under the paternalistic guidance of the employers."[37]

Increasingly at issue, then, by the mid-nineteenth century, as R. W. Connell has pointed out, was not the simple allocation of work but "a gender-structured system of production." This system was not defined simply by class relations but by increasingly rigid ideas about masculinity and femininity and their application at the point of production. These ideas

thus became "a deep-seated feature of production itself."[38] Further, they res-
onated well beyond the workplace, as McClelland has brought out, and
"legitimated a new figure, the working-class citizen." This citizen was male,
endowed with property in labor, and the family provider. On the basis of
these traits, attained through hard work, he gained independence and
respectability, and on these grounds his authority rested.[39] While we have
explored this figure previously in relation to the cotton district, outside that
region and later in the century his presence may be seen as more command-
ing, particularly where female labor, low-waged and devoid of status,
became an issue.

By the last quarter of the nineteenth century, two industries examined by
scholars, lead-working and mining, have served to illustrate the hardening
of the categories of men's and women's work and thus the boundaries
between them within this increasingly gender-structured world of industry.
In each instance a public outcry was raised against female labor, seeming to
suggest a natural development of opinion reflecting concern for their conditions. Yet in each instance an examination of the discourse makes it clear,
as Jane Long has argued in relation to the campaign against women's
employment in the white lead industry, that the discourse itself "contributed to the construction of the 'problem' of women's work."[40]

The question of women's participation in the workforce by this period
hinged upon how the female worker was constructed, upon dominant ideas
about femininity and masculinity, as may be readily seen by briefly examining the two industries, drawing upon the work of Long and Angela John.
Similarly, we will see in our discussion of the metal trades in Birmingham
and the Black Country the significance of ideas regarding manhood and
womanhood in relation to female labor, leading to the pursuit of policies to
exclude women from certain work. Yet this discussion will also serve to
reveal the limits of and pressures upon this discourse which served to undermine such policies.

The lead work and pit-brow controversies

In the early 1880s, according to an Inspectors' Report, there were 4,479
female surface workers employed at Britain's coal mines, constituting 4.58
percent of the total workers so employed.[41] Interestingly, this number actually reflected a recent sharp decline in such employment of girls and women
in south Staffordshire and, in Yorkshire, "a virtual taboo on all their colliery
employment."[42] In west Lancashire, however, in 1886 when a controversy
surrounding their employment fully erupted, female surface workers
accounted for 21.58 percent of the total so employed in that region. Num-
bering around 1,300, they represented approximately 32 percent of all
females employed at collieries.[43]

At the pit brow, girls and women worked at a variety of tasks, including
filling wagons and loading barges, but primarily they were engaged in labor

involving the sorting of coal.[44] Here steady improvements had been made in recent years. New tipplers, which workers used to tip the coal on to a screen for sorting, were introduced in the 1870s and 1880s. Picking belts were also introduced for the purpose of separating the dirt from the coal as women sorters, standing on either side of the belt, picked out the dirt with their hands. No matter how they were employed, however, the labor was dirty, long, and required the worker to keep up a rapid pace.[45]

In reaction to these conditions of labor, one "wealthy coal contractor," Ellis Lever, wrote a letter to the *Times* in the spring of 1883 which "enunciated his disgust at the work of the pit brow women."[46] It was work, he concluded, "unsuited for females,"[47] an opinion with which the *Labour Tribune*, "organ of the miners, ironworkers, nut and bolt forgers, &c., of Great Britain," appeared to concur. Miners in those areas where female labor was not allowed were convinced, the *Tribune* reported, "that such employment tends to demoralization, and therefore will not allow their daughters to be so degraded. A woman accustomed to such work," these miners maintained, "cannot be expected to know much of household duties or how to make a man's home comfortable."[48] "The natural sense of the propriety and fitness of things" dictated women's exclusion from "certain employments," declared an article from the *Leeds Mercury* reprinted in the *Tribune*. And until "women can safely be left to decide what work is fit for them," the article continued, "we cannot evade our responsibilities in protecting women even against themselves from employment which, from their coarseness and their conditions, revolt the national feeling of propriety."[49] The *Tribune*, and apparently many miners, were convinced that "the banishment of this evil is only a question of time."[50]

At the center of this opposition to the labor of the "pit-brow lasses" of Lancashire was their attire, described as "as near an approximation to the dress of the masculine miners as can be."[51] To the blackened and dirty faces of the women and girls so employed was then added the scandal of wearing trousers, which were said to minimize the distinction between the sexes.[52] The female pit workers thus came to be viewed, states Angela John, as part of a "sordid," "potentially destructive" environment, "to be especially pitied as they represented the reverse of the feminine ideal."[53]

Ideas about femininity and the gender of work clashed sharply with the stark reality, the employment of women at the coal pit, and it was on this basis that the miners' union came to the support of an amendment to the Coal Mines Regulation Act Amendment Bill in 1887 which would prohibit female employment in surface work, excepting those who were already so employed. Another more comprehensive amendment was also proposed, calling for the exclusion of all girls and women from such labor.[54] Harshly affected by an ongoing depression themselves, the miners generally believed that the jobs available should be held by men. But equally important was the distinctly unfeminine nature of that work, labor that was dirty, not clean, that was rough, and not delicate, that was heavy and not light. Such conditions experienced by women workers threatened to turn the Victorian sense of gender order on its head.

Similarly in Newcastle, widespread opposition to the employment of women and girls in lead works emerged in the last quarter of the nineteenth century. Here 600 women were engaged in labor which brought them into direct contact with poisonous white lead. Already in the 1860s, health concerns began to be raised, leading to passage of an Act in 1878 that prohibited the labor of children as well as all females under the age of 18. In addition, the Factory and Workshops Act passed in 1883 set minimum standards for cleanliness and diet as well as requiring that sick employees receive medical examinations. Such legislation, however, did not adequately address particular concerns regarding female workers who were shown to experience high miscarriage rates and whose breast milk was poisoned by lead exposure, leading to a high rate of infant deaths. As a result, further investigation into the industry and the effects of white lead poisoning was undertaken in the early 1890s by doctors and the Newcastle press, as well as the government. Inquests were held into the deaths of women workers, leading to a widespread call for their exclusion from the industry which was enforced in 1898.[55]

In the course of investigations into the industry, however, as in the case of the pit-brow lasses, the issues were not confined to objective conditions of work. Rather, the women workers themselves were characterized in a negative fashion, described as weak and immoral and likely to be drinkers. The victims of lead poisoning were considered to be not the good and honest workers, but those who failed to take the precautionary measures necessary to protect themselves. Forced to defend themselves against such attacks, the women pointed to economic necessity as the reason for their being so employed, emphasizing that it was not to facilitate the leading of "free and easy lives" as charged.[56]

Women workers, laboring under such conditions as the lead workers and pit-brow lasses, as well as the rural Northumberland bondage workers considered by Long, were cast in such a negative light because, she has pointed out, they disrupted the Victorian framework of belief in progress and improvement. Society was to move forward on the basis of sharp distinctions of gender, and workplace conditions represented a vital and visible expression of just how womanhood and manhood were perceived. Conditions at work were thus indicative of an ordered, or disordered, society. Women outside the framework imposed consequently "became portentous signifiers of disorder" and had to be excluded from the settings in which they labored, which were drawing such attention.[57] Consequently "purely economic interpretations [of their conditions]," contends Long, "were overwhelmed by constructions about disordering female sexuality, both in broad social life and in the specific sites of workplace, workhouse and public streets."[58] And it was on this basis that attempts were made to exclude them from the workplace altogether.

Yet Long is also mindful that, while attempts "to fix female identity" were rife, simultaneously "the variety of material conditions and the individual responses of women illustrated that idealised visions of how women should behave and what their priorities should be, were subject to constant processes of negotiation."[59] A complex web of tensions, conflicts, and ambiguities thus surrounded the issue of female labor. For instance, a conflict often existed between the needs, and perhaps desires, of the women themselves and the ideal of what constituted womanhood and femininity expressed through the dominant discourse. In the case of mining, regional differences in the miners' circumstances led to variations in their views regarding the efficacy of female labor. And further, the late nineteenth century witnessed the emergence of a feminist movement with views about women and their rights, to be discussed further below, that did not necessarily fit comfortably within the established Victorian framework. A strategy of excluding female labor from the pit brow, then, unlike the case of the lead workers where clear health issues were involved, was sharply contested and did not meet with success.

In the course of the ensuing debate over female surface workers, the feminist journal, the *Englishwoman's Review*, was quick to point to the discrepancy between ideals of masculinity and femininity and what constituted "men's work" and "women's work," on the one hand, and the reality of working-class life on the other. In coming to the defense of women's position in the workforce, the journal noted that, despite concerns expressed in the *Labour Tribune* and elsewhere regarding female labor at the pit brow, that labor was no heavier than that of laundresses and some kinds of factory work. Further, the coarseness of the women's lives and their inability to follow domestic pursuits were not unique to the pit-brow lasses. Their homes were not worse than "the one-roomed den of the starving mothers of families who . . . work at matchbox making," the *Review* declared. And the corruption of their morals by the language of the men was no more of a problem on the pit brow than "in any trade or occupation where women meet the coarse of the other sex."[60] And of course the concern of the men for their jobs and wages only served to illustrate the degree to which self-interest was involved.[61]

The right of the women to a livelihood further emerged as a central argument of the pit workers and their defenders. Mrs Margaret Park, Mayoress of Wigan where the pits at the center of the controversy were located, emphasized the lack of alternative opportunities for the girls and women to earn wages. When young, such labor enabled the girls to work alongside their friends and, when faced with the loss or illness of a husband, return to the work made it possible for mothers to maintain their families, she contended. Mrs Park then went on to wax eloquently about "how nobly our Lancashire women do this, and how patient and self-sacrificing they are in their endeavours to keep themselves and families from starvation and the workhouse."[62]

A leading feminist, Lydia Becker, declared along the same lines:

The confiscation of their wages would mean for them either starvation, dependence on charity, or the breaking up of home and family ties by dispersal to other districts in search of employment. How this would conduce either to morality or domesticity [she pondered] is for those who would drive women to these cruel alternatives to explain.[63]

At a meeting attended by Rev. George Fox, with the rector of Ashton occupying the chair, a petition "praying the House of Commons to reject any clause which would do the pit-brow girls the great injustice of depriving them of their only means of livelihood, was adopted enthusiastically."[64]

The self-interests of the ruling elite must be placed in perspective in considering this particular discourse in defense of the female pit-brow workers. Mrs Park, having a "local reputation as the leader of movements to help the poor," was clearly, as John puts it, "at pains to emphasise her altruistic concern for the women and detachment from the coal industry."[65] The patronizing character of her comments is evident as she referred to the girls as "robust and healthy" and especially called attention to the healthy nature of their work, being in the fresh air with "all the bright surroundings of the country about them."[66] For the vicar of Pemberton, who worked alongside Mrs Park, self-interest was clearly involved since his position in defending the women was in the interest of the coal companies, who offered him considerable assistance in the establishment of day and Sunday schools.[67] Yet the views expressed were representative of an emerging viewpoint, particularly promoted by feminists who, according to Angela John, "couched the pit-brow argument in absolute and uncompromising terms" regarding women's right to a livelihood. Furthermore, in putting forth this argument, the feminists enjoyed considerable support from the women themselves as well as some miners.

The female surface workers, as Angela John has demonstrated, laboring as a team and contributing to the welfare of their families, were conscious of their identity as pit-brow lasses. While, in the community of Wigan, the female mill worker appeared to hold a higher status, and consider herself above the pit workers, the latter did not necessarily see things that way.[68] Indeed, it appears that "while it was rare to find a woman leaving the pit to work in the mills, it was common enough to witness the opposite."[69]

The spring of 1886 thus found these workers attending the meetings convened and addressed by the clergy, Mrs Park, and Lydia Becker, and receiving their remarks with "loud cheers" and "lively and earnest" demonstrations.[70] The following year, after introduction of the Amendment calling for a prohibition on female employment in surface work, Mrs Park and the vicar were able to organize a deputation of women to meet the Home Secretary. Prominent among the supporters of this effort were leading feminists including Millicent Fawcett, Ada Heather Bigg, Clementina Black, as well as Lydia Becker.[71]

Some miners as well were increasingly lending support to the women, attending meetings on their behalf and subscribing toward a fund to support the London deputation.[72] Most significantly, John points out, at a miners' conference in Manchester in 1887, a representative from Lancashire indicated that, due to the support for the women's cause in that district, "he could not feel justified in advocating their exclusion."[73]

Miners' leaders Thomas Burt and Benjamin Pickard were from areas that did not employ female labor and were strongest in their opposition to female employment. In Lancashire, however, the earnings of girls and women employed at the pit brow were viewed as "a vital source of income," one on which the community depended. More specifically, daughters of the miners themselves were employed at the pit surface. The Lancashire miners' own economic interests thus conflicted with the position taken by their own union and a split among the miners emerged.[74]

This division became apparent in the pages of the *Labour Tribune* early in the controversy when the paper gave an account of the meeting in Pemberton addressed by the Mayoress of Wigan,[75] reporting her positive outlook on the work of the pit-brow women. Also reported was the comment of a miner present at that meeting in March 1886, suggesting that if the colliers were canvassed on the issue, presumably in the Lancashire area, 90 percent would be against legislation prohibiting female labor.[76] And, appearing alongside the article from the Leeds paper reprinted by the *Tribune*, opposing such labor, was a reprint from the *Birmingham Daily Post,* a well-established opponent of legislation restricting the employment of women. In a clearly sarcastic tone, the *Post* reprint maintained that, in the case of the attempt to prohibit female labor in bolt and rivet shops, "a little enquiry sufficed to show that the agitation originated with the male competitors for this class of work, and that the motive underlying it was not so pure and disinterested as parliament was asked to believe."[77] The question to be considered, then, was whether the same was true in this case.[78]

While printing the views of major supporters of the proposed legislation, including Ellis Lever,[79] opponents' views were well represented in the April issues of the *Labour Tribune.* An article reprinted from the *Colliery Guardian*, referring to the strong opposition to the legislation "all throughout the district," commented that the labor of the women was not of an "arduous character" while they gained wages of 9s. to 10s. per week. "To compel the colliery women to relinquish this means of employment would be a very great hardship," the *Guardian* declared, particularly given that they themselves had expressed no such desire.[80]

In May, the *Tribune* reprinted a reflective article from the *Weekly Dispatch* recognizing that there were "partisans of both sides," with women workers and some trade unions in direct opposition. As for the women, the *Dispatch* indicated that they "have made out a good case for themselves, and rebutted all of the general charges against their behaviour and morality," concluding that "they appear to hold quite as high a place as the factory hand or the drudge of domestic service in the social scale."[81] While the "town-bred man" would be shocked at the sight of their labor, "the impression soon wears off," the writer declared, "and the dress and work of the women seem to become a parcel of the pit-brow surroundings." While the work "is as rough and hard as that usually performed by men," the reporter maintained, the hours were deemed "not long" and many of the women, having worked from 6 a.m. to 4 p.m., were able to devote themselves to their domestic labors the rest of the day.[82] Further, "the economic argument does not tell either way," the writer argued, since the women employed were the wives and daughters of colliers and, thus, with their dismissal, it was unlikely that the household would be any better off.[83]

In this instance, the writer still concluded that expressed concerns with regard to public health and morality were "quite sufficient to justify the intervention of the State."[84] His argument, however, with the modifications noted above, appeared tepid compared to those of the outright opponents of legislation appearing in the same issue of the *Labour Tribune*. A "pit-brow lass" herself, for instance, was described as "decidedly prefer[ring] colliery to factory work, and [being] quite indignant that anyone should seek to deprive her and her fellow workers of their employment." And with similar conviction, a reprint from the *Wigan Examiner* declared the garb of the pit-brow girls to be "eminently suitable for the work" and drew a sharp contrast between the "ruddy" complexion of the pit-brow girl and the "sickly, pallid countenance of the factory worker."[85]

With the introduction of the legislation a year later, the *Labour Tribune* appeared to be fully supportive of the women mine workers, opposing legislation prohibiting their employment. An article reprinted from the *Liverpool Mercury* called attention to the "great dislocation industrially and socially" that such legislation would cause, with thousands being sent adrift. "But the strongest point," stated the article, "is that these young women are now honestly earning a reasonable living by their own exertions, and ... much suffering to themselves and their families would be the inevitable consequence of their dismissal."[86] When the Act that was passed failed to include a provision excluding female labor from the pit brow, the *Labour Tribune* quoted the *Woman's Suffrage Journal*, warning of the threatened effects of such legislation. "The industrial rights of women," declared the *Journal*, "would have received a blow as serious for the pit-bank industry as a law forbidding the employment of girls in factories would be for women's work in textile industries."[87]

Despite appearing sympathetic to the prohibitive legislation at first, the *Labour Tribune* thus in the end offered considerable support to the cause of the pit-brow lasses. Significant as well is the expression of that support, which not only served to defend the immediate interests of the female surface workers, but directly contested predominant understandings of gender as applied to the woman worker. While the labor of the women was acknowledged as "rough and hard," even similar to men's, that reason was now deemed insufficient to exclude female labor altogether. The girls and women themselves were not viewed as necessarily degraded or demoralized by the work or their masculine garb. Rather, the trousers were now defended as "eminently suitable for the work." And perhaps most significantly, it was not the work of the women that was viewed as threatening in the comments appearing in the *Tribune*, but the loss of that work. "Honestly earning a reasonable living by their own exertions," the pit-brow lasses were to be admired for the support they lent their families, enabling them to realize at least a subsistence living.

The Victorian gender order was destabilized by the very presence of the woman worker, particularly in such settings as mines and lead works. It was also, however, directly challenged by a discourse which deemed that presence acceptable, necessary, and even admirable. And of interest as well is the alignment of forces behind that discourse. On the surface it first appears that we are dealing simply with gender antagonism, of feminists and women workers allied against "the miners." However, as was brought out above, support for the pit-brow lasses cut across not only class but gender lines as well. Regional differences among the miners, rooted in varying household economies, led to a division in their approach to the cause of the female surface workers.

As M. M. Bakhtin writes, "a unitary language gives expression to forces working toward concrete verbal and ideological unification and centralization."[88] But that language, that discourse, Bakhtin maintains, lives and develops in a larger context in which forces reside that threaten that unity.[89] Despite the prevailing discourse surrounding the appropriate labor of women, the boundaries set were not always adhered to in practice. Whether and where they were employed depended on numerous factors including regional identity, leading Horrell and Humphries to call for "detailed analyses of institutional changes at occupational and regional levels" when discussing women and work.[90]

As we have seen in the case of the cotton industry, as well as mining, a certain fluidity was in evidence with regard to "women's work." Notes Ulla Wikander in relation to the pottery industry in Sweden, "the *social* construction of male and female work . . . continuously takes place inside a tradition, which might be opposed and changed." While perceptions existed of separate technologies for men and women, there was no consistent practice. Rather, boundaries were "fluid and random" over time and in the aggregate.[91] The type of work deemed suitable for women was a principle on which work was generally allocated. For instance, in the inter-war period when the assembly line was introduced, involving forms of labor traditionally associated with women, they came to be identified with the new technology. Yet Miriam Glucksmann, the historian of women assembly-line workers, points out that such "principles never had an existence above or beyond historical circumstances and were not found in a pure form or in the abstract." The "detailed structure" of the sexual division of labor "varied according to each concrete case."[92]

Neither were dominant ideas of masculinity, particularly suggesting that men were the sole providers, fully determining in terms of the allocation of work or universally applicable. The existence of a hierarchy among men, as well as their varying circumstances,[93] clearly underpinned ideas regarding the work women did as well as gender relations. While the independent, respectable artisan might well oppose the employment of women, to many men whose families, as well as the larger community, were dependent on the earnings of their wives and daughters, such a position was a luxury. This reality served to complicate and challenge dominant gender understandings, leading to a defense of women's work in circumstances otherwise considered unacceptable. It is thus to the process of negotiating "women's work" in the small metal industries of Birmingham and the Black Country that we now turn.

5 Gender divisions and class relations

The Birmingham metal trades

As early as the mid-nineteenth century, female labor in the Birmingham small metal industry was common, varied, and acceptable. Definite ideas regarding what constituted "women's work" prevailed, resulting in a rigidly sex-segregated labor market. The Brassworkers' leader, W. J. Davis, in particular, was determined to maintain this sharp division, questioning the extension of the labor of women and girls beyond its established confines by suggesting that such labor was illegitimate as it came into competition with that of men. This discourse, however, came under pressure from a variety of sources, most notably the early feminist movement, which stressed freedom of contract in relation to all adult labor.

The ramifications of the conflict between male artisans and the early women's trade union leaders, however, extended well beyond simple gender antagonism. On the surface it appears that established understandings regarding the work of women and men, despite feminist opposition, remained in place well into the 1890s as the Brassworkers were able to prevent the extension of female labor into those areas monopolized by men. However, these gender-based divisions were closely linked to class relations that were themselves in flux. As employers introduced mechanization and extended the use of sweated labor, existing labor agreements were threatened. While some attempt was made by male union leaders in this context to begin to organize women workers, they met with little success. Davis in particular then continued to take his well-established, gendered approach, pursuing exclusionary policies with regard to women's work while forcing an agreement with employers, made possible by an economic upswing, limited to skilled male workers. However, I argue, while such a policy appeared to be effective at the time, its success was likely to be temporary due to alterations in the nature of work itself. Gender understandings came under pressure from the material circumstances surrounding them.

Women's work in the Birmingham metal industries

As early as the sixteenth century, Birmingham emerged as a center of the iron trade, manufacturing knives, nails, and cutting tools. During the eighteenth century the city became known for the manufacture of guns and swords as well as "toys," meaning buttons, buckles, and trinkets. With the destruction of the forests that provided charcoal, however, iron was increasingly imported and the manufacture of finished iron generally migrated to south Staffordshire to be close to the Severn ports. Birmingham itself then became a center for the manufacture of finished products that required a considerable amount of labor, particularly skilled.[1]

In these circumstances, male artisans were often able to exercise a relatively high degree of control over trade practices. In times of crisis, according to historian Clive Behagg, they were able to invoke the "custom of the trade," meaning "informal 'understandings' between workers, against which the process of change could be measured and judged."[2] By appealing to such "understandings," skilled workmen were often able to resist changes in methods of work and thereby protect their own interests by maintaining the existing hierarchy. As early as the 1830s, however, the independence and control enjoyed by male artisans were threatened by the demands of the market, which dictated the lowering of production costs by the introduction of new technology. As industry was reorganized and restructured, the large manufacturer came to dominate the various trades. But rather than absorbing the smaller production units, the latter actually proliferated as the large firms gave out work to the small firms, particularly to do the finishing work on the final products.[3]

In this setting, girls were equally employed with boys in many processes of the metal industries, while women were increasingly substituted for men. Wrote Sub-Commissioner Grainger in his report to the Children's Employment Commission of 1843, "I saw in some manufactories women employed in most laborious work, such as stamping buttons and brass nails, and notching the heads of screws." He estimated that girls and women, generally between the ages of 16 and 24, constituted 80 to 90 percent of all those employed in screw manufactories. In general in Birmingham, between 1841 and 1851 males over 20, as a percentage of the workforce, declined from 63 to 52 percent.[4]

Writing in 1857, J. S. Wright claimed that female employment had become an institution in the city and declared that the town owed "its position to the ready supply of cheap labour afforded by women and girls."[5] In the jewellery industry, he estimated that 1,000 women were employed in soldering links of gold and silver chain, while 200 worked in polishing. The tinned and japanned ware trade employed 500 to 600 women, according to Wright, in press work and in blacking which involved coating the product with tar varnish.[6] Approximately 1,200 women were employed in manufacturing metal buttons, eyelets, and buckles, while about the same number worked in the newly established steel-pen factories.[7] The work in the button and steel-pen trades consisted mainly of cutting out and forming discs or blanks of metal by means of a press. Wrote Wright, "This is, in large work, very laborious, each blow requiring the whole strength of a woman."

However, he indicated that fatigue arose "only from the long-continued unvarying motion" which he estimated amounted to 14,000 to 20,000 strokes per day among "practised workers."[8]

In the brass trade, which Samuel Timmins declared to be the chief industry of the metropolis, women accounted for nearly 1,000 of the approximately 5,000 adults employed in 1861, while girls and women combined constituted about one-quarter of the total employees.[9] Here they were employed in stamping and piercing, as well as lacquering, the final stage in the production process, which was established as an all-female trade. In long, heated rooms, the women and girls applied the lacquer to articles, which had been heated, with camel-hair brushes. As the spirits evaporated from the hot surface, a thin layer of varnish was left behind, serving the vital function of protecting the item from the atmosphere.[10] The new trade of iron and brass bedsteads attracted considerable female labor in lacquering as well as japanning. Here girls and women accounted for approximately one-sixth of the 2,500 employed.

While at mid-century a minority of married women engaged in paid labor, hundreds of families were kept from want, as Wright indicated, by the mother's earnings.[11] In a letter to the *Morning Chronicle* in 1850, a man who had worked as an operative buttonmaker for fifty years, whose mother and father had preceded him in the trade, declared that his mother had tried to see to the support of the family without working for wages. But his father's wages were too small, as the family became mired in debt from spending on furniture and the father's frequenting the gin-shop.[12] As a result, the worker now turned "gentleman," occupying "a highly respectable position in the town," said his mother "did double work – in the shop and at home. I have known her to sit up till three or four o'clock in the morning, after a hard day's work," he lamented, "washing and mending our wretched clothes."[13] He described his mother, who had eleven children, as "a perfect slave," rushing home from work at midday to get dinner for his father and working until the day before her confinement, returning within three weeks.[14]

Particularly in instances where men were out of work, their wives sought employment, as Jemima Toules, aged 23, told the Children's Employment Commission. Echoing the testimony cited above, she indicated that women often worked, if necessary, "till the time of their confinement; and generally returned in three weeks after it." This comment was repeated by others, including a woman, aged 34, engaged in brass-foundry, whose husband had been out of work for three years and whose daughter worked alongside her. In such instances when there were infants, they were left in the care of little girls or female relations, preferably the grandmother, or were "put out to neighbours."

As Wright noted, however, the labor of wives was not limited to times of crisis. Rather, he stated, "when the husband's earnings were ample, we have known women return to the workshop, to escape the loneliness of their new mode of life."[15] Employers such as Joseph Gillot and Josiah Mason, both pen manufacturers, even located their works in the jewelry and gun districts respectively to take general advantage of such female labor, provided by wives as well as daughters.[16] Gillott, who employed 500 to 600 in his factory already in 1850, further attempted to entice girls, who were over 14, and women by taking a paternalistic approach to his employees. He selected those who had been to day and Sunday school for employment, and required a recommendation of good moral conduct, steadiness, and cleanliness from a Sunday school teacher, clergyman, or other person deemed respectable. Gillott also established a sick club for the employees, while the girls and women themselves established their own shoe and boot and shawl and dress clubs to which they contributed two pence and three pence per week, indicating some degree of commitment to continue working.[17]

In general, girls and women chose to work in such factories or workshops, rather than domestic service, despite the often harsh conditions and strenuous labor. In such labor as lacquering, the skill was readily acquired. Some commentators further suggested that, in addition to being "tolerably well paid," with earnings of approximately 8s. to 10s. per week, girls and women gained some degree of independence, which one referred to as "freedom instead of thraldom," despite laboring twelve hours per day.[18] Wrote Wright, "The more direct control of their wages, the opportunity afforded for gossip, and, above all, the liberty a shop-girl has to spend time after work in the evening as she chooses, are allurements that cannot be resisted."[19]

The general use of girls and women as a "reservoir of cheap labor," Dennis Smith has concluded, was of considerable value to Birmingham families, who were, as a result, less dependent on the male breadwinner than those of the neighboring industrial center of Sheffield.[20] The sharp differentiation between the labor of men and women, suggested by the above examples, made this even more true, making it more likely that, at a time of crisis in the husband's trade, female labor could carry the family through.

As a result, it appears that the labor of women and girls was generally non-controversial. Little training was necessary and, if strength was required, that was of little moment. Rather, it was the repetitive movements that may have led to exhaustion, but such labor was identified with "women's work," thus apparently making it acceptable despite the strain involved. Further, paternalistic measures were put in place to undercut any suggestion that, by being so employed, women had transgressed the bounds of womanhood. They remained under the control of male employers concerned about their character. And they were good girls, suggesting that the labor itself could not be inappropriate.

That girls and young women gained control over their earnings, and thus a degree of liberty and independence through such employment, was grudgingly acknowledged but clearly disparaged. A separate female culture, apart from male control, was seen to be emerging, marked by such purported trivialities as gossip. The independence and companionship the girls and women realized were put down as "allurements that could not be resisted," not expressions of selfhood, in contrast to the importance of labor and liberty to the male artisan. They were simply tolerated, that is, until the work in which female labor was engaged came into conflict with the work culture of the male craftsman.

The Brassworkers and gender conflict

Such a conflict emerged most sharply in the Birmingham brass trade in the 1870s and 1880s. At that time W. J. Davis, perhaps the most eloquent spokesman for the skilled male worker of the period, was serving as general secretary of the Amalgamated Society of Brassworkers, which had been founded in 1872. Writing of the establishment of the brass trade in Birmingham in the mid-eighteenth century, Davis declared that that city, "in a population of metal workers, possessing hereditary aptitudes descending from father to son during many generations, was the destined home of the new industry."[21] According to Davis, the craftsman in brass of that metropolis was expected to produce not only works possessing utility but, especially under the artistic revival of Augustus Pugin, objects that contained within them "meaning, language, inspiration."[22] With art and ornament thus joined with utility, the resulting products represented to Davis not only an "expression of the culture of the day, but a means of raising that culture."[23]

It was clearly the male artisan, who traditionally passed on his skill to his son, who was the bearer of that culture. He represented "male honour," based not only on the qualities of hard work and skill, Martin Wiener has suggested in an intriguing discussion of the case of a jewelry stamper who murdered his wife in Birmingham. Now, that honor was increasingly associated with discipline and rationality, as well as peaceful family relations, as a decline in tolerance of violence became evident.[24]

Davis' approach to union organizing and the settling of trade disputes directly expressed this outlook. Early in his tenure as general secretary of the Brassworkers' Society in the 1870s, Davis was able to put in place a framework for negotiating disputes based on conciliation and arbitration in the chandelier and general gas-fittings trade.[25] This system depended on a high degree of organization among both employers and workmen, the suggestion being that a "community of interests" existed between them, based on a recognition of and appreciation for the skilled workman's abilities and status. To Davis it was evident that it was in the interests of both sides to maintain that status, founded upon the high quality of the goods produced.[26]

As early as 1874, the Brassworkers were reporting considerable satisfaction with their relations with their employers as a result of Davis' approach. They noted in particular that "a growing good feeling" could be detected on the part of their employers toward themselves.[27]

Your representatives know of no instance [stated the *Annual Report*] in which your interests have been ignored by a refusal to hear the representations on your behalf. The conciliatory attempts have been most successful in settling disputes involving vital principles between employer and employed.[28]

Inherent in these statements of self-congratulation, however, were definite assumptions regarding who constituted "the employed," whose interests were being represented, and the "vital principles" that were at stake. The gendered nature of these assumptions became eminently clear in the course of that year when Davis led a strike at Smith and Chamberlain in protest against women replacing skilled male workers.[29] In 1881, he expressed his views on this matter in the course of a later dispute with that same firm. Writing to the *Birmingham Daily Post*, Davis declared:

This Society has never asked that firm to discharge women who were employed in legitimate occupations. We recognize the right of women to perform the duties of wrapping up, lacquering, etc. What we oppose (& many employers also oppose) is the employment of women to turn at the lathe & file at the vice . . .[30]

What clearly concerned Davis was not the employment of women *per se* but "the frequent attempts to displace the labour of men with that of women, & in departments . . . that are only fit for the male sex."[31] To Davis, the "legitimate occupations" in which women were engaged had been established by a custom which simultaneously recognized the exclusive right of the male artisan to exercise his skill in those occupations that were "fitting." The brass trade proved to be capable of defending this viewpoint during this period as Davis was able to maintain a male monopoly on employment in the skilled areas of brass manufacture.[32]

In the Trades Union Congress, however, a controversy in which Davis became involved had been brewing since 1874 regarding the question of female labor and its regulation. Seven years earlier, the Factory Acts Extension Act had been passed, extending provisions of existing factory legislation to several industries in addition to textiles and, most importantly, to workshops as well, meaning places of manufacture that employed less than fifty people who were not part of a family unit. The TUC was now pressing for consolidation and extension of these Acts, since the Act of 1867, unlike earlier legislation which restricted the working day to a twelve-hour period, allowed for employment between the hours of 5.00 a.m. and 9.00 p.m. and failed to cover all children, young persons, and women employed in manufacturing establishments.

Within the early British women's movement, as Rosemary Feurer and others have pointed out, the passage of any such legislation that placed restrictions on women and did not apply to men was considered "anathema."

Concerned with the expansion of economic opportunities for women, early feminists considered such gender-based legislation "a hindrance to the economic advancement of their sex." No matter how limited the proposed legislation, according to its feminist detractors, it served to restrict women's freedom of contract and place all women in a secondary position in terms of the labor market.[33]

Such a position on the part of the women's movement readily brought it into sharp conflict with Davis and the trade unions. In early 1874, the Trades Union Congress refused to receive a deputation from the Vigilance Association seeking to discuss the proposed Factory Act Amendment Bill and any legislation affecting women's work. In response, the Association forwarded a memorial to TUC delegates registering its opposition to all "restrictions on the labour of adult women to which the labour of men is not subjected."[34] While expressing sympathy with attempts to shorten the working hours of both men and women, the memorialists argued that such a reform could be realized without legislative interference and that "for women, as for men, the most advantageous condition is freedom in the disposal of their labour." However, to apply special restrictions to women only was to "perpetuate the existing injustice of treating a woman as an irresponsible being, incapable of judging and acting for herself."[35]

The Women's Protective and Provident League was then established, under the leadership of Emma Paterson of the Bookbinders, for the precise purpose of organizing trade unions among women, thereby serving to demonstrate that the protection of the state was indeed unnecessary.[36] It determined to send delegates to the TUC itself later that year to raise objections to the proposed legislation directly. In her comments at the conference, Paterson declared, "She would rather see [women] suffer the evils of overwork to make them fully understand the unsatisfactory state of their position, and how necessary it was for them to form unions for themselves." In retort, Henry Broadhurst, the general secretary, indicated they would all be glad to see unions formed among working women, but he believed the legislation proposed could only improve their situation. He further added the comment that "the proper position of married women was the home."

This dispute intensified in 1877 with the Parliamentary Committee of the TUC supporting a proposal, to be discussed further in the next chapter, that girls under the age of 16 be prohibited from employment in chain and nail works. W. J. Davis spoke in support of this proposal at the TUC, indicating that women in Birmingham were employed at "harder work than making chains." There existed "proper avocations" for women, he contended, but, with reference to the brass trade, "it was degrading when they were employed in factories at the lathe or file bench."[37] Paterson stated simply, "Women should be allowed to earn their own living without undue restrictions." She even added that "it was a degrading thing for a woman to be hunted about by a factory inspector."[38] In this sentiment Paterson was joined by Augusta Brown of the London Shirt, Collar, and Underlinen

Makers, who maintained that "exceptional legislation for women was bad and degrading in its effects."[39]

Not surprisingly, these remarks met with considerable opposition from TUC delegates who felt they "ought to lend a protecting hand to the women," as a Birmingham delegate stated.[40] Declaring that "much good had been done by Mrs. Paterson and other ladies in forming and maintaining unions," Broadhurst contended that restrictions were necessary due to "the greed of those who would work their mothers and sisters like dogs or slaves for the sake of gain." Further, he continued, "it was their duty, as men and husbands, to use their utmost efforts to bring about a condition of things where their wives should be in their proper sphere at home, seeing after their house and family."[41]

This debate had particular resonance in Birmingham, with Davis on one side while the feminists found allies among the employers. In particular, Arthur Chamberlain of Smith and Chamberlain gas-fitting and brass-foundry, whose hiring of a girl for a job considered "men's work" had sparked the strike led by Davis in 1874, voiced support for Paterson's views.[42] "Having long had the theoretical belief that women could do a certain class of work to their advantage," Chamberlain told the Factory and Workshops Commission, he had simply taken the opportunity presented by the ensuing strike "to give them a chance" to work at a lathe on small articles of brass, work heretofore universally deemed "men's work."[43] Due to existing legislative restrictions on women's entry into "many occupations," Chamberlain argued to the incredulity of at least one commissioner, they were now forced to take jobs that were not suitable for them. He was simply attempting to find them appropriate positions that would expand their opportunities, unhindered by government interference now depriving them of their right and ability to seek suitable employment.[44]

The self-interest and opportunism of Chamberlain were unmasked when he admitted that women earned only 7s. to 12s. in polishing compared to the male wage of 30s. to 50s. When confronted with this discrepancy, he responded with the rejoinder that it was intense competition among women in this instance that served to lower their wages.[45] Clearly economic gain and a supposed championing of the rights of women were conveniently merged for Chamberlain, as he attempted to offer women more of a "chance." But beyond this, his apparent alliance with the feminist cause, coupled with the opposition he encountered from the Brassworkers, serves to expose the links between gender conflict and class relations.

Gender and class

During the 1870s and 1880s, brass wares were increasingly being manufactured on the basis of newly introduced machinery, higher worker productivity, and the increased employment of female labor.[46] In brass-foundry, in particular, stamping, a process employing girls and women, was increasingly replacing the skilled labor of casting. By the early 1890s, machinery on which both male and female laborers were employed was widely introduced in common gas fittings. Polishing was becoming a growing trade employing "strong lads and youths" who overstocked the trade. Dipping and bronzing, processes which the brassworkers considered to be rooted in a scientific understanding of metalworking, were "degraded to little better than … cleansing" while the workers so employed, including girls and women, were exposed to dangerous conditions, being insufficiently protected from the chemicals used.[47] Additionally, sweated labor became increasingly common as garret masters employed their own families and undersold established firms, thus acting as employers of such labor, as it came to be defined.[48]

Employer/employee relations throughout the industry, as a result, proved to be strained, exposing the fragility of existing understandings with employers nurtured by the Brassworkers. Already in 1877, the Brassworkers' *Annual Report* noted that a "great number" of members were out of work.[49] By 1880, both the chandelier trade and workers in brass-foundry had been forced to accept a 5 percent reduction.[50] By the mid-1880s, many disputes were occurring between masters and men. In this context, Chamberlain's introduction of female labor, at cheaper rates, proved to be simply part of a larger strategy, undertaken under conditions favorable to employers, to undercut existing agreements between employers and the Brassworkers. This conclusion is supported by the fact that Chamberlain remained outside the Employers' Association which negotiated with the Brassworkers[51] while his firm sought to adopt a price list 25 percent below the lowest in the trade. Further, the firm established its own trade benefit society from which members of the Brassworkers' Society were barred, leading to numerous discharges among those refusing to enter into the company plan.[52] The question of concern to us, then, is how issues of gender figured into such strained employer–employee negotiations, thereby potentially placing pressure on existing understandings regarding women's place in the workforce as well as assumptions with respect to their organizational capacity.

At the time serving as factory inspector for Sheffield, W. J. Davis was somewhat removed from conditions then affecting the Birmingham brassworkers. However, in his capacity as factory inspector, he addressed the issue of sweating, condemning its practice in testimony before the Lords' committee on the subject, thereby suggesting an acute awareness of its detrimental impact on labor in general. Referring to tailoring and other trades in Sheffield, he maintained that sweating "produces an unskilled class of workmen, resulting in the formation of a surplus industrial market becoming impotent at the approach of, and a ready prey for, the sweater."[53] Upon returning to Birmingham and leadership of the Brassworkers in 1889, Davis quickly became aware that such tendencies were in evidence in the brass industry, as changes in production processes served to reduce "the opportunities of younger men to become skilled and efficient artisans."[54] He thus came to see himself, according to his biographer, as rescuing "a skilled industry from the disgrace of being unable to command good profits for the manu-facturer and fair earnings for the workman."[55] Davis then called upon members of the Society to replace "the struggle for scanty subsistence, for a status in which all who wish and are able to labour could, by industry, main-tain themselves, their wives, and their children in comfort and happiness."

Davis' approach to the combined threats of mechanization, female competition, and sweated labor was then to attempt to re-establish the "good feeling" that appeared to exist between masters and men when the Brassworkers' Society was first formed, based on organizing the male artisans and establishing a system of conciliation and arbitration with employers. He and the Brassworkers, in March 1891, thus called for the establishment of a Board of Conciliation that "would afford a practical solution of matters in dispute between employers and employed, [assuring] that the future pros-perity of the trade as a whole could be regulated and controlled with advant-age by mutual negotiation."[56]

Initially, the Employers' Council responded favorably to this appeal, calling on all manufacturers to unite and cooperate with Davis' efforts. As a result, a Conciliation Board was established the following year.[57] Further, the workers themselves, who had recently been widely engaged in outbid-ding each other and acquiescing in price reductions, now returned to the Society. Consequently, its membership increased to nearly 8,000 from a low of 2,000.[58] Apparent success was then realized, as an agreement was reached with a number of employers re-establishing the 15 percent bonus negotiated in 1872.[59]

The tenuous nature of that success, however, was readily apparent. As the *Daily Post* noted:

> At present, unfortunately, the sole aim of the small general brassfounder seems to be to push trade by producing something cheaper than anybody else, and as a means to this end labour is squeezed and cheapened to the utmost practicable extent, in defiance of all contracts and arrangements between the leaders of the trade and the Brassworkers' Association.[60]

Any agreement among employers and men was thus potentially undermined by the infamous undercutter. Further, the introduction of female labor, which was increasing in the brass trade as indicated by the examples above, was already proving destructive to both the position of male artisans and their attempts at organization in other small metal trades.

Founded in 1855, the Gold Beaters' Trade Society had apparently col-lapsed by the early 1890s following the employment of girls in leat-work, involving cutting sheets of gold into leaves and affixing them in books. It was reported that their entry into this aspect of the trade had "disorganized the men & eventually broke up the Union."[61] Among the Spoon and Fork Makers, Filers, and Polishers, constant wage reductions led to several strikes and the founding of a union by W. J. Davis in 1890. The employers' response was to introduce Emery wheels on which girls were employed, doing work previously carried out by skilled male filers.[62] With the growing demand for cheap silver jewelry on which women were widely employed, the Goldsmiths' and Jewelers' Society witnessed a fall in membership and was unable to make significant gains for its skilled members, as the women remained unorganized.[63]

Organized skilled male workers responded by attempting to prevent female labor from being introduced into a number of trades, at least in those areas monopolized by men. The Society of Galvanizers and Turners, for example, went on strike against women's introduction to the trade and refused to admit them to their Society.[64] The bedstead trade, where approximately 3,000 women were employed, took a somewhat different tack and organized the women into their own union. The paternalistic approach of the male union leader, who was also head of the men's Society, was evident, however, as he indicated that he had no doubt "that he could get all the 3000 women in the trade into the Society if he had time to look after them."[65] Further, women working in the trade were employed in painting, transferring, lacquering, and wrapping, "all of which operations [were] allowed by the men to be women's work" and thus considered non-threatening. When attempts were made to introduce women into other departments "regarded as the men's," the Bedstead Workers' Society "interfered & stopped them," a strike generally being unnecessary.[66]

Briefly in 1890, it appeared that the organized Birmingham trades, with Davis' participation, were generally prepared to initiate a different approach and attempt to organize women workers. Following recent trade disputes involving pen workers and tailoresses, the city Trades Council held a meeting of female operatives, chaired by the president of the Council, A. R. Jephcott. Also present were representatives of the Women's Trade Union League from London, including Emilia Dilke, as well as Davis who was apparently accompanied by his wife and daughter.[67]

Reference was made at this meeting to a pen workers' society formed recently but which had not lasted due to intimidation. One woman had been discharged for simply being seen with a prominent trade unionist, while another met a similar fate upon attending a deputation to the Trades Council. Such action pointed to the weakness of the women, leading to an expressed determination on the part of the Council to assist them in organizing.[68] A resolution was passed at the meeting, declaring:

> That this meeting is of opinion that the formation of trade societies by the female operatives of Birmingham would be advantageous to the workers, would raise their position in the industrial world, and would improve their everyday working condition; that those present agree to form such societies, and to give in their names for that purpose; and that a committee be appointed to take steps for carrying this resolution into effect.[69]

Speaking to the resolution, Davis declared that the mere fact of forming a society would insure improvements if they "only stood together." According to some people, Davis continued, skill alone would mean good wages, but he maintained that "was a fallacy. Combination only could get a fair day's wage for a fair day's work."[70]

It appears, however, that this attempt at combination among the women workers of Birmingham failed to meet with any lasting success. Further, in the brass trade itself, despite Davis' recognition of the evils of the sweating system, the Society failed to challenge it directly. Rather, the Brassworkers continued to follow the practice of attempting to restrict entry into certain sectors of the trade, often undergoing mechanization, by calling for putting an end to the introduction of juvenile labor and upholding the gender division of labor and their control over it.[71] While recognizing that "in this thickly populated country ... employment should be found for women," they declared in their *Annual Report*:

> there should be a line drawn somewhere, but the drawing of it should not be left in the hands of a class – that of the employer class – or it will be drawn in a way that will be anything but equitable to the six millions and a-half of male adults, who do pretty well all the work of this country.[72]

If they were "more fairly dealt with," the *Report* added, they "would be able to maintain their wives and daughters without the degrading labour that some would put them to."[73]

In order to see that the brassworkers were "more fairly dealt with," Davis further continued to pursue their traditional exclusionary policies through participation in a government inquiry into their conditions. The report of the committee, on which Davis served, focused on the illness associated with the casting process known as "brass founders' ague." As a result of long hours of work at the mixing or pouring of metal and the preparation of molds, casters often experienced "shivering, vomiting, and acute depression," especially at the end of a day's work and over weekends and holidays, resulting from the fumes emitted. Confronted with widespread evidence of such suffering among casters, the committee recommended that "the most serious efforts ... be directed by manufacturers and artisans alike" to alleviate these effects of their employment, moving toward "securing a proper construction of casting shops, supplemented by a system of ventilation conducted on scientific principles." As a means of enforcing such standards, they recommended that each employer be required to obtain a "certificate of fitness," assuring that the place of employment met government specifications.[74] Having found women employed in casting shops at the process of core-making, necessary for the production of holloware, the committee further concluded that their employment "should be absolutely prohibited,"[75] although this step was not recommended in the cases of dipping and lacquering, where women had long been employed. This last provision is of particular interest here, especially when we look further at the context in which it was put forward, with Davis' participation.

The report of the committee of inquiry into conditions existing in the brass trade was issued in 1896. The following year saw a revival of trade in the industry which led the Brassworkers to issue a circular to employers, applying for a 10 percent advance. Initially the employers were unresponsive. However, Davis then followed up his proposals with a private letter to some principal employers indicating that, failing an agreement, he would "lead a movement which would not only lay bare and expose the terrible state of brassworkers, but disclose to the world the sweating which existed in the trade."[76] A general meeting of employers then followed at which Davis proposed a general 5 percent advance; a 20 percent bonus; application of the advance to Society members only; and formation of an Employers' Association. An agreement was then reached under which all gained the 5 percent advance while, to receive the additional bonus, non-union men had to join the Society. Four thousand, it was reported, complied.[77]

Despite the restructuring of the industry taking place and the threat posed by the sweating system, which Davis clearly recognized, his tactics remained unchanged. According to Davis' biographer, with the bonus representing an added incentive for workers to join the Society, Davis believed that this would, in turn, place pressure on the sweaters to comply with the rates agreed to by the Employers' Association, since workers would be forced to refuse employment at a lower rate. The resulting unity among employers would then enable the Society to put in place a minimum rate, an objective of Davis' since 1893.[78] A public agitation directed at the sweating system itself, and the extreme exploitation of labor that it represented, would thus be avoided.

According to Davis, the key to this agreement lay "in its restriction to those who won it and will maintain it." "The curse of our trade is the under-cutter," he declared, "who by the most dastardly means brings down wages and prices, and so filches orders from those who conduct their business in a fair and honourable way."[79] Yet he refused to take on the undercutter directly either by means of a public agitation or by directing his organizing efforts at sweated and female labor. Simply by working with the "honorable" employers, the implication was, skilled men could attain and maintain the status and economic security they deserved, as the undercutter was presumably forced out of the trade. A cornerstone of this approach was also apparently the maintenance of the gender division of labor. Women were to remain unorganized while excluded from traditionally "men's work" such as casting, and the artisan was to earn sufficient wages to support his wife at home.

Fundamental to Davis' approach to maintaining the strength and position of the Brassworkers, then, was his continued adherence to gendered notions regarding skill and the "proper avocations" of girls and women. As Keith

McClelland has pointed out in relation to the male skilled worker in general, the Society member's position thus continued to rest "on the exclusion from or subordination of women within capitalist relations of production and the dependency of women within the household."[80] Many men as well, if they agreed to work for the sweater at reduced wages, remained outside the purview of Davis' organizing efforts, which thoroughly relied on the "honorable" employers. A narrow vision or construction of class, as well as gender-based strategies of exclusion, thus continued to be central to Davis' approach to industrial relations.

Yet as was demonstrated above, industrial production and organization in general were in the midst of a transformation, based on an expansion in mechanization and an increase in the number of sweaters and sweated labor, including youth, men, and women alike. As a result, employer–employee relations in general were strained at best as many workers proved unable to maintain their organizations and forestall the introduction of cheap labor. In the brass industry itself, Davis apparently found it necessary to use the threat of public exposure of the sweating system and the major employers' apparent own complicity in it to obtain an agreement.

Despite Davis' apparent organizing successes, then, class relations were not grounded in a solid foundation. Embedded as they were in the existing structure of class relations, neither were current understandings of gender, particularly involving what constituted men's and women's place in the workforce. Such understandings were transcended by the reality of changes in the nature of work that served to place pressure on them. Our analysis, then, must venture beyond a recognition of the gendered nature of existing class relations to examine the dynamics of class and gender as process and their interrelationship. As employers pursued their interests, in this case by mechanizing production and seeking cheap labor, in opposition to the interests of the Brassworkers, existing agreements were threatened. Long-held assumptions and understandings of both class and gender, imbricated in these very agreements, were at least potentially undermined as a consequence. The effectiveness of exclusionary policies toward women as well as the inattention to organizing unskilled men would thus come under increasing scrutiny.

Enmeshed in material relations that were constantly in flux, understandings of gender were themselves unstable and subject to the pressure of change. While constructions of gender were inscribed in economic and class relations, as evidenced in the brass industry, they were subject to alteration as those relations themselves underwent a transformation. The picture we have presented here, then, which stresses the degree to which class unity was fractured by gender among Birmingham metal workers, should not be considered a static and unchanging snapshot but a series of moving frames. Imbricated in the transformation of class relations taking place were also re-workings of understandings of gender and gender relations. In the Black Country metal trades, existing cultural constructions of gender as well as gender relations were under stress as well, from differences in industrial organization and conflicting community interests. Following a consideration of such issues in nail- and chainmaking, we shall examine the process by which gender understandings and gender relations were re-worked in each of these settings.

6 Gender, class, and community in the Black Country

"By 1660," writes Marie B. Rowlands, "the Midlands had all the features of an expanding economy based on rural industry."[1] The agricultural system itself, based on inheritance through primogeniture, served to promote the growth of industry. Under that system, manorial controls were weak, making woodland, wasteland, and heathland widely available for settlement. Laborers and younger sons were then frequently able to combine subsistence farming and industrial production, while landowners benefitted from profits from manufacturing as well.[2] Based on rich resources of coal and iron as well as water power, production was largely devoted to metalworking, which was enjoying a period of expanding markets due to increasing internal trade and travel, agricultural improvements, and rising standards of domestic comfort. Such products as nails, locks, edge tools, agricultural implements, and saddlers' ironmongery as well as pewter and brassware proved to be in considerable demand. During the civil wars, the ironmasters particularly prospered. Enjoying such a solid foundation for continued growth, by this period the industrial parishes of south Staffordshire were more populous than the agricultural.[3]

The area came to be particularly noted for its diversity in the size of communities, types of products, and modes of organization, as well as levels of wealth and poverty. It was the small family-based unit of production, however, that came to dominate as localities increasingly specialized in particular products with which they became associated. While the workforce was large, production continued to rely on "the persisting importance of high-level skills of hand, brain and eye."[4] Within the family, tools were passed down from generation to generation. And when sons reached adulthood, having been trained in the trade, they frequently established workshops contiguous to those of their families. They then provided the resources for their descendants that would enable them to carry on the family trade.[5] The family, its continuity and solidarity were thus critical, Rowlands contends, to the stability of the metalworking trades in the West Midlands. It "provided for continuous recruitment, educated new generations in empirical skills, and dignified labour with a sense of purpose and pride."[6]

By the 1760s, a worldwide market for Midlands goods had been established, with the greatest increase in exports occurring in wrought brass and
copper as well as nails. The port of Bristol on the Severn provided ready
access to the American colonies as metalwares became the largest export
commodity after textiles.[7] Further, the South Staffordshire economy was revo-
lutionized by the introduction of iron smelting by coke rather than charcoal.
The accompanying introduction of rolling mills made it possible for domes-
tically produced pig iron to replace imported bar iron, while puddling furnaces were introduced for the purpose of transforming pig iron into wrought
iron. In the late eighteenth century, the area that became known as the
Black Country came to supply 32 percent of the national output of pig iron
as the traditional industries continued to expand.[8] Until the 1850s, the area
was the leading producer of iron sheets and plates for use in construction,
including shipbuilding; bars for chains and cables; and nail rods and tin-
plates.[9]

The manufacture of chains of all sizes was carried on in a small area of one
to two square miles around Dudley, Cradley, and Cradley Heath, and to a
more limited extent in Walsall where harness chain was produced in connection with saddlers' ironmongery. Heavy chain manufacture became increasingly significant at mid-century, especially around Dudley, in response to a
growing demand in shipping, mining, and agriculture.[10] Nail manufacture
as well was a major industry from the eighteenth century. In general, Rowlands points out, the Midland hardware trade was able to exploit new
opportunities, using resources of leadership, skill, and capital, which was
effectively invested although often small. The community itself provided the
resources it needed not only to survive but expand.[11] Population growth
during the mid-nineteenth-century period, rooted in the strength of coal
mining and the iron trades, was astounding, increasing from 211,323 in
1831 to 473,946 thirty years later.

Despite the apparent economic strength of the area in terms of production
and trade, however, by the mid-nineteenth century it came to be known for
its poor living conditions, particularly housing and the lack of sanitary
measures, as well as the purportedly low social and moral character of the
population.[12] Houses were reported by the *Morning Chronicle* to be dilapi-
dated due to the sinking and shifting of the earth. Drainage facilities in the
towns were inadequate and filth and waste were allowed to accumulate near
the dwellings. Seepage into the soil meant that wells were often contami-
nated. Outbreaks of infectious diseases were not uncommon, and the death
rate was high, as was the infant mortality rate. The area also had a bleak,
actually black, appearance, from which it got its name, due to the coal being
near the surface and thus mined in shallow pits, as well as the many chim-
neys and iron furnaces belching smoke throughout the region. The sun was
practically shut out and gardens were unknown. As a result of such circumstances, the towns and villages were almost entirely working-class, with no
significant middle class taking up residence.[13]

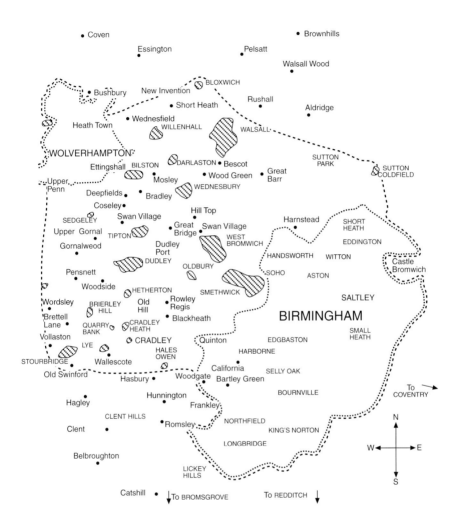

Figure 1 Map of the industrial development of Birmingham and the Black Country, 1860–1927.

According to the *Morning Chronicle*, it was generally accepted that "the workers in metal are proverbially thirsty." St. Monday was said to be widely observed, at times extending to Wednesday.[14] A high rate of illiteracy was typical throughout the area, with half the children receiving no schooling in the 1840s.[15] Larceny was the most frequently reported offense, involving "clothes taken from the washing-line, home or workplace; sheets, blankets and utensils taken from lodgings; coal taken from the domestic coalpile;

poultry taken from a hutch in the yard; money or a watch stolen from the person."[16] Metal and tools were often taken from iron works, while a practice locally known as "black gleaning," whereby people would take discarded coal piled in heaps at the pit mouths for themselves, was widespread.[17] In the majority of cases involving coal, women were the guilty parties, leading commentators to conclude that, in the large towns, there was emerging "a breed of aggressive, violent, drunken, lawless women, as prone as their menfolk to crime and disorder."[18]

Indeed, the general state of the population was widely condemned by contemporary commentators. But the actions of the people that received critical comment must also be seen as ways of confronting a harsh existence. While workers took advantage of formal procedures under the law to gain back any property taken from them, they also shared a sense of traditional "rights to such little private property as they had" to enable them to make a living and provide for their families. Taking coal from the pit mouths and metal and tools from the workplace was thus accepted.[19] A generosity of spirit was also widely in evidence during periods of individual and collective suffering. Wrote R. G. Hobbs, on a "Midland tour" for *The Leisure Hour* in 1872:

> there are individual instances of the possession of some remarkable qual-
> ities, or of qualities ... possessed in a remarkable degree. These have
> been seen ... in self-sacrificing kindness to neighbours; in self-denial,
> involving the privation of necessary food, for the sake of giving some-
> thing to missions, the erection of a church, etc.[20]

Such times became commonplace from the 1860s. At that time, coal mining and iron production began a decline which became a permanent feature of the iron industry after 1874. Iron workers' wages fell 70 percent over the next dozen years, accompanied by a depression in the coal industry. Due to a high level of unemployment and under-employment, George Barnsby has estimated that over half of Black Country families experienced a living stan-dard below the basic level of comfort while 20 percent fell below the minimum to maintain life. The severity of the effects of the depression in trade varied from town to town and was relieved somewhat in the early 1870s with the outbreak of the Franco-Prussian War.[21] However, the sense of a general and widespread impoverishment in the area is clear.

It was in this setting during the 1870s that female labor in nail- and chainmaking, to be considered in this chapter, became a prominent issue. As in Birmingham, the male artisan tradition, and male union leaders, clashed sharply with leaders of the feminist trade union movement over the issue of the employment of women, its morality and legitimacy. And here, too, eco-nomics and the organization of capital complicated the apparent gender con-flict that emerged. However, the conflict itself took a different form due to the differing nature of industrial organization and labor market structures existing in the Black Country communities, both in comparison to Birmingham and in relation to each other.

The domestic manufacture of nails and chains was not organized on the basis of a strictly sex-segregated labor force. Juveniles, women, and men often worked alongside each other doing the same or similar work. Unlike the general situation in Birmingham, whole families and even communities were in some instances dependent on a single form of employment, into which female labor was fully integrated. However, labor market structures varied. When the chainmakers of the community of Walsall, who had been able to organize, maintain their craft status, and exclude women from the trade, attempted to restrict or exclude female labor in general, then, a conflict ensued which took on the appearance of simple gender antagonism. Feminists appeared to gain the support of women workers in opposing restrictions on female labor. However, the division was not simply along gender lines. The rhetoric of the male artisan employed by the Walsall men expressing their ideas regarding work and womanhood failed to resonate in the nail- and chainmaking communities as a whole. Male workers from the Dudley Wood district generally defended women's position in the trades. Rhetoric embedded in the experience of one community thus proved to be in tension with the experiences and needs of others, thereby serving to illustrate the necessity to examine not only the prevailing discourse but its links, or lack of them, with those experiences. The need to re-negotiate gender difference, in terms of class interests, was becoming increasingly apparent. It is this dynamic, then, among understandings of gender, the organization of capital, and class and community interests that is to be examined here.

Female labor in the manufacture of nails and chains

Nail manufacture was a prominent industry in the Black Country from the seventeenth century, employing 35,000 to 40,000 by 1780.[22] At this date, in contrast to the previous century, the labor of women and children was common as "every pair of hands in the family was needed, a few more nails producing a little more money."[23] No other occupations for women were available and it was generally agreed that the manufacture of lighter nails did not require any special strength or skill.[24] As a result, in 1830, it was estimated that 50,000 were engaged in nailmaking in east Worcestershire and south Staffordshire, with women accounting for approximately one-third of the total in the former region.[25] As the industry expanded over the next decade, the rate of increase in the employment of women was 120 percent, as the employment of females aged 15 to 25 came to account for two-thirds of employees in that age group in Staffordshire alone.[26] As children's employment declined in the 1860s, women and girls came to account for generally one-half the laborers.[27]

While some degree of skill was certainly necessary in nailmaking, it was a

Figures 2–5 Illustrations from the *Handbook of the Daily News Sweated Industry Exhibition*, compiled by Richard Mudie-Smith, London, Burt & Sons, 1906.

Source: British Library of Political and Economic Science, LSE.

Figure 3

Figure 4

trade that was comparatively easy to pick up.[28] The tools of the trade were simple, with the work requiring only a hearth, a leather bellows, a hand-hammer, and a treadle and spring pole that operated the oliver, or large hammer, that cut the heavier rods and formed the points and heads. As a result of the simplicity of the trade, in communities such as Halesowen it has been claimed that "nearly every cottage possessed a one-storied nailshop in the backyard."[29]

Figure 5

Figure 6 Women chainmakers at Harry Stevens Chains, Cradley Heath, *c.* 1912.
Source: Sandwell Public Library.

The work itself required careful attention, quickness, and dexterity. The rods were kept hot by the fire which was constantly kept going by a puff or two of the bellows. A nailer would snatch a rod from the fire and, with a few sharp blows of a hand-hammer on the thinner rods, form a point which was then inserted into a tool and twisted, severing it from the rest of the rod. The nailer then operated the foot treadle which brought down the hammer that formed the head of the nail. The rod worked on was returned to the fire, another rod grabbed, and the process repeated.[30] Wrote Rev. Harold Rylett in 1890 of the long-established hand industry, "The dexterity and speed with which the operation is performed are amazing, for the iron is heated and the nail made in much less time than will be occupied in reading this description of the process."[31] He estimated that "a clever girl of sixteen or eighteen" could make 2,000 to 2,500 nails in a ten-hour day, depending on their size.[32]

As demanding as such work on smaller nails was, Rev. Rylett claimed that "we have not touched bottom in the nail trade until we have seen how spike nails are made," work which he considered "the cruellest occupation in which women and young girls are employed in this country."[33] Here two people worked together, commonly a man and young girl, first using the oliver to cut the iron rods into five-inch lengths. The general method described by Rev. Rylett was for the girl to get "close behind the man, generally holding him by the waist," as they jumped together on the treadle, bringing down the oliver two or three times until the required length was cut off. In some instances when the iron was particularly thick, Rev. Rylett indicated that he had seen as many as four or five young men and women jumping together on the treadle, and added, "a more brutal and loathsome spectacle I never witnessed in my life."[34] Following this operation, the workers moved to opposite sides of the hearth where the heads and points of the nails were formed. Stated Rev. Rylett:

> It is humiliating to see a girl thus occupied. But I have seen a girl of eighteen "heading" as well as "pointing." I shall never forget the sight. Suddenly turning into a well-known yard in Halesowen I saw this young woman with arms and bosom bare, grimy, profusely perspiring, and working like a tigress. It was simply revolting.[35]

In 1866, it was estimated that a male first-class nailer could earn 22s. to 25s. per week, while the minimum rate was perhaps 7s., earned by youths and women. From these rates, however, deductions were made for firing, tools, and shop rent amounting to approximately 2s. 6d. per week.[36] Wages were further reduced since nailers would generally not be able to put in a full week's work due to the time spent fetching the iron rods and taking the nails to the warehouse of the master or middleman, known as the fogger.[37] Due to domestic duties, the women's work week would often be shorter, serving to bring down their wages even further.[38] Moreover, the nature of the work, particularly operation of the oliver, was especially harmful to women's child-bearing capacity as they suffered ruptures and miscarriages brought on by such labor.[39]

Yet it was clearly the unfeminine nature of the work itself that Rev. Rylett found offensive. While women and girls had been engaged in such work for one hundred years, now they were identified with animal prowess while concern was expressed regarding their bodily exposure. The conditions of the labor, as in mining and lead works, were now considered unacceptable.

Conditions in the chainmaking industry, and reactions to it, were similar. In the early 1870s, approximately 3,000 people were engaged in the trade, 1,000 being women who were employed in domestic manufacture in the Dudley Wood district.[40] Wrote the author of a pamphlet on women chainmakers in 1877, "a very few miles from Wolverhampton may be found hundereds [sic] of young girls – almost children in many instances – middle aged matrons, and wrinkled old women engaged in one of the most laborious and unwomanly of occupations."[41] Here he reported seeing many pregnant women and others who had recently given birth hard at work. One such woman he described as looking "pale, wan, and emaciated, but she was blowing her bellows and forging her links as well as her scanty strength would allow, while her baby wrapped in some rags, was lying on a heap of ashes in a corner."[42]

Ten years later, during a major strike, the Special Commissioner for the *Sunday Chronicle* recorded a number of scenes, among the women who had settled with their employers, of young babies present while the women worked.[43] At a mass meeting of perhaps 2,000 striking female chainmakers, many babies were in evidence, since women often continued their employment following the birth of their children.[44] Probably typical was a scene painted by a reporter for the *Labour Tribune* in 1888, upon entering Cradley Heath, of a man and his wife in a small workshop:

> They were making chain, and working as hard as they could. Three little children half-clad were perched upon the hearth while their parents rapidly put in and drew out the iron they were making up into chain, and the sparks flew from the tiny anvils all about the children.[45]

Alongside such scenes appeared instances, such as that reported in the *Sunday Chronicle*, of a home where a 30-year-old man was working alongside his mother, aged 70, "her shrivelled form bent almost double," working the bellows for him. Said the woman proudly, "I've been a good 'un in my time, too, but I've got past it now!"[46]

The organization of the domestic side of the industry was similar to that in nailmaking. Outworkers went to the employer's warehouse where iron rods were supplied. The workers then returned to their homes, where they had from one to as many as eight fires to work, or took their rods to a workshop rented out at a weekly rate by a middleman. In the latter case, tools and fires were provided at a cost of a 25 percent wage deduction. A male worker would often employ his wife and children in such shops or they would work together at their home. With the work requiring continuous labor, involving cutting off lengths of iron rod, heating, and welding them, they worked ten to eleven hours per day at piece-rates based on the hundred-weight of chain produced.[47]

With the majority of the population trained to follow the trade when young, an oversupply of labor became evident in the early 1870s. Lacking any alternative employment opportunities, girls and women of all ages were so employed. Further, women working at their own forges often married miners and puddlers who then, in periods of partial employment, took to the trade themselves.[48]

Throughout the period, as Sheila Blackburn brings out in her important study, an increase in the number of middlemen was evident. With little capital required to establish shops with a number of fires, they took advantage of the ample labor supply of men, women, and children, causing the trade to become even more overcrowded. The chainmakers were thus "obliged to take whatever they were offered to gain work,"[49] and wages fell dramatically, amounting to 6s. to 7s. per week in 1877, a rate 20 to 50 percent below those paid in the north of England as well as Wales and Walsall.[50]

In both the chain- and nailmaking industries, there were frequent protests and attempts at organization to resist reductions in wages. Already in 1820, George Barnsby reports, labor unrest had occurred among the nailers resulting from a cut in wages brought on by a depression in trade. A parade in Stourbridge attracted "thousands of distressed work people of both sexes," whose appearance was reported to be "deplorable and calculated to excite the deepest commiseration."[51] As early as the 1830s, the hand-wrought nail trade was affected by competition from machine-made nails, resulting in an abatement of wages, or a bate, as the practice was called.[52] While some masters indicated that they were simply forced to follow others who had reduced wages, it was clear, write Kings and Cooper, "that the foggers and the little masters were already calling the tune."[53]

In 1842, a year marked by depression and widespread labor agitation throughout the country, a major strike among Black Country miners occurred. Chartist agitation and organization in the area were also extensive, as Charter Associations of both men and women were established in Cradley and Netherton, while a Female Association was founded in Dudley.[54] But, George Barnsby indicates, "trouble first came from the nailers" whom he refers to as "the most depressed section of workers."[55] When the nail masters introduced a 20 percent bate, "15,000 nailers marched on Dudley, captured some of the nailmasters en route and attempted to seize the Dudley masters."[56] Again, in 1848, in the midst of a depression in the iron trade, "The nailers, as usual, suffered longest," writes Barnsby. After a two-week strike, however, the masters were "forced to discontinue the reduction in wages due to the great demand for nails."[57]

Between 1838 and 1863, it has been estimated that there were five general strikes in the nail trade and numerous partial ones involving the men and women employed throughout the industry.[58] Among chainmakers as well a number of strikes took place, the largest occurring in 1859 when a union was established with the support of their counterparts in Newcastle.[59] From that summer, Barnsby writes, "the relationship between masters and men [*sic*] deteriorated so rapidly that within a few months the cutting of bellows in nail and chain shops was reported and a virtual state of war declared on nail and chain masters."[60] The action included a chainmaker being "assaulted with a hedge stake" and "an alleged attempt to blow up a nail shop" whose proprietor was not a member of the Nail makers' Union.[61] At the same time, employers were increasingly bringing charges against workers for petty thefts from the workplace in an attempt, states David Philips, to enforce a strict understanding of property rights as opposed to traditional communal rights to which the workers often appealed.[62]

The next five years were generally marked by "the most extraordinarily bitter industrial battles" but, states Barnsby, for the most part "the period belongs to the domestic workers, nailers and chain-makers, who fought for their very existence at this time."[63] The truck system, which referred to the paying of workers in provisions rather than money wages, a practice common in both industries, became a major target of attack. A number of workers brought charges against their employers who often were required to pay fines by the courts. Finally, in 1863, an eight-week strike among nailers, against not only a 10 percent wage reduction, but against the truck system itself, took place, apparently leading to an agreed price list.[64] This agreement was threatened only five years later when there was again considerable strike activity. However, these protests resulted in at least the Bromsgrove masters agreeing to a return to the price list negotiated in 1864, a decision that was marked by a "celebratory tea" among masters and men.[65]

By the early 1870s, while the chainmakers' union had apparently been broken,[66] the Bromsgrove Nail Forgers Protection Association had been established and managed to negotiate an increase in wages in the town. However, not all employers adhered to the wage list agreed to and a bitter strike resulted in 1877.[67] Three years later, George Green of the firm of Eliza Tinsley and Co. convened employers in the trade to establish a Board of Conciliation and Arbitration for the settlement of wage disputes, but again an insufficient proportion of masters were involved while undercutting was common.[68] Further, the hand-made nail trade itself was in sharp decline as competition from the Belgian trade increased, while machine-made nails were beginning to dominate the market, particularly on the large dock contracts. In addition, the American and Australian markets were lost abroad.[69] By 1888, John Burnett estimated that 2,000 workers, half of whom were women, continued to work in Halesowen in the hand-made nail trade, manufacturing nails for horse and mule shoes. Overall, Burnett claimed that 15,000 hand-nailers, half of them women, were in employment.[70] Accompanying this decline in the hand-wrought nail trade was an influx of women nailers into chainmaking from the 1870s, serving to add to the overcrowded conditions in that trade, described above.

Clearly by the final quarter of the nineteenth century, both the chain- and nailmaking industries centered in the Black Country were in a state of crisis brought on by the interrelated problems of an overcrowded labor market, an increase in middlemen, low wages, and, in the case of nailmaking particularly, competition from foreign manufacturers as well as mechanization. Despite valiant attempts to deal with these issues through strikes, price lists, and a system of conciliation and arbitration, no resolution of the prevailing crisis appeared in sight. In this circumstance, the issue of women's work was taken up by Parliament.

Women's work, Parliament, and the Walsall Chainmakers

A factory inspector's report issued in 1875 drew particular attention to the conditions under which women labored in these industries. It especially called attention to the apparent advantage idle husbands took of their labor. While the women "toil and slave," often working hours beyond the legal limit, the factory sub-inspector, Brewer, reported, "the ought-to-be bread winner is luxuriating in some public-house."[71] He went on to cite a number of examples, including that of an anchor smith, capable of earning £3 per week, who had deserted his family, forcing his wife to keep children out of school to work at the forge. "The poor woman, at last getting wearied out," Brewer reported, "threw herself on the parish, who prosecuted her husband, and the justices sent the man to gaol."[72] In a similar vein, the pamphlet writer who visited the area in 1877 offered the experience of one woman who "had a husband living, and in the village somewhere." Asked, "Didn't he do any work," the woman responded, "No, he didn't, except, perhaps, one or two days a week, when he had no money to drink – then he'd go to work fast enough; but she had to keep the house and the children."[73]

The Royal Commission on the Factory and Workshops Acts convened in 1876 followed up on the inspector's report by giving prominence to the Black Country metal industries, particularly soliciting testimony from representatives of the chainmakers of Walsall. In this community of about 50,000, only 300 men worked in chainmaking. However, that labor was carried on in a setting that differed sharply from that existing in Cradley Heath.

In the Black Country, the manufacture of ironmongery articles, such as nuts and bolts, screws, latches, hinges, and gunlocks, was often centered in workshops of craftsmen who were recognized for their time-honored skill in metalworking.[74] Walsall in particular had a reputation for "excellence of workmanship," with its main industry being leather manufacture and saddle- and harness-making. Here chainmaking was associated with the craft of saddlers' ironmongery and, as such, had retained its exclusively male workforce.[75] The chainmakers of Walsall were also part of a larger network of organized crafts with a society recognized by the employers. Thus in the fall of 1871, when trade had revived following a slump during 1866–8, they were successful in gaining a 20 percent increase in wages, having presented their employers with a list for such an advance.[76] By 1876, their wages averaged approximately 30s. per week compared to 8s. earned by women in the Dudley Wood district.[77]

Despite such favorable conditions, however, the chainmakers of Walsall were vulnerable, largely due to the depression generally affecting the iron trade. As early as June of 1872, a request for an advance by the chainmakers had been met with a negative response from the employers who indicated that inaction at that time "was the best means of retaining the trade, and thereby securing employment for their workmen." They further noted that they had orders on hand that would last six months and feared that such an advance would serve to limit additional orders, particularly since merchants were currently only purchasing quantities necessary to meet immediate demands.[78] In denying the chainmakers' request at that time, then, the employers claimed they "were actuated by the most kindly feeling" towards the chainmakers and reached their decision "only from a sincere desire to promote the interest of the workmen, by retaining the trade in the town." Apparently there was some question as to whether the trade would remain in Walsall, with a charge being made by some that the objective of an Act of Parliament, requiring the testing of cable chain, was "to drive the chain trade out [of] Walsall and send it to Cradley."[79]

The Walsall men had reason to feel that their trade and their earning power were less than secure. By 1874, the 2,000 workers employed in the town in the iron industry generally were feeling the harsh effects of the depression in trade, although the town in general, due to its diversity of trades, marked the downturn from the end of 1876.[80] Consequently, by that date the chainmakers felt particularly threatened when they saw work produced in the Dudley Wood district, at the prevailing low wages, intermingled with their own and sold at a considerably lower price. In these circumstances, they singled out the subcontracting system and its widespread use of juvenile and female labor prevailing in the Dudley Wood district as the main source of their difficulties.[81] The Walsall chainmakers also pointed to other working men, "the self-indulgent drunkard – very often a collier, or maybe a puddler . . . who, tempted by her being able to work, has married a female chainmaker, in hope of leading an easy, idle life." As a result of such a practice, they complained, whole families are trained in the trade, and the number thereby engaged "is doubled and quadrupled until the trade is over-run by those who ought never to have been in it at all."[82]

In general, the Walsall men complained of a system that compelled men to work at the same low wages as women and children, obliging them "to make such a large quantity of work to earn a bare subsistence that they have no time to do full justice to their work, the incentive to good workmanship being crushed out by excessive competition." "Through the instrumentality of women and children," Samuel Stringer of the Chainmakers Association declared, "the markets are glutted with cheap but very inferior work."[83] As a remedy, he proposed that the Factory Acts, rather than the less stringent Workshops Act, be applied to chainmaking, "because one of the first effects of it would be to cause women and children's labour to be gradually eliminated from the trade." Eventually, he predicted, women would even "be ashamed to learn how to work at such a trade."[84]

To hasten this end, the Association further called upon the Parliamentary Committee of the Trades Union Congress to support an amendment to the proposed Factory and Workshops Consolidation Bill prohibiting "the employment of females under sixteen years of age working at chain- and nail-making."[85] Upon presentation to Parliament, this amendment failed, although the Bill passed generally met with approval from the TUC.[86] Despite this setback, however, the Walsall Chainmakers continued to pursue their cause over the following years, concluding "that the employment of women and children in such a trade as that of chain-making, is unjust to legitimate workmen; that it tends to demoralise the women engaged in it, and is a gross outrage on the civilization of the nineteenth century."[87]

By 1883, the cause had become a crusade as the Walsall Chainmakers attempted to take advantage of the comparatively good times, due to foreign demand, enjoyed by the saddlery and harness trade, to which they were connected.[88] In their efforts, they gained the support of the South Staffordshire and East Worcestershire Trades' Council and Richard Juggins, whom Eric Taylor has described as "the voice of the Black Country craftsman" during this period.[89] As secretary of the Nut and Bolt Makers' Association, established in 1870, Juggins had pioneered in reaching an agreement with employers establishing a list of prices and standards of quality for the trade.[90] Now he turned his attention to the effort initiated by the Walsall Chainmakers, concerned with the threat they perceived to their superior craftsmanship posed by female labor, to restrict or exclude that labor from the trade.

Appearing before the TUC Parliamentary Committee in February 1883, Juggins, accompanied by Thomas Harrison of the Chainmakers, presented samples of the heavy iron on which girls and women of all ages labored. Apparently the Committee was particularly struck by their "description of the half-nude state of the women engaged in the work, in company with men in the same state of undress." The Committee thus concluded that, "if anything like the condition of things described exists, it is a disgrace to the nation" and supported the introduction of legislation prohibiting the employment of girls under the age of 14 at iron forges.[91]

Upon returning to the Black Country, Juggins and the Trades' Council defended the proposed legislation at numerous meetings held throughout the nail- and chainmaking districts and in letters appearing in area news-papers. Referring to his involvement over a period of twelve years "in improving the social and moral position of the operatives in my own and other trades," Juggins declared that he was now "anxious . . . to remove what I believe to be the great cause of their present sad condition . . . female and especially juvenile labour."[92] By "putting a stop to the immorality which was known to take place in the workshops,"[93] Juggins hoped the working people of the Black Country would be placed "upon an equal footing with the artisans of other trades."[94]

A deputation of chainmakers from Newcastle and Sunderland visited the district in 1883 and added their voice to the call for the proposed legislation along the same lines. They expressed their displeasure with the men of the region for even allowing women in the trade and called for the abolition of female labor on the grounds that such competition was injurious to all.[95] The president of the South Staffordshire and East Worcestershire Trades' Council responded, declaring that "they were all agreed that efforts should be made to prevent female labour in the nail and chain shops."[96]

As he pressed his agenda in the following years, Juggins returned to the theme of the questionable morality of female labor, proclaiming the work of girls as blacksmiths to be "a disgrace to the female sex" as it was "contrary to their nature."[97] In 1886, during the course of a major strike among chain-makers lasting several months, he declared that he had "reluctantly" con-cluded "that the first and real cause of all our local evils is female labour."[98]

> The unnatural employment of women at the forge [Juggins continued] has been most detrimental to the interests of wage-earners in all these trades. From the Trades Unionist point of view, such female labour should no[t] only be condemned by the public voice, but should be pro-hibited by legislation, just as we have by legislation prevented females working in the mines.[99]

Where "juvenile labour and female slavery recede," he optimistically pro-claimed:

> fresh and unlooked for occupations spring up, and those who have been nursed in the lap of luxury at the expense of those who have been living a life of slavery . . . [are] compelled to throw in their lot with those who have been oppressed, and not complain of those who desire to bring about such needed alterations.[100]

To Juggins and his allies in the Trades Federation and among male chain-makers of the North, the skilled craftsman, organized and maintaining a recognized status in the trade, represented the "legitimate" workman, as the Walsall Chainmakers declared. Women's work in the same trade, carried on alongside men under such conditions as those described above, however, contained within it different meanings, which were closely linked in the discourse of the male artisan. It was deemed "a gross outrage on civilization," "a disgrace to the nation," "a disgrace to the female sex," "unnatural," and assumed to lead to immorality at the workplace. Divisions between the work of men and women in the discourse of the Walsall craftsman had become naturalized. To witness women working alongside men in their own craft offended the Walsall Chainmakers' well-established sense of order and threatened their masculinity, built upon their property in skill and their exclusive practice of their craft and control of it. Since the exercise of that control was thus founded upon gender segregation, the intermingling of the sexes, as well as their work, was seen to undermine that control and the respectability that accompanied it. Add to this circumstance the presence of female sexuality fully exposed and revealed, and civilization itself, and the standards of morality on which it rested, were in danger.

At the same time, female labor represented low-wage competition, further adding to its illegitimacy. And that competition was not only gendered, and thus not neutral, but was intimately bound up with the nature of the work itself and its lack of suitability for women. As Thomas Harrison of Walsall stated in a comment that could not better illustrate how the issues involved were thoroughly intertwined, "I believe that many of the workmen have as much regard for women's rights as most men or women . . . but we do decidedly object to them working at such unfeminine and unwomanly work so as to interfere with our wages."[101]

Once female labor came into direct competition with the labor of the Walsall men, the long-standing position of girls and women in the nail- and chainmaking trades, of which many men had taken considerable advantage, was proclaimed to be immoral and against nature. The men then, Sheila Blackburn argues, "simply made what was essentially a wage issue into a sex problem."[102]

Such a conclusion, however, is not fully satisfactory since it fails to come to terms with the extent to which the sex of the worker and the issue of wages, meaning particular views of femininity and masculinity, were always dynamically interwoven in the discourse of the male artisan. The views expressed by Juggins and the Walsall Chainmakers clearly led to gender conflict. But, as in Birmingham, the issues transcended such antagonism. Not only were understandings of what constituted womanhood thoroughly embedded in the apparently economic ideology of the craftsmen of the Black Country. But as has been suggested by some remarks of the Walsall men quoted above, what constituted masculinity was at issue as well. Here a clear consensus is evident among Juggins, Broadhurst, and the chainmakers of Newcastle and Walsall. Not only was masculinity identified by property in skill but also by the exercise of authority in the workplace and the home, meaning upholding a sense of morality and order, as they defined it, and preventing female labor in circumstances where the labor of men would suffice to support the family. Seeing the puddlers and miners as lazy, rough, and thus unmanly led to conflict between men and communities, as well as between women and men, as detailed below.

Gender conflict in the Black Country metal trades

Women chain- and nailmakers of the Black Country were acutely aware of the extent to which their families depended on them. In one instance, at a meeting in 1883 arranged to oppose the possible exclusion of women from these trades, this awareness led to some humor when one woman declared, if such a policy were put in place, "There would be no marriages." Her comment was followed by laughter.[103] But of course the necessity of women's work was a serious matter and their labor was clearly vital. Rather than being confined to a period of their youth prior to marriage, women worked throughout the life cycle, as indicated earlier. Even where husbands worked at other trades, earning adequate wages, wives continued to labor, purportedly neglecting their domestic duties, leaving their children alone or in the care of someone else, or keeping them "in some corner of a smoky, draughty, unhealthy workshop, open to every wind that blows." Their labor in a single day often exceeded the limit imposed by factory and workshop legislation, at times reaching fifteen hours "while the 'master' only puts in eight hours a day in the pit."[104] Where possible, children assisted, with girls apparently remaining at home "helping mother" rather than entering domestic work.[105]

Despite these deplorable conditions and long hours, evidence emerges of a sense of identification with their work among the women workers. In reference to chainmaking, a reporter for the *Labour Tribune* called attention to the "hereditary skill" that "enters very largely into the trade." Describing the work in some detail, he wrote:

> The proper heat has to be maintained, and then since the iron is very light in the small chain it must be manipulated with great rapidity and dexterity. From the moment of cutting off the bit of iron that is to form the link until it is properly heated, bent, linked, and welded, less than half a minute is occupied in the case of what is known as No. 1. And in this brief space of time the worker has to take the iron out of the fire, and put it back again, and use the anvil twice. It is simply astonishing what a degree of dexterity is required and attained . . .[106]

Women understandably exhibited pride in such skill. Thus the woman of 70 mentioned above, working alongside her son, may have been "shrivelled" and "bent almost double" but she had no doubt that she had been "a good 'un" in her time. Another woman, also visited by the *Sunday Chronicle* correspondent, explained "with some volubility the mystery of her craft," while another responded to her husband's smug comment that "thou'rt not so brisk as thou wast once," with the rejoinder that "there's plenty o' men as can't do so much as a woman."[107] Chain- and nailmaking were clearly skills in which the women took pride. But perhaps of greatest importance in this respect, and this to some extent is conjecture, is not only their own identification with their work, but the importance they placed on passing on that skill to their daughters.

Aware of the value of their labor and that men could not always be counted on, the women were, we can safely surmise, especially concerned that their daughters be able to support themselves. Having no other trades to turn to, and being generally resistant to working as domestics, they would need to be trained in the only work available, chainmaking. Legislation that prohibited their training at an early age could reasonably be viewed as undue interference in an important aspect of family life and the culture of the community: the transmission of skill from mother to daughter. The legislative restrictions proposed in this context were highly controversial to say the least.

Feminists of the Women's Protective and Provident League (WPPL), whom we encountered in our discussion of women's work in Birmingham, quickly came to the conclusion that the intention of the legislation, aimed at the prohibition of the labor of girls, was actually directed toward women as well. The *Englishwoman's Review*, representing the ideals of "the emerging emancipated middle-class woman,"[108] thus confronted the issue on this basis and quickly came to the women's defense. "Why," the journal asked, should "hard-working women . . . be compelled to forego their already insufficiently paid labour, while the men – husbands and fathers – who spend their time and money in low pleasures, were to be unmolested." Such a measure, they concluded, represented yet "one other instance of the careless way in which legislation is proposed for women."[109] Rather than considering such measures philanthropic and in the interest of working women, the journal suggested that it was the interests of men that were being served by eliminating competition from their female counterparts.[110]

At the 1877 Trades Union Congress, Emma Paterson indicated that she was "startled" at the attempts under way to exclude female labor from agriculture and chainmaking.[111] According to Paterson:

> the fires used for the purposes of the work were not hotter than ordinary fires, and the work she considered was not too hard for the females employed at it in the Black Country. Women should be allowed [Paterson concluded] to earn their own living without undue restrictions.[112]

Having staked out such a position six years previously, it was not surprising that the WPPL again entered the fray in 1883 as Juggins and the TUC stepped up their campaign for restrictive legislation. That spring, Ada Heather Bigg of the WPPL wrote a letter to the *Times* declaring, "The whole movement to restrict female labour in the Black Country is the outcome of an agitation partial in extent, and interested in character."[113] Rather than being concerned with the hardships of women workers, the *Women's Union Journal* concurred, those supporting legislative restrictions were simply looking after the interests of the men.[114]

The *Englishwoman's Review* chided other newspapers such as the *Daily News* and the *Standard* for putting forth the "picturesque side" of philanthropy with their tales of "daughters of tender years working at their mother's side," realizing earnings, after rent for shop and tools, as low as 2s. 6d. per week. What other occupations could the women be engaged in, the journal asked. "Are they to become barmaids, or to go to the workhouse, or to do worse?" With regard to the labor of girls, they asked if it wasn't better that they could "keep at home, under maternal supervision, rather than seek for situations alone and unprotected."[115] Such comments sparked a heated response from Henry Broadhurst of the TUC who took aim at the privileged backgrounds of the "refined and educated ladies" of the WPPL. Had they "been born to a state of perpetual toil for wages which at the end of a week are often little in excess of the cost of a pair of dainty gloves," Broadhurst railed, "their fine reasoning would have taken a different turn."[116]

Yet it does appear that, at least to some degree, women chain- and nail-makers were receptive to the feminists' position. They were prominent at meetings held among workers in the Black Country where resolutions were passed expressing such a view. One such resolution declared that "the making of small chains and nails is not injurious to the health of girls or boys . . . and [added] that the parents of girls cannot keep them until the age of fourteen without work."[117] At a meeting of nailmakers addressed by Edith Simcox of the WPPL, she called upon men and women to join together to improve their wages rather than press for further legislation. With this message, she apparently gained full support among the female operatives who resolved that "further interference with the work of girls in nailmaking is unnecessary and undesirable."[118] Among the men, however, Simcox confronted opposition, with a nailer, apparently from Halesowen, calling for women's work to be abolished so "that they could cook and wash and bake and attend to their families" rather than work for wages that were 50 percent of men's for the same work. Separate votes among men and women were then taken, with the men alone resolving to support "further legislation with regard to the restriction of female labour."[119]

On the basis of such experience, Emma Paterson charged the TUC Parliamentary Committee, which was pursuing the legislation, with acting as if men were the best judges of women's wishes. The WPPL, in contrast, had sought the opinions of actual women working in the small metal trades. When they had done so, Paterson contended, they had found support for their opposition to legislation, with women generally objecting to the proposed Bill on the grounds that it was ultimately directed at their work as well, although only the labor of girls would be prohibited.[120] "However unsuitable such work may appear to be," the *Women's Union Journal* concluded, "we must look at the question from the working woman's point of view."[121]

In May of 1883, the proposed Bill was defeated in the House of Commons by a vote of 124 to 44, with members arguing that the desire to raise men's wages was the real purpose of the agitation.[122] Some also maintained that, with growing competition in the labor force, it was necessary for people to learn such trades, where the labor was deemed to be comparatively light anyway, at an early age. Perhaps Charles Dilke put forward the most effective argument by pointing out that, of 896 nail and chain shops, only nine employed female children and thus would be affected by the Bill, a contention with which the Trades Union Congress took sharp issue.[123]

Such an overwhelming defeat, however, did not bring an end to the agitation. Rather, Juggins called for the re-introduction of the Amendment Bill before the Trades Union Congress later that year and the year following. At the Congress of 1884, he indicated that he did not wish to interfere directly with female labor but suggested that those trades "best adapted" to it "should be encouraged for females, and not those that were adapted only to males, such as those of blacksmiths and of working in shops."[124] The *Women's Union Journal* then accused Juggins of being "less guarded" before his own members of the Nut and Bolt Makers' Association. Here, apparently, rather than expressing concern regarding interference with female labor, he suggested that, since the nail and chain trades were oversupplied with labor, the solution was to "rid [them] of [their] female element . . . and let men do the work that belonged to them, and so rid the country of this lasting disgrace."[125] In response, the *Journal* intoned, "We advise Mr. Juggins to invite the women to join his trade union, instead of trying to 'ameliorate their condition' by the harsh and undeviating operation of a law forbidding them to work."[126]

With these comments the WPPL called upon Juggins to deal with the work of women by taking economic measures, by organizing them, rather than judging its "suitability." Yet they too were aware of the popular appeal of legislation restricting the work of girls and women in such trades as nail- and chainmaking, and recognized a necessity to address it. Ada Heather Bigg, in an article for the *Fortnightly Review* based on a three-day visit to nail and chain shops in Rowley, Blackheath, Old Hill, Cradley, Cradley Heath, and Lye Waste, even acknowledged that there were "evils" that were "indisputably" connected with them.[127]

> Many of the shops were dark and close [she noted], the homes squalid, the sanitary arrangements unpleasantly defective, the strain on the physical powers severe, the hours of work unduly prolonged, and the nailers naturally ill content with their lot, and ready to welcome as a boon any measure that held out promise of relief.[128]

Accompanied by George Green of E. Tinsley and Co., a large employer of female labor in the wrought nail trade, however, she also indicated that she saw the full range of conditions existing in the district and was allowed to canvas the issue of female labor "from all points of view."[129] Other shops she then described as "light" and "airy" and "the homes clean, the women cheerful and robust." And she further concluded that there was nothing "objectionable" or "so physically exhausting or so peculiarly unwomanly in the making of small nails and chains." "The fires roar, the hammers clink, the sparks fly, and women and men toil together at the anvil," creating a "spectacle [that] is a rude shock to the idealiser of woman." But it was the low wages that were responsible for "such evils as do exist," Bigg concluded.[130]

Several women workers, Bigg reported, expressed to her their preference for such work over domestic service. And the visiting commentator herself, having tried to operate some of the olivers, declared that such work was no more of a strain than operating a sewing machine with a foot treadle.[131] Noting that their labor was generally confined to four days per week, Bigg further waxed eloquently regarding the setting (her own garden plot) in which the women carried on their work, which she believed contrasted favorably with that of the factory operative. And on Saturdays, when the women nailers gathered in the warehouses to receive their wages, Bigg proclaimed, "you see a comely, respectable set of working women, robust and strong, without being in the least masculine." She even admitted that she was so "favourably impressed with their appearance," she "might almost have forgotten how desperately hard the whole family had to toil for such small wages as were then being doled out to them."[132]

Here Bigg took on the critics of women's work, but it is interesting to note the extent to which she did so explicitly on their terms, indicating it wasn't so "peculiarly unwomanly" as suggested. Some of the shops were "light and airy," located in gardens (which seems particularly unlikely), she assured the women's detractors, making them "suitable" settings for the labor of women – in other words, not that unfeminine. Further, the picture conveyed by hammers clinking and sparks flying suggests a lightness, a playfulness that again detracts from the strength involved in the labor itself. And of course the women could appear "comely, respectable" upon the occasion of collecting their earnings. Here Bigg called upon a central feminine image, explicitly contrasting it with the "masculine" qualities of strength and robustness that the women also displayed, thereby reassuring critics that they had not been fully de-feminized.

Despite such attempts to address the issues involved regarding women's work, however, the lines were clearly drawn as a dispute broke out at the Trades Union Congress of 1887 between WPPL representatives and Richard Juggins. Here the latter introduced a resolution calling on the Parliamentary Committee to oversee the introduction into Parliament of

> such amendments to the Factory and Workshops Act as shall prevent the employment of females in the making of chains, nails, rivets, bolts, or any such articles that are made from iron or steel, such work not being adapted to their physical constitution . . .[133]

In response, Clementina Black, a delegate for the WPPL, acknowledged that the conditions under which women worked in these trades were undesirable. But at the same time, conditions in such work as matchbox-making were equally deplorable, yet no one thought of forbidding women from being engaged in such labor because men were not so employed and consequently did not suffer from the competition of female labor. Declaring her resentment at "the attempt of one class of workers – especially a class whose interests were concerned – to impose restrictions upon another," Black maintained that men should instead "join in helping [women] to combine in order that they might receive the same wages for the same work."[134]

Such antagonism appears to have culminated in 1891 when the passage of legislation restricting female employment in the nail, rivet, and chain trades was again sought. At a "crowded meeting of operatives" held in Old Hill, sharp divisions became apparent when the chairman asked if the meeting approved a proposed Bill prohibiting employment of girls prior to the age of 16. Provoked by the question, the girls and women present "rose *en masse* and waved their handkerchiefs" to signal their opposition while the men launched a "counter demonstration" of their own.[135] The meeting then passed, with a number of dissentients, a resolution presented by Ada Heather Bigg declaring, "That this meeting deprecates all legislation which will have the effect of driving women out of the nail and chain trades."[136]

It thus appears that, while Juggins continued to assert that it was a "disgrace" for women to be employed in making large chains and in the working of olivers, the women themselves "strongly object[ed] to the proposed restrictions."[137] The suffragist Millicent Fawcett was even able to organize a deputation of women chain- and nailmakers to appear before the Home Secretary and voice their opposition to legislative interference. This deputation included girls of 16, as well as a woman aged 57 who had worked at the trade for nearly fifty years, had fourteen children, "and strongly deprecate[d] any interference with the women engaged in the chain and nail industry."[138] In response and suggestive of the depth of the apparent conflict between men and women workers, the *Labour Tribune*, organ of the Miners, Ironworkers, Nut and Bolt Forgers, &c., of Great Britain, lamented:

> That was a very discreditable cause which the deputation of female chainmakers, who visited London ... had in hand. A praiseworthy effort has been made to introduce more civilized conditions into the lives of these poor women, to prevent them working iron beyond their strength, and to restrict the hours of employment to a reasonable limit, and those women have gone to tell the Home Secretary how much they are attached to the degrading slavery of their daily existence.[139]

For well over a decade, it appears, the chain- and nailmaking trades of the Black Country were characterized by gender antagonism as male union leaders continually sought women's ultimate removal from the trades, over the women's strong objections. Yet the extent to which gender was also being re-negotiated is brought out by the above comment appearing in the *Labour Tribune*, the journal which we examined previously in connection with the dispute over female pit-brow workers. Then the *Tribune* came to the defense of the women workers, although that did not appear to be their position at first as they joined the miners outside Lancashire in deploring the labor of women and its interference with their domestic pursuits. Now, a striking difference emerged between the rhetoric of Juggins and his allies, which we have examined, and that of the journal, which was not only associated with the miners but apparently with Juggins' own trade, the nut and bolt forgers, as well. While the paper referred to the lack of "civilized conditions" surrounding the labor of women chainmakers, reminiscent of Juggins' rhetoric, it was clearly their exploitation with which they were concerned, "working iron beyond their strength" for hours beyond "a reasonable limit." Issues of femininity appear to have become secondary as the discourse of the male artisan, desirous of the exclusion of female labor, proved, as in the case of the female surface workers, not to be universally applicable.

In the Black Country outwork industries themselves, the increasing role of middlemen forced the population to become heavily dependent on female labor, whose availability had itself been a strong incentive for the increase in middlemen. As a result, the interests of entire communities sharply diverged from those of the Walsall chainmakers. A coalition thus emerged, consisting of employers and working people alike, male as well as female, in opposition to the legislative agenda set by Juggins and the Walsall men. Clearly what was at issue was not apparently conflicting interests of men and women, or even wages, but the precise manner in which gender – ideas of womanhood and manhood – was embedded in the economic relations of these communities.

Gender and community

When the agitation for the proposed legislative restrictions on female labor was at its height in early 1883, a series of meetings attended by male and female workers was held throughout the nail- and chainmaking districts. At that time, Benjamin Billingham, chairman of the Cradley Heath and District Chainmakers' Association, joined forces with George Green of E. Tinsley and Co., whom we have met in connection with Heather Bigg's tour, as well as the JP, W. Bassano, and the local vicar,[140] to rally opposition among the working people to the proposed legislation. Expressing his resentment at the interference of Juggins and the Walsall men in the affairs of the district,[141] Billingham declared that the abolition of female labor would be ruinous to the trade since the production of smaller chains was now the staple industry of the area and depended heavily on female labor. If such labor was eliminated, it would be impossible for a man to make a living since orders for larger sizes were sent only where smaller sizes were also made.[142]

This argument was reiterated by the JP, Bassano, who presided at a meeting of 1,600–1,700 workpeople held in Old Hill. Citing the example of the Kidderminster carpet industry, he warned against opposition to female labor. In this instance, men had struck work against the introduction of machines for making tapestry carpets on which female labor was to be employed. In response, the manufacturer withdrew the machines, and that sector of the industry, as a result, was lost to Bradford where women were employed. Suggesting that if a trade was monopolized by men, it would eventually be lost to the area, Bassano expressed his fear of such an occurrence in the Black Country nail and chain trades.[143] Since women had no other employment available to them in those areas, he asked what would happen to widows and families where men had been injured, and concluded that "no Government had a right to pass a bill taking away the only available labour from such an enormous body of population."[144] Billingham echoed this sentiment, suggesting that the issue regarding women's employment in chain- and nailmaking actually came down to a lack of alternative employment opportunities.[145]

The men of the Cradley Heath district, however, did not limit their defense of female labor to the argument that it was available and necessary to the survival of the community. They also challenged the claim that it was by its nature immoral. Testifying before the 1876 Royal Commission, chainmaker Richard Fosbrooke maintained, "there is not a decenter trade on record for females than what small chain making is, especially where a man has got his own children under his own roof, it is better than being in a factory, and mixed up with all sorts."[146] "For his own part," Billingham declared at a meeting of workers reported by the *Advertiser*:

> he did not think there was any class of women more respectable, more decent, and more healthy than those in the chain trade. (Applause.) Chainmakers, to a great extent, composed the congregations of the churches and chapels of the district, and the children of chainmakers filled the Sunday schools . . .[147]

In response to a series of articles in the *Daily Gazette*, Billingham further pointedly remarked, "The women of Cradley Heath and district are the equal of the Walsall women both in cleanliness and decency."[148]

Employers in the area, not surprisingly, were able to take advantage of such sentiments. Thus, in February of 1883, George Green led a deputation, which included Billingham and a delegation of chainmakers, to a meeting with H. B. Sheridan, MP, and declared that "employers and workmen generally were all agreed as to what [they] wished to lay before him."[149] Neither workers, male or female, nor manufacturers, he claimed, considered legislative interference to be in their interests. Juggins and the Walsall men had begun the campaign in hopes that putting an end to women's employ-ment would increase demand for their labor and bring higher wages. That this was their aim and concern, rather than the conditions under which women labored, was clear, Green strongly suggested, since the Walsall men were not seeking interference on behalf of their own wives and daughters working in leather factories.[150] To Juggins' claim of immorality existing in the chain and nail shops, Tinsley and Co. responded with apparent, and carefully expressed, outrage. Such a charge represented a "gross slander," the company's representatives declared in a letter to the *Advertiser*. Further, they cleverly added, it suggested that the working men of one trade were pre-suming to take it upon themselves to slander the men *"and women"* of another![151]

That Green was following his self-interest and that of his company is obvious. The female workforce at Tinsley's was said to be perhaps double that of the male.[152] Lamenting that circumstance, a delegate to the South Staffordshire and East Worcestershire Trades' Council stated:

> It was a fact that men had to mourn in consequence of women being engaged in making goods that were sold at Tinsley's warehouse at a reduced price. . . . [I]f the women refused to do the work at the reduced price [he continued] they were told, "You can do as you like; we can get others."[153]

The case of John Price offers further evidence of the degree to which Green was able to exercise control over his employees and the working people generally through the use of heavy-handed tactics. In a letter to the *Adver-tiser* signed by Juggins and other delegates to the Trades' Council, Price, an employee of Green's and president of the Nailmakers' Association, was iden-tified as a long-time champion of the effort to curtail female employment. In a recent speech he had pointed to its inhuman character and its injurious impact on the employment of men in the small metal trades, reducing it in some cases by as much as 40 percent.[154] After the speech, Juggins and the other letter signers claimed, Price was confronted by Green and since that time had been a "weak vessel."[155] Indeed, in a letter to the *Advertiser*, Green quoted Price as declaring that legislative interference would be ruinous to the nailmaking districts.[156]

Such evidence clearly suggests that the coalition that emerged in opposi-tion to legislative restrictions on female labor, at least to some degree, was held together by outright intimidation. Nevertheless, it effectively forced Juggins and the Walsall men on the defensive as they gradually became aware of the extent of the opposition they faced. At first, it appears they assumed that general agreement existed among the workpeople in support of the proposed legislation.[157] However, when Billingham failed to appear at a meeting of the Trades' Council to which he was invited, Charles Williams, president of the Council and secretary of the Nailmakers' Association, recognized that his absence indicated that "something was wrong." Green was apparently succeeding at "pos[ing] as a Liberal in the district," Williams caustically suggested, "purposed to do all he could for the good of the working classes."[158] The Council was also forced to recognize the degree of support being galvanized among women in opposition to legislative interference. "Females would in time find that the Council was their friend," one delegate noted,[159] apparently aware that Green and Billingham were succeeding in appealing to what the women perceived as a threat to their earning power and their interests.

Juggins, the Trades' Council, and the men of Walsall were thus forced to re-examine their position on female labor in a broader context. As we saw above, Juggins clearly stated that he supported its prohibition. Yet he also joined with Thomas Harrison and Charles Williams of the Nailmakers' Association in writing a letter in response to Green's claim that the aim of the movement was the abolition of female labor altogether. Instead, the letter writers claimed, the objective was its restriction.[160] Williams reiterated this outlook, in a meeting of nailers from Sedgley, stating that his Association did not want to abolish female labor but to restrict it "to prevent women from doing men's work," a comment that was greeted with cries of "hear, hear" at a meeting of male and female nailmakers.[161] The aim of the movement, stated Juggins, was simply "to restrict women making work totally unfit for their sex," to enforce the Workshops Act, and prevent the employment of young children.[162] Accordingly, when a delegate to the South Staffordshire and East Worcestershire Trades' Council declared that "the females who made nails deprived the men of their rights," another delegate responded, "they should all be careful not to make exaggerated remarks."[163]

Despite some apparent contradiction on the part of Juggins regarding his approach to female labor, the aims of the movement seem clear, to prohibit women from "men's work" and to confine them to work that was "fit," thus recognizing that female labor was often acceptable. As Samuel Stringer declared in his testimony before the Royal Commission of 1876, voicing the views of the Walsall chainmakers, "I really should not be so blind as to think that [women] should be sent to the right about altogether, having nothing else to fall back upon."[164] It was generally agreed that in Walsall, unlike the Dudley Wood district, the women had "something much better" to do than chainmaking, according to Stringer.[165] Here, the leather industry followed the more common sexual division of labor, with men employed in the skilled trade of cutting while women labored, often on an outwork basis, in stitching where they were not in competition with men.[166] The entire community, particularly those such as the chainmakers engaged in saddlers' ironmongery, depended on the leather industry and thus on female labor. And this situation was perfectly acceptable.

The move to prohibit or restrict female labor in chainmaking seemed then to uphold existing divisions of labor which found acceptable women's employment, but only that which was fitting to their sex. Yet the rhetoric as to the issue of women's work, as in the case of the *Labour Tribune*, was being altered in important ways, as suggested by perhaps the most accurate statement of the position of Juggins, made by the union leader at a conference of representatives of nailers and chainmakers. Here he declared that "he should be glad if there was a law to prevent females from working in nail and chain factories. [But] [i]f they were to have improvements they would have to try for them gradually."[167]

Juggins thus continually opposed married women's work, but he also recognized the limits of such an appeal. Accordingly, the issue of "improvements" of conditions of work began to supersede the discourse of morality and legitimacy. Womanhood, in the lives of some working-class communities, meant not doing work that was suitable but labor that was available on which the community depended. It meant training daughters so that they could come to their mother's aid, and also to assure that they would be able to support themselves. Perhaps just as significant was a re-thinking of manhood. Often it meant not property in skill but working alongside wives and daughters at the home and in the workshop to assure the family's survival. Masculinity as defined by the craftsman, in control of his craft and entry into it, was not universally applicable.

Understandings of gender were beginning to unravel, at least to a degree, as the artisan culture clashed with "a plebeian culture based on community ties between families and neighbours, not on the ties established between workers in a journeymen's association."[168] Here the community and the families that comprised it, in this instance, rather than being threatened by female labor, depended upon it for their very existence. "Custom and community," exemplified by the labor of girls and women in nail- and chainmaking, thus "continued to hold sway"[169] in those districts, serving to bring about the conflict described above.

When Juggins and the men of Walsall began to pursue their legislative agenda, tensions surfaced. Their attempt to transfer their own outlook regarding "women's work," its "legitimacy" and "morality," confronted entrenched female labor as well as communities dependent on that labor. As we have seen during this same period, such conflict was not unique. In many of its facets, the controversy concerning female surface labor in mining, discussed above, bears a striking resemblance to that of the Black Country women metalworkers. Indeed, Angela John suggests that attempts to exclude women from working at the pit brow were influenced by and followed upon similar attempts described above in chain- and nail-making.[170]

Understandings of gender and gender relations within working-class culture were clearly in a period of flux. How to reconcile ideas of womanhood and women's work, in an industry that by its nature was "unfeminine," became the issue.

Female labor and its meanings

The artisanal tradition ascribed certain meanings to the labor of women, particularly that in competition with men. Basically, female labor was viewed as "unnatural," "illegitimate," and "immoral." Such an outlook clashed sharply with the feminist perspective which basically defended women's right to employment. Further, women workers themselves appeared ready to defend their own right to earn a livelihood. They took pride in their craft, recognized the significance of their role in the workforce to their families' well-being, and realized the necessity for their daughters to be trained in the only work available to them. In communities such as Cradley Heath and Wigan, labor not generally considered "women's work" was taken up by female laborers and became part of the landscape. By their very presence, the discourse of the male artisan was placed under pressure and destabilized.

Moreover, the construction of class inherent in the artisan tradition served to exclude some men as well. In some instances, as in Birmingham, mechanization drove many out of skilled labor, where they had achieved some degree of status, often into the ranks of the sweated laborer. In some industrial centers, such as Cradley Heath, the organization of production and capitalist relations, increasingly centered on the role of the middleman, forced wages down while bringing girls and women into the workforce in increasing numbers. In neither case did an appeal to the immorality or illegitimacy of female labor hold meaning for the men working alongside women and girls, for their labor, increasingly cheap and deemed unskilled, was looking more and more like their own and less like that of those putting forth a rhetoric of exclusion. Rather than seeing their own position in the workforce undercut by female labor, they, their families, and communities were increasingly dependent on it. They did not see themselves represented in such rhetoric.

While language may be viewed to some degree as a constitutive force, as it functions to convey the meaning of experience and thus shape it, it also emanates from and is embedded in particular experiences. But experiences are varied and diverse and transcend that discourse, and consequently may themselves actually serve to challenge hegemonic discourses situated within a limited framework of experience. The subjective experience of those on the margins, those who have been voiceless, thus often contains elements of resistance to the hegemonic discourse, thereby serving to reshape it.[171]

Discourses promoting the exclusion of women from certain labor were thus being destabilized and challenged by workers outside the artisan tradition by the period of the 1880s. Foundations for a re-working of gender understandings were being laid which would, in turn, affect gender relations as well. The potential implications for class interests were far-reaching for, even as cultural constructions of manhood and womanhood continued to divide working-class culture, class formation proceeded apace. Now this process was accompanied by a growing recognition of mutual interests across gender lines, despite inequality and often strained relations between men and women. In what follows, we will examine the metal industries to 1912 in this light.

7   Negotiating gender difference in the small metal industries

As the previous two chapters have demonstrated, exclusionary practices and policies toward female labor in the small metal industries in both Birmingham and the Black Country were becoming increasingly controversial. Community interests and the organization of capital and class relations, as well as the continued and in some cases growing presence of women in the workforce, were serving to place pressure on an artisanal discourse that constructed class in such a way as to exclude women and many men as well. In this context, evidence of a re-working of understandings of gender and gender relations among the working classes, to be examined in this chapter, emerges.

Increasingly, some male union leaders took an interest in organizing among women. And as they did so, the women's trade union movement itself began to reconsider and alter its own approach to female labor, moving away from an emphasis on freedom of contract and toward more consideration of the impact of that labor, and the competition of women, on workers in general. A coalescing of forces across gender lines in support of legislation covering conditions of labor as well as organizing among women workers became evident in the Black Country.

In Birmingham, however, it appears that tensions prevailed, particularly as we follow the narrative of the Brassworkers into the twentieth century. Even as women's work expanded in the metal trades, unionizing efforts continued to be limited, while attempts were made to prevent women from working in certain trades altogether. Indeed, W. J. Davis of the Brassworkers continued to follow exclusionary strategies, even as relations with employers remained strained and agreements restricted to members of the Society broke down under the system of arbitration.

In this context, the Brassworkers finally confronted the practice of employing sweated labor, prevalent in the industry, as that practice in general was gaining considerable public attention. But even though Davis saw female labor as a source of sweating, the crusade against it did not concentrate on that labor but instead focused on the male laborer, forced to work for undercutting employers at low wages. The crusade was thus marked by an approach toward class that recognized common interests between such male workers and members of the Brassworkers' Society, suggesting a more inclusive strategy in terms of organization than that followed previously, one that could be readily extended to women as well. And indeed, the major labor upheaval of 1910–13, beginning with the chainmakers' strike, was marked by widespread unity among workers across gender lines. Yet at the same time wage agreements reinforced the subordinate position of women as their wages were set at a lower rate, raising again the issue of the significance of gender difference in working-class culture.

Gender and gender relations in chainmaking

In the small metal trades of the Black Country, antagonism on the basis of gender actually appeared to intensify to some extent in the mid-1880s. At that time the correspondent for the *Sunday Chronicle* estimated that, "granting perfect health, a robust constitution, and incessant work the whole week through," a young woman could earn 4s. while a young man took home only 1s. more.[1] Such wages, it was estimated, approximated half of those received fifteen years previously, and could readily be traced to a rapid influx of female labor into the trade as the men departed for other occupations. According to the West Bromwich *Free Press*, the trade union organized in Cradley Heath and prominent during the events of 1883 was also a casualty of this trend, having broken up after a series of strikes during which the women apparently remained at work.[2]

Confronted with such rapidly deteriorating conditions, while witnessing the success of a nailmakers' strike, the chainmakers determined to go on strike themselves during the autumn of 1886, with the major target being underselling masters. Ultimately this strike involved the entire trade in an action which proved to be one of the greatest and most memorable struggles in which the chainmakers were ever engaged.[3] The strikers demanded "that it shall be *possible* for a woman to earn eight shillings and sixpence, and a man thirteen shillings for sixty hours' work."[4] Female labor and its effects on wages gained considerable attention throughout the labor struggle, with Richard Juggins making some of his strongest statements on the matter in this context. At a mass meeting held in November, for instance, he declared:

> what I say about all this is that it is a result of female labour, and especially of juvenile female labour. . . . if it hadn't been for the terror exercised by the masters on the women in times past rates would never have sunk so low as they have. As the Devil got into Eden and tempted Eve the first [Juggins railed], so the masters began their reductions with the women, and the men had to follow.[5]

Addressing mass meetings, Juggins effectively intermingled money and morals, calling for the separation of the men and women, girls and lads at the workplace, which he believed would lead to an improvement in working conditions, as "the decencies of life" would be observed. But "to work this change," he argued, "they must be paid – paid well enough to give them some semblance of a home, something better than rags to cover their naked-ness, something better than garbage to feed on."[6] As things stood, however, the work of women must be "condemned by the public voice" in the inter-ests of morality and the wage earners alike.[7]

With Thomas Homer, now president of the revived Cradley Heath Chainmakers' Association, sharing the platform with Juggins at meetings of strikers, it appears that agreement may have been reached on the issue of female labor, despite the dispute of three years earlier.[8] According to the West Bromwich *Free Press*, Homer joined Juggins in attempting to impress upon women chainmakers that, if they refused to work beyond the age of 14, general wages would increase. The hope clearly was that, if the labor of girls was prohibited, young women would be "averse to engaging in such unfeminine employment."[9]

Community differences regarding female labor, outlined in the previous chapter, thus appeared to recede over the course of the strike, as the union leaders seemed to agree to support the withdrawal of girls and women from the trade. Indeed, the strike itself seemed to symbolize a new-found unity among the chainmakers as Richard Juggins, defender of the chainmakers of Walsall, now emerged as a hero to the people of Cradley Heath. Accompa-nied by Juggins on his tour of the chainmaking district, the Special Commissioner of the *Sunday Chronicle* described "grimy children" and "eager-eyed men and women" gathering in the roadway as they approached, appearing "to know and to reverence my conductor, judging by the earnest-ness of the salutations with which he is greeted."[10] Such a welcome was cer-tainly a far cry from the resentment expressed a few years earlier when many criticized Juggins and the Walsall chainmakers for their apparent attempts to force women out of the industry. As for the men of Walsall, they were suffering a sharp decline in wages, to 18s. per week, due to the cheapness of chain from Cradley Heath. Yet their response at this time was to lend support to the strike, amounting to a weekly contribution of £50.[11]

Such support was indicative of the new degree of unity established among a number of trades, including the Walsall Chainmakers, through the recent founding of the Midland Counties Trades Federation under the leadership of Richard Juggins. With the establishment of this Federation, the various trades were able to assist each other, as well as unaffiliated workers, in their labor disputes throughout the Black Country. The Federation thus came to the support of the Cradley Heath chainmakers, a step that had important implications, although not immediately obvious, for women workers, but in quite the opposite direction from that suggested above. For despite Juggins' emotional appeals stressing the immorality and injurious effects of increased female labor on the trade, and apparent unity on this point with Homer of Cradley Heath, the newly established determination among workers to improve wages and conditions meant a shift away from exclusionary strategies. Now, instead, steps were taken to organize the women alongside the men, implicitly suggesting an acceptance of their position in the trade.

Indeed, 2,000 men and women chainmakers had gone on strike together, while the union organized in Cradley Heath under the leadership of Thomas Homer united them in one association. In this situation, Juggins himself explicitly called on the women to "stick to it . . . for without it they [were] doomed, body and soul."[12] A mass meeting of perhaps 2,000 women and girls was held in November, prompting Homer to claim, "The best feature of the business is the firmness of all, both men and women."[13]

In the following months, such "firmness" was apparently severely tested. Despite having gained an agreement with employers assuring an average weekly wage for men of 15s. and for women, 8s. 6d., that agreement was soon undercut by "renewed encroachments on the part of the masters" who apparently took advantage of girls and women in particular. According to the *Sunday Chronicle*, they were "more liable than men to be imposed upon by the resolute and artful tyranny to which they [were] exposed."[14] The methods employed were described in some detail by the *Chronicle*:

> The fogger selects the most weak-minded and likely subject for his purpose – perhaps the woman with most children – and informs her that he has resolved to revert to the old rates, that a number of her companions are secretly accepting such terms, that he is only making for stock, and, in short, she may take the iron or leave it.[15]

Having succeeded with one or two, he then used them "to work upon the feelings of their comrades" with the result, claimed the reporter, that "a majority of them have fallen into the net."[16]

By April 1887, Homer and the Chainmakers' Association responded to this "artful tyranny," resolving "to call out every man and woman on their books" to resist such methods. Individual women as well took action, with some suing the manufacturers who took deductions from their wages, allowing them to fall below the agreed rates. One Sarah Ann Cox was able to win such a case, with the judge ruling that the general trade price must be paid. Strengthened by such unity, an apparent agreement, with some increase in wages, was reached.[17]

At the same time, grounds for an agreement among women workers, feminists, and male union leaders were apparently beginning to emerge regarding the issue of legislative restrictions on female labor, despite the sharp conflict of 1883, described in the previous chapter. Despite their apparent general opposition to the legislative proposals put forward at that time, it appears that women workers' views regarding all such legislation restricting female labor were not as clear-cut as previously implied. On more than one occasion during the agitation of 1883, women workers spoke up to propose that, in accordance with existing legislation that was being evaded, women's work be confined to the hours between 7.00 a.m. and 7.00 p.m.[18] Further, even at a meeting of female workers in the nail and rivet trades that was chaired by the local vicar, who opposed legislation limiting female labor, those present expressed support for legislation limiting their work to quarter-inch rivets. They also made a point to make it clear that it was only the complete abolition of female labor to which they were opposed.[19] Accordingly, at a meeting at which the feminist Edith Simcox spoke, although the women voted for a resolution opposed to legislative interference, in the course of the discussion a woman spoke up to defend the proponents of the legislation, denying that their intention was to prohibit female labor altogether.[20]

In so far as legislation was designed to limit their hours and size of work, rather than placing age limits on entry into the trade, women were often supportive. Thus we might suggest that the sharp divisions reported between men and women, and claimed by the feminists, were often more apparent than real. This appears to have been the case in 1891 when men and women did indeed, as described in the previous chapter, demonstrate sharp differences over the issue of legislation restricting female labor. Yet a closer look reveals that the divide generally involved the attempt to prohibit the employment of girls before the age of 16. While women generally were opposed to such a measure, evidence also suggests that many were supportive of restrictions on the size of chain they worked, limiting them to No. 1 or quarter-inch chain. Even the *Daily Post*, a consistent opponent of the legislative restrictions proposed, had to admit that the deputation of female chainmakers organized by Mrs. Fawcett to oppose all restrictive legislation may have been "picked specimens and not fairly typical of the womanhood of the Black Country" who often "admit that there are some sizes [of chain] too heavy for them."[21] A ballot taken by the National Amalgamated Federation of Chainmakers and the Chainstrikers' Association in Cradley Heath, Old Hill, and the surrounding area, indicated that overall 1,779 operatives "were of the opinion that iron a quarter of an inch in thickness was large enough for a female to work, and 242 were against the proposal."[22]

Women chainmakers undoubtedly desired the assistance of their daughters and wanted them to be trained in the only trade available to them. On this basis, they opposed legislative interference aimed at prohibiting the entry of girls into the trade. At the same time, however, they expressed a sense of their own right to a better life as well. They thus voiced support for legislation restricting hours and the size of chain they could work. Further, a simultaneous reassessment was taking place among feminists with regard to protective legislation and the "rights" of women workers, suggesting the possibility for negotiation among women workers and men and women union leaders involving ideas of gender and women's work.

Female labor and its impact

In her work on feminism and protective legislation, Rosemary Feurer concludes that the pit-brow workers' deputation to the Home Secretary, discussed previously, represented "the finale for the ideal of the unity of all women against protective legislation before the curtain of class fell on the old ideal of sisterhood."[23] Increasingly, the women of the WPPL, in contrast to many feminists, recognized the weakness of women in the workforce as long as they remained unorganized "without trade feeling and sympathy."[24] Especially important for our purposes was the recognition within the organization of the effects of this weakness on labor in general, "in dragging down the value of labour and in diminishing excellence of work."[25] Declared the *Annual Report* of the WPPL in 1888, "The damage done to the interests of working men by the undue cheapness of women's work is evident."[26] The more work traditionally carried out by men is transferred to women, at a cheaper rate, the *Report* pointed out, "the more essential it becomes for women to support themselves and their families, and the more eager becomes the competition among them."[27]

Concerns for the rights of women workers, as expressed by feminists generally, thus began to be superseded within the WPPL by the issue of female competition and its effects on wages. "Where wages were already low and conditions hard," declared Clementina Black, secretary of the WPPL from 1887, "the entrance of women into the labour market has served to intensify competition and increase these evils."[28] Thus, maintained Emilia Dilke, "the special difficulty of the labour question, as far as women are concerned," is indeed much the same in all directions," the major question being, "How are we to prevent them from lowering the current rate of wages in the trades they seek to enter?"[29] Answering her own query, Dilke contended, "Trades Unionism alone can come to the rescue in this matter." Through such association, she maintained, "each woman gradually learns that her individual action is important to the well-being of all" while "the just objection to and fear of their labour felt by men will disappear."[30]

In such industries as chain- and nailmaking, Dilke decried the extent to which unregulated competition between women and men brought down the general level of wages, although, like Heather Bigg, she did not "consider the labour either objectionable in itself or unhealthy."[31] The character of the industry was not the issue. In white lead manufacture, where women and their children suffered the effects of lead poisoning, the competition of female labor similarly served to bring down wages, Dilke contended, citing a Sheffield factory where women received "but half the wages" of men although engaged in the same work.[32] In another setting in the same industry, she sought to encourage combination among the women as a means to address, and hopefully remedy, such grievances and inequities. However, here the competition, limited only to that among women and girls:

was so keen, and the amount of training required for its adequate perfor-
mance so small, that, supposing all the women engaged in it had been
organized, and had used the extreme argument of a general strike to
enforce their demands, such a course was bound to be ineffectual.[33]

Stated one girl, "our places could all be filled up within a fortnight," with
"any smart girl" learning all that was necessary in one week's time. Though
their numbers were small, their situation was "monstrous," Dilke declared,
concluding that they were in "dire need of the protection and consideration
of the State."[34]

When women and girls take up "the father's trade," Dilke warned, they
are "paid as an extra" and the results are "suicidal" as the employers increase
the number of female laborers at the expense of the men. She pointed to
such an instance of what she called "betrayal" by the women when they took
jobs at lower wages in the Halifax carpet-weaving industry when the men
went on strike against threatened reductions. Similarly in Sheffield, women
file-makers began taking in work at home and training girls in the trade,
thereby undercutting the men's ability to earn a livelihood.[35] "No one can be
surprised, as long as women behave in this way," Dilke contended, "that
men should endeavour to keep the higher branches of industry in their own
hands."[36]

What Rosemary Feurer calls the "ideological construct of freedom of contract" was beginning to lose its appeal, it appears, as the WPPL gave tacit
support to legislation covering conditions of women's work by supporting a
campaign for the introduction of women factory inspectors.[37] A clear shift in
the direction of support for protective legislation was also signaled by the
organization's support for the extension of the Factory Acts to laundries in
1890.[38] Further, it was becoming increasingly clear by the late 1880s that,
whereas feminist organizations were nowhere to be seen when it came to
such major events as the matchmakers' strike, the male-led trade union
movement was increasingly responsive to calls to organize women workers.[39]

This shift in outlook on the part of the WPPL, it appears, may have had
direct implications for the small metal trades of the Black Country. In June
of 1888, the *Women's Union Journal* reprinted an article from the Walsall
Observer reporting that attempts were being made to organize a society
among women in the saddlery trade in that community.[40] Here women were
widely employed as stitchers where they earned wages less than those of
men, who were employed in cutting, and also were forced to pay for lighting
and heat as well as rent for the room in which they worked. On behalf of the
WPPL, Clementina Black spoke to a meeting of the women, expressing her
views on the necessity for women to organize. Referring to the history of
strife between men and women in the workforce, she emphasized that such
competition had only served the interests of employers, and that a better
feeling increasingly prevailed, as men were now giving willing assistance to
the women. This point was reinforced by a male representative from the

leather workers of Manchester. Originally, he indicated, he had supported the exclusion of women altogether from the job of stitching because stitchers from Walsall had gone to Manchester and taken work below the trade price. Now, however, he was supporting the effort to organize the women.[41]

Whether the chainmakers of Walsall were aware of this meeting or of Black's presence in the community is not clear. Nor is it clear whether Black may have met with Richard Juggins on this occasion. But what is apparent is that a basis for agreement had been reached between the two union leaders regarding an approach to female labor. At the Trades Union Congress of 1888, Juggins not only supported but seconded a motion presented by Black stating, "That in the opinion of this congress it is desirable, in the interests both of men and women, that in trades where women do the same work as men, they shall receive the same payment."[42] In supporting the resolution, he commented that, in his district, "they had come to the conclusion that nothing but better pay for the women workers could do anything to cure" the general low wages and poor conditions.[43]

A new approach on the part of Juggins to legislative restrictions was also evident, suggesting a further basis for agreement with the women's trade union movement whose views were also evolving as indicated. The previous year, we will recall, a dispute had erupted at the TUC between Black and Juggins when he proposed the complete withdrawal of girls and women from the small metal trades. Now the Midland Counties Trades Federation, with Juggins' support, passed a resolution more limited in scope, urging the Parliamentary Committee of the TUC to work for passage of a measure prohibiting girls and women "from working either on nails or chains above certain sizes," to be determined by law.[44] In its report of 1888, the Committee supported this recommendation.[45] Juggins further reiterated his support for such a measure in testifying before the Lords Select Committee on the Sweating System, stating that he would restrict the size of iron worked by women to a quarter-inch. In taking this position, he hastened to add that he had "the authority of a meeting of females" engaged in the nail and rivet trades which "agreed that no women should be allowed to make a larger size than a quarter inch diameter."[46] Thomas Homer as well concurred with Juggins with regard to restricting the size of chain worked by girls and women.[47]

Indeed, according to the report of the Board of Trade issued by John Burnett in 1888, the strong feeling expressed previously on the part of some men, calling for the virtual exclusion of female workers from the trade, had been generally superseded by a call for their restriction to lighter work. Both Homer and Juggins told him that all were agreed that a prohibition on female labor was "impossible as other industries presented no opening to females, and they must do something."[48] As Homer stated, it was "no use objecting to it under present circumstances."[49] Burnett thus reported that the men and women as well of the chain- and nailmaking districts denounced the widespread presence of female labor in these trades. But they were "practically between two fires on this point."[50] The men recognized that the labor of their wives and daughters was lowering their own wages, and to the point that they became dependent on the very wages that were threatening their own livelihood! The people were thus, as Burnett eloquently stated, "between the devil of cheap labour competition and the deep sea of family poverty."[51] As a result, he concluded, "the social reformer who should seriously propose in the Black Country that female labour in nail or chain making should be prohibited by law would have a bad time of it."[52]

Only the exclusion of married women remained on the agenda for some. As Thomas Homer pointed out, only in south Staffordshire, as far as chainmaking was concerned, "the women have got to take a share and part of the work like the men." Women often had to contract with employers themselves, especially those whose husbands were employed in other trades, and, as a result, agreed-upon piece-rates were violated.[53] Neither were limited hours adhered to as "many a brute in human form ... would make his wife work day and night if he could."[54] When Juggins then indicated that, "The object in restricting [female labor] as far as possible is to keep the married women out," Homer agreed "on principle." "When the woman turns into the shop to work," he claimed, "everything in the house is entirely neglected."[55] Rather than returning to a "clean and tidy" house, the husband was driven to the public-house "which would not be if the women were better domesticated."[56] An arrangement that kept wives "entirely out of the chain shop" was clearly preferable to the union leader who considered it "a disgrace that a man cannot earn enough money to keep his wife." Many men in his district, he indicated, agreed and would be "pleased" for their wives to remain at home.[57] Yet when asked if he would propose a prohibition on married women's labor, Homer responded, for the reasons suggested by Burnett, "I should not like to say that that would be my proposition."[58] Before the Royal Commission of 1892, he indicated that he would be "glad" of such a measure, but stated, "I do not ask for that to be brought about."[59]

The issue of competition from female labor had to be addressed. As Juggins stated before the Select Committee, "when the married women turn into the domestic workshops they become competitors against their own husbands," leading to the need for two wage earners "to earn what the man alone would earn if she were not in the shop."[60] But the issue could not be addressed by calling for the exclusion of girls and women from the trade. Rather, Juggins now claimed that the "principal remedy" for the deplorable conditions existing in the small metal trades lay "in the abolition ... of the whole system of working in domestic or family workshops."[61] They clearly served to promote competition among workers, thereby causing wages to decline.[62] Agreeing, John Burnett declared, in his report for the Board of Trade, that the domestic workshop "is the root from which spring most of the evils of the nail and small chain trades."[63] Under a factory system, he maintained, the middleman would disappear, while underselling and underbuying would be reduced, to the benefit of the workers and the well-being of their families.[64]

Gender issues then appeared to be set aside as female labor seemed to recede as an issue. As we will recall, the very legitimacy of the labor of girls and women in chainmaking in particular had been thrown into question by male workers identifying with a craft tradition. Now that labor was legitimated by the move away from exclusionary policies and toward support for measures that would mean improvements in working conditions for all, but particularly girls and women, thus implicitly recognizing their position in the workforce.

At the same time, however, the question of "woman's place" did not totally disappear as an issue, as Homer made it abundantly clear what he perceived a wife's role to be. Further, by supporting measures restricting women to lighter work, male union leaders attempted to undercut competition from female labor by separating out their work.[65] Women clearly continued to be considered secondary laborers.

Through the introduction of more humane measures at the workplace, however, their work was now to be reconciled with understandings of what constituted womanhood. And that work was increasingly recognized as a mainstay of the nail- and chainmaking industries, however reluctantly. The discourse of the male artisan had been placed under pressure and undermined. Where it failed to resonate, to link up effectively with the experiences of the people themselves, it frankly fell flat on its face. The discourse itself was thus reshaped to take in female laborers as chainmakers, with implications for class as well as gender. The experiences of the people transcended the discourse that constructed class as male, that saw class fractured by gender. Through a coalition of forces composed of women workers, feminists, and male trade union leaders, understandings of class came to be more inclusive, expanding to include women as well as men outside the craft tradition. As the threads followed in this chapter began to come together, they coalesced in an approach to female labor that, at one and the same time, embodied gender difference but encouraged class cohesion as well. Such reworked understandings had important implications for organizing efforts within the chainmaking trade.

Organizing women

In October 1889, Lady Dilke of the Women's Trade Union League, formerly the WPPL, addressed a large meeting in Cradley Heath, mainly attended by women. Present at the meeting were Thomas Homer of the local Chainmakers' Association and Richard Juggins, appearing in his role as secretary of the Midland Counties Trades Federation. Referring to the history of women's trade unionism, Lady Dilke indicated that, in previous years, men in the leadership of the union movement had not been favorable to the organization of women and had attempted to address the issue of women's work through legislation. In recent years, however, she argued, echoing the views of Clementina Black expressed to the Walsall leather workers, feelings had changed. She herself, as well, as was indicated above, had come to understand the fears of men based on the use employers made of female labor in bringing about wage reductions. She thus desired to see women acting in concert with men as a means of addressing such fears, suggesting that their interests must be identical with those of their husbands, fathers, and brothers. For women to do otherwise, and act in such a way that tended to reduce men's wages, Lady Dilke considered "unjustifiable and immoral." She accordingly expressed her pleasure at the opportunity that existed among the chainmakers for women and men to organize together and encouraged women's participation, particularly at the time when trade was apparently good.[66]

Along with the agreement reached by Black and Juggins at the 1888 TUC, this address appears to symbolize the importance now placed on organizing men and women together in the small metal trades of the Black Country by male union leaders. Evidence from the following years further suggests that ongoing ties with the Women's Trade Union League (WTUL) were established on a reasonably firm foundation. In 1890, 8,000 nail-makers, including men, women, and girls, were confronted with a 10 percent reduction in wages and the introduction of machinery which employers used to force greater productivity from the workers. A strike ensued in the fall of 1891 supported by Juggins and the Midland Counties Trades Federation.[67] In the course of the strike, Juggins called for support from the WTUL, asking Miss Abraham to visit and speak to a gathering of workers in Bromsgrove.[68]

Over the following years, however, considerable division existed among male leaders representing different sections of the chainmaking industry, forcing the issue of women's work off the agenda for a time. In 1893, for instance, while the newly formed National Amalgamation was supporting strike action, the Cradley Heath Society appeared to be in disarray.[69] Further, the purported leader of whatever organization did exist, Thomas Homer, intervened in the efforts made by the Amalgamation to obtain an advance by notifying the employers that his Society did not intend to support the request, thereby serving to undermine whatever unity might have been possible.[70] The chainmakers also became involved in a dispute with Juggins and the Midland Counties Trades Federation, who refused to support an ongoing strike, charging that, although they had provided assistance previously, the chainmakers had left the Association.[71] By January of 1895, the *Women's Trade Union Review* was declaring that trade unionism was "practically a dead letter among the workers of Cradley Heath."[72]

Employers were naturally able to take advantage of such divisions. However, by the fall of 1895, trade had improved and new attempts were made to organize and gain increased wages, with the various sectors of the industry working together to gain their objectives.[73] Thomas Sitch, secretary of the United Chainmakers, representing male factory workers, apparently worked closely with James Smith of Cradley Heath, as the two collaborated in devising a strategy to gain an advance among the outworkers, to be followed by a push among the factory workers for an advance as well.[74] By October, it was reported that a majority of outworkers, apparently, had succeeded in gaining an advance, leading to the factory workers giving notice for a 7.5 percent rise in wages.[75] However, while the dollied chainmakers – a branch of the trade monopolized by men – received an advance as of the first of February 1896, girls and women as well as some men employed in the country-work and hammered chain branch had to give notice that they would strike for an equivalent advance.[76] While a number of masters conceded the advance, many did not, forcing the dispute to continue, with the strikers reportedly displaying "a strong determination to continue the struggle." In this, with trade on the upswing, they were supported by weekly levies from those operatives who had received an advance.[77] The divisions of previous years had apparently been overcome, illustrated further by the founding of a new association, the Cradley Heath and District Best Chainmakers' Association, which affiliated with the Midland Counties Trades Federation. At its banquet in October, James Smith declared that the chainmakers had been able to achieve advances of 20 to 30 percent over recent months.[78]

Most importantly for our purposes, accompanying the new-found peace among the various sectors of the trade was a renewed emphasis on the organization of women workers. Speaking to the Best Chainmakers, J. Taylor, who succeeded Juggins upon his death as secretary of the Federation:

> urged all young men that if they secured benefits themselves they should look after their downtrodden sisters, and see if they were receiving a living wage. He deplored women['s] labour, [he continued] but he considered whilst they remained in the chain trade it was the duty of the men to endeavour to improve their position and make their future life more pleasant and happier than it had been in the past.[79]

In November, a meeting of the Hammered Chain and Country-work Makers' Association was held in Cradley Heath for the purpose of organizing female workers. It was estimated that approximately 400, mostly women, were in attendance. At the meeting, James Smith indicated that only 20 percent of the country workers were currently organized and referred to complaints having been made of a "want of sympathy on the part of the male workers towards the female workers." However, if the women would join, with the Association affiliated with the Midland Counties Trades Federation, Smith emphasized that "they would all be members of the same Federation, and the one section would not only have the sympathy and help of the others, but of the other federated trades as well." If they had previously been united, he further pointed out, they might have been able to gain an advance, with work being plentiful.[80]

Smith also announced at this same meeting that he and Benjamin Hingley, MP, had met with the Chief Inspector of Factories to ask that the Particulars Clause be applied to the chain trade. Under this legislation, which had been passed without designating the trades to which it applied, each employer would be obligated, Smith explained, to post a list of prices in the warehouse, stating the size of work on which each female chainmaker was employed and what she was paid for it. The women were clearly skeptical, with one declaring, "They won't do it." But here the established ties between the union leaders and the WTUL came into service, for present at the meeting was a representative of that organization who served as secretary to Lady Dilke. She was able to refer to the successful operation of the Particulars Clause in other trades, including the cotton and woolen industries as well as her own trade, tailoring. She particularly emphasized the importance of the workers being organized in realizing such gains.[81]

Apparently some progress was made in the following year, with a general meeting of chainmakers of all branches occurring in Cradley Heath in October 1897. Here Thomas Sitch announced that a 15 percent advance, mainly benefitting male and female hammered chainmakers, had been achieved.[82] The traditional disunity of the trade, however, was often pointed to, with Sitch mentioning that many societies had been founded in the hammered chain trade, but they had not been continuously supported by the workers, particularly once an improvement in conditions had been achieved.[83]

James Smith also brought out the "greater difficulty" in organizing women workers and the problem of "wring[ing] contributions from the women."[84] Of particular interest with regard to women workers, however, was an exchange that took place between Smith and T. Jones, president of the Midland Counties Federation. Stated Jones:

> He was one who believed that a woman's place was in the house, and not in the workshop, and especially not married women. [Comment met by cries of] Hear, hear. He considered that every man ought to have a sufficient wage to keep his wife and family, and if the trade was not good enough for that the sooner it was done away with the better. (Cheers.)[85]

Smith responded, declaring that "Mr. Jones was labouring under a wrong impression," that "the female operatives did not work at chainmaking simply because they loved it" but, the suggestion was, it was necessary and expected of them. According to Smith, then, "the primary object of the meeting was to organise the female operatives." Since the men had succeeded in gaining an advance, he stated, "now what was wanted was [for] the women to materially better their position." Recently, Smith pointed out, most masters had agreed to an advance without a strike, which had never happened before among the hammered chainmakers. What was needed now was "to keep the society going." John Taylor of the Federation concurred, stating, "As long as they had female operatives in the trade, in his opinion it was their duty to see that the conditions were altered."[86]

This exchange brings into sharp relief the re-negotiating of gender difference that had occurred within the small metal industries in the Black Country over the previous twenty years. Despite the continued presence of a discourse that constructed women as wives and mothers, their position in the industry had to be recognized, given legitimacy, and improved. Even as class interests were fractured by gender, and tensions and inequities were evident, a degree of unity was increasingly apparent as well. The extent to which a similar process was in evidence in the Birmingham small metal trades is considered in the following sections.

Women workers and organizing efforts in Birmingham

In 1901, according to the official census, over 25,000 women in the Birmingham district were employed in metalworking. Finding it necessary to earn incomes immediately upon leaving school, girls and women between the ages of 15 and 20 joined the workforce at a rate 80 percent higher than the national average already in the early 1890s, as they drifted into employment largely determined by the district and home from which they came.[87] Among married women, it was estimated that approximately 19 percent were employed, a large portion of whom were widows.[88] Again, their employment depended on their family circumstances, with wives of artisans generally not seeking paid employment, while others worked to supplement the family income.[89] In certain neighborhoods, however, where metalworking dominated and poverty prevailed, the labor of women outside the home was common. According to a survey taken by Dr. Robertson for the Medical Officers of Health in the municipal wards of St. Stephen and St. George, 54 percent of women who bore children in 1908 went out to work.[90]

The work in which women and girls were engaged was increasingly varied. According to the study of Edward Cadbury, M. Cecile Matheson, and George Shann, "the subdivisions of labour [were] almost endless, to such an extent [was] differentiation of process now carried." As an example, the authors of this invaluable study offered the example of a brass knob on a bedstead which could go through as many as six processes before reaching the manufacturer, with no two processes being carried out "by the same girl, one might almost say by the same class of girl."[91] In general, female labor could be divided into work in various surface processes and in press work, labor that had been traditionally considered "women's work," as well as lathe work, which had recently been undertaken by women and girls and, as such, had become a focus of controversy, as we will see below.

Press work, where the machine forced the metal into shape as it moved up and down, was generally considered unskilled work. While requiring considerable attention in the placing of the metal, particularly in the presence of a power press, a girl could learn the job in a week, being taught either by the foreman or "the next girl."[92] In the steel-pen trade, which alone employed approximately 7,000 women, constituting 85 percent of the trade, much of the work involved such labor, thus typifying, according to the British Association for the Advancement of Science, the industrial position of a majority of women workers. Here, the Association surmised, it took an average worker approximately three to four months to master the necessary skills. In nine months, it was estimated, a girl would have become "absolutely dexterous."[93]

In the surface processes, a range of skill involving the labor of women and girls was in evidence. The dipping of common black bedsteads was considered a particularly "rough and dirty trade." The bedsteads were dipped into a well of black paint into which the women had to put their hands, removing the paint with petroleum or turpentine. Additionally, the workers had to "pass in and out of the hot drying-room, carrying the bedsteads to and fro," an occupation which Cadbury and his fellow authors considered more suited to "strong youths." Japanning or blacking of smaller articles, closely related to dipping, also represented a class of work that was "not particularly skilled" and was often carried out in small domestic sheds, since only annealing furnaces and ovens and the japanning fluid were required. Hand burnishing, however, which also remained a home industry, was considered an "excellent," "highly skilled" trade in which girls and women were employed. Here a girl was apprenticed for two years due to the care and skill required in the process of removing the polish from such articles as buckles, clasps, and brooches. In hand-lacquering, another trade recognized as skilled, the coloring mixture was brushed on and, in many instances, gone over several times to make the surface "absolutely even," giving the impression that it had received only "a brilliant polish."[94]

Working at a lathe, women were employed in cutting, worming of screws, forming, polishing, machine burnishing, and lacquering, labor said to require "every degree of skill that machine work can demand of women." Forming appeared to be among the simpler tasks, requiring only that the items be held against the revolving forms on the lathe. In machine burnishing, however, where women were replacing men in the lighter branches of the trade, "great skill and judgment" were required, while grinding in the pen trade was ranked as "one of the better-class trades for women." Polishing with the use of a lathe in some cases was forbidden to women and girls by the rules of men's unions, particularly since it had not traditionally been women's work.[95] In the 1880s, attempts to introduce women into polishing in fact had been unsuccessful, with the work often proving to be too heavy. Now, however, women were often employed on lighter work where they often "picked it up" from a shop-mate. Yet a degree of skill was certainly involved since, as Cadbury *et al.* indicated, the worker had to "adapt to every change of shape that fashion or progress may dictate" as the proper color was finally attained.[96]

Conditions under which the work described above was carried out seem to have varied as much as the work itself. "Fair conditions" apparently existed in many press shops since the work itself was basically clean. However, many such shops were "crowded, oppressively hot," and lacking in cleanliness. The machinery also introduced an element of danger, causing "hundreds of Birmingham women show[ing] maimed and scarred fingers as the result of their service in the press shops." Accidents of this nature, Cadbury *et al.* concluded, could often be due to carelessness. But at the same time they noted that "the incessant noise of the machinery, the excessive monotony of the work, and, above all, the long hours ... too often spent in an ill-lighted and ill-ventilated atmosphere" could not help but have a deleterious effect on the degree of alertness the workers exhibited.[97] In lathe work, the shops themselves were "nearly always dirty, frequently dangerous, and generally more or less unhealthy." Japanning was "always dirty work," with much depending on the kind of shop in which the worker was engaged. While domestic workshops, where it was often carried on, were frequently associated with the evils of sweating, "a better class of girls" was often able to work with friends and neighbors in such a setting.[98]

Such variety in both the labor and the conditions under which girls and women worked led Cadbury *et al.* to suggest that sharp class distinctions were to be found among them. In general, they considered warehouse work to be a refuge of girls from the poorer classes, but who were seeking a degree of respectability. Among metalworkers, the large machines were said to be worked by girls considered rough. Some work, such as polishing, was also considered degrading.[99] At the same time, however, probably because working conditions were often poor, there was a constant demand for workers, and wages could reach 18s. per week, compared to 12s. for those working hand presses and engaged in japanning. In the jewelry trade, where the work was generally clean and light and the girls said to be carefully selected for the trade, earnings in polishing and finishing could reach 18s. to 25s. per week, while those in the skilled trade of lacquering averaged 15s. to 20s. per week.[100] Competition for those trades considered respectable, such as hand burnishing, could often be intense, keeping wages at a level comparable to those in lacquering.[101]

In the pen trade, married women were commonly employed, at times having worked as girls in the same factory.[102] Generally they were "obliged to work to make up the family income," as was the case of Mrs L. who was visited, as were the others considered here, by the British Association for the Advancement of Science. She was currently a grinder who had worked for sixteen years, having returned to work after marriage when her husband became ill from consumption. The family of Mrs H., who was employed in the same work, lived on her earnings as her husband was also consumptive and was able only to earn a casual wage by hawking the tin skewers he made. In yet another family, where the husband had died, the mother and daughter, aged 22, worked as grinders, supporting the family in a home which the visitors determined to be quite comfortable.

In all of these instances, the women were the bedrock of the family. As Mrs L. stated, "factory work for a married woman means that the husband is ill or lazy" and it was "untrue that a woman goes back for pocket money or amusement or because she dislikes being at home." These women were particularly vocal regarding conditions at work. Visited before the application of the Particulars Clause to the pen trade, the women generally complained about deductions and fines for the waste of material. With the male toolmakers responsible for taking care of the machines and adjusting them to different pens, Mrs L. further complained of the employment of boys who had not completed their apprenticeship. "The boys never seemed to know what was wrong with the 'bobs' until you pointed it all out to them," she declared to her visitor, obviously proud of her knowledge. The main complaint apparently involved the size of the lot into which the pens were divided. Women generally thought they were increasing and complained that they were not allowed to count the gross themselves. Problems with the foremen, which were considerable under the "piece-master" system that prevailed, were also mentioned. Commented Mrs H., "Mr S. he sacks you and sits on you too – some only sits but he sacks too."

Despite such grievances, organization among the working women of Birmingham proved difficult, although some attempt was made in the pen trade. As we have seen, the Brassworkers opposed the extension of female employment into new areas of work and, where it did exist, resisted confronting the issue by failing to address the question of sweated labor while organizing only among the skilled male workers in the trade. However, in 1896, the Birmingham Trades Council began to take up the issue of the employment of girls and women. At a meeting reported in the *Birmingham and District Trades Journal*, a delegate, Lewis Goodman, referred to "the cruelty to young women which took place because of their long hours of labour," and indicated that there were a number of cases that had been brought to his attention. In one instance, he reported, two young women had worked for twenty hours overtime in one week without receiving compensation even for the full week. In other instances, women were working to between 10.00 and 12.00 p.m., especially on Fridays, while others were laboring for a half-day on Sundays. Another delegate particularly deplored the sweating of women and girls associated with the pen trade who frequently took their work home to be sorted. He also claimed that in certain instances they were "at the mercy of many unprincipled overlookers."[103]

Goodman declared that he saw it as "their duty as trade unionists and as men" to try to eliminate the sweating conditions that prevailed in many trades. He further added that he believed, in apparent contrast to W. J. Davis, that the way to go about it was to see to the appointment of additional factory inspectors, including women. The Council then passed a resolution in support of such a measure.[104]

The following year, the Trades Council also gave its support to organizing among women workers. In conjunction with the meeting of the TUC in

Birmingham in 1897, the president of the Trades Council, A. Keegan, chaired a public meeting of women workers at which the Penworkers' Union was founded.[105] The organ of the Women's Trade Union League, the *Women's Trade Union Review*, indicated that at that time they were virtually hopeless with regard to any possibility of organizing among women in Birmingham, due to the apparent attitudes among male leaders. Perhaps referring to W. J. Davis and the Brassworkers, the *Review* claimed, "The competition in the Birmingham trades, a most serious problem, was combated by ignoring it."[106] However, following the meeting attended by WTUL leaders Lady Dilke and Gertrude Tuckwell, they were convinced that Keegan had "recognised the vital principle that industrial problems are the same for both sexes, and that the only way in which they can be solved is by united effort."[107] Writing in the *Birmingham and District Trades Journal* a year later, Keegan, who was serving as president of the fledgling Penworkers' Union, indicated that many of the women saw the value of combination. The results in this trade where a concerted effort was made, however, were limited.

The process of penmaking was described by a *British Mail* correspondent. It began with the shredding of steel sheets into long strips or ribbons which were then given out to cutters where began "the first of the many processes for which the nimble and delicate fingers of women [were] found of inestimable service."[108] The worker passed a ribbon through a machine and cut out pen blanks by a rapid succession of blows of a punch in the shape of a pen. Slits in the sides of the pens were then made by operation of a press which made the perforations, while the distinctive markings of each manufacturer were impressed by a heavy stamp-hammer operated by the foot.[109] Describing this process in some detail, the *Mail* correspondent painted a word-picture of the marker, who:

> takes a handful of pens all lying confusedly from a heap at her left hand, and with a dexterous palming motion, marshals a little procession of them between the thumb and forefinger in parallel order, presenting the foremost in a convenient position to be seized. The right hand travels backwards and forwards to the stamp about twice in a second, each time taking a pen, turning it over point foremost and right side up, and placing exactly under the descending punch, which she causes by the motion of her foot to give a constant succession of blows in regular beat, almost as quick as they could be counted.[110]

Such labor, employing a punch, press, and stamp-hammer, had long been considered "women's work," and was never viewed as competition by male workers. The labor itself utilized attributes identified with girls and women in the workforce, "nimble and delicate fingers" as well as dexterity. The quick movements suggested a clean, light, and airy atmosphere, serving to conjure up somewhat cheerful mental images. The "regular beat" of the machinery was an indication of an orderly process as were the disciplined hand and foot movements described. More serious reflection, however, yields a different picture, of constantly repeated motions, carried out with split-second accuracy. Accordingly, despite the support of many of the workers, Keegan reported that the majority were so "deadened" by such labor they "turned a deaf ear" to appeals to join the ongoing organizing effort.[111]

Nevertheless, the union was able to realize some success despite the limited participation of the workers themselves. Specifically, it gained a ruling compelling employers from making certain deductions from wages.[112] Further, as a result of agitation, the pen workers were brought under the Particulars Clause of the Truck Act, which required that the number of gross in each lot of pens be posted.[113] Referring to such successes, Keegan appealed to the importance of "the moral effect" the founding of the union had on the penmaking industry. "Employers will not do what they did only 18 months ago," he declared in a letter to Mrs. Muirhead, Honorable Secretary of the Penworkers, dated May of 1900.[114]

Employers, in fact, were apparently sufficiently disturbed by the very presence of a union that they at times expressed an intense displeasure at its existence and took measures to prevent its further development. The manufacturer who had invented the grinding machine considered the grinders "particularly troublesome," probably the backbone of the union. In January of 1900 he indicated, as a consequence, that he was looking forward to replacing those now earning wages of from 10s. to 13s. per week and more with girls "fresh from school at an initial wage."[115] The following October, six machines were being worked by girls aged 14 to 16 at a maximum wage of 10s.[116] "Owing to Lady Warwick having stirred up the girls to agitate," Josiah Mason's introduced a self-acting grinding machine.[117]

According to Keegan, one firm, apparently looking to undercut the union, established a thrift club to which the workers contributed 2d. per week, with the firm doubling the amount at the end of the year. Acts of intimidation were also employed, with the firm offering £2 for a summer holiday to anyone who would leave the union.[118] Gillott's, a firm that had at an earlier period taken a paternalistic approach to its employees, now employed very young girls at wages apparently lower than the average, according to Keegan, and put up a notice indicating that any girl joining the union would be dismissed.[119] Such measures apparently had an effect. As early as 1899, Keegan reported to the Trades Council that a ladies' committee was putting forward an appeal "to establish [an] indemnity fund to restore wages to the victimised penworkers."[120] Three years later the secretary of the union reported that membership had fallen to three, partly as a result of the tactics of the firm offering the summer holiday which led to 300 members leaving the union.[121]

In other industries, women continued to be unorganized as their employment at low wages understandably raised the ire of male union leaders. In the tinplate trade, for example, women did the press work, which the men "were quite willing to allow" since they "did not take kindly to the idea of spending their lives in putting pieces of tin under a press."[122] But the manufacturers then found that women could do soldering as well and, moreover, "that they did it with a degree of neatness ... which comparatively few of the men could attain."[123] Women were also employed in riveting as well as the production of hurricane lamps, which brought them into direct competition with men in one firm. When union officials objected that women were being employed on "men's work" in such instances, the firm gave notice to the men and took back only "those who were willing to work according to the wishes of their employers." Eventually, however, the firm concluded that the men were unnecessary altogether and proceeded to employ only female labor at 14s. to 15s. per week as compared to 35s. to 40s. for male labor.[124] In response, the secretary of the Operative Tin-Plate Workers declared that women were difficult to organize and indicated the union did not admit them since "it would be necessary to permit a system of 'preferential rates' which the men would object to."[125]

For the most part, as these examples suggest, as wage workers and as wives and mothers, the women of the Birmingham working classes generally had to depend on their own resources. And here the degree of independence and control they were able to realize, as Carl Chinn brings out in his richly textured analysis, as well as the degree of care they gave their families within the constraints that poverty and gender subordination imposed, are clear.[126] While often giving their families their "only chance of getting enough for house rent, clothing, and fuel" by working for wages,[127] mothers were devoted to the care of their infants as well. In 1908, upon passage of the Notification of Births Act, Dr Jessie Duncan, serving as the Medical Officer of Health, visited mothers in St Stephen's and St George's Wards when their babies were one week old.[128] At that time, Dr Duncan invited the mothers to bring their babies to an Infant Consultation for inspection and weighing. She reported that she was gratified with the results, indicating that many women "who are at work have their children sent up regularly for inspection and weighing, and some take an afternoon off their work so that they may know how the child is progressing." Dr Duncan even expressed encouragement that "drunken women" and those with illegitimate children came regularly although they were "not bribed in any way, not even with the customary cup of tea."[129]

When mothers of infants had to work outside the home, adequate provisions for them were generally made, as they were commonly left in the care of an adult family member or neighbor.[130] The infant mortality rate also was not deleteriously affected by women with young children going out to work, although breast-feeding was rarely possible under such circumstances. Income brought in by the mother often prevented poverty, although the infant was denied the nutrition provided by breast-feeding. At the same time it was the presence of poverty, more likely if the mother did not bring in a wage, that was determined to be responsible for high rates of infant mortality.[131] Stated a 1910 report on the industrial employment of married women, "It does not very much matter whether the mother is industrially employed or not or whether the infant is breast-fed or not, if great poverty exists the infant suffers from want of nutrition."[132] The effects of breast-feeding in poverty, on the one hand, and working and not breast-feeding thus "cancelled each other out," according to Chinn, despite the best efforts of the mothers.[133]

What comes across most strikingly in Chinn's analysis, largely centered on Birmingham, is the devotion of working-class women to their families at the same time that they gained sufficient confidence to exercise a degree of independence themselves. As Chinn states, "If poverty could not defeat these women, then neither could middle-class men impose their masculine concepts of womanhood on them, and nor could their husbands dominate them."[134] The streets and courtyards were dominated by the women and became the centers of community life. A Saturday night out to have a drink with other wives, apart from the menfolk, was indicative of a certain "freedom of action" which they allowed themselves following a week of work in, and often outside, the home.[135] The paid labor of women, however, as it came into conflict with ideas of what constituted womanhood, continued to be controversial.

W. J. Davis, the TUC, and women's work

In the brass industry, W. J. Davis continued to voice his opposition to some female labor, stating that "men are perfectly right to resist women being put on to do hard and unsuitable work."[136]

> we consider it demoralizing for women [Davis wrote to B. L. Hutchins of the BAAS in 1902] to work as polishers, as the process is dirty, unhealthy, and altogether unfit for women, & no real friend of the [Brassworkers'] Soc[iety] would advocate that such objectionable employment should be carried on by any but men. . . . I only wish there would be a stand made against giving such work to women & girls.[137]

Interestingly, Davis went on to argue that he would support women working in groups, as Hutchins had apparently suggested, thereby removing the "objectionable competition" that resulted when women were paid lower wages for the same work undertaken by men.[138] If "work was given to women fitted to their special gifts [which presumably would not include polishing] it would remove the present degradation of female labour," he concluded. Such a result, however, was not expected by Davis because, he declared, "the main object of employing women is to bring down the wages of men."[139]

These remarks were made by Davis in the midst of a campaign he had been waging for a number of years to establish a minimum rate in the brass trade. His purpose in gaining an agreement on such a minimum with employers, Davis indicated in 1899 at a meeting of Brassworkers, was to assure that "no workman who possesses average ability shall work below it" while, at the same time, the trade was regulated in such a way as to "recognise skill, dexterity, or ingenuity at their true value."[140] He then went on to propose a grading of workers under which the piece- and day-workers would be paid a minimum rate assured that the skilled laborers would be paid at a rate agreed to with the employers.[141]

Davis recognized that a number of obstacles stood in the way of such an agreement, including the manner in which the trade was organized into a plethora of subdivisions as well as the widespread employment of juvenile, and increasingly female, labor.[142] These workers remained unorganized and received lower wages as a matter of course. To address this issue, J. Ramsden of the Brassworkers proposed that all underhand labor, employed by piece-workers, be brought into the Society. If this were carried out, he declared, "victory will be ours."[143]

This approach, however, was not pursued at this time, while the employers, responding to Davis' proposals, went on the offensive, declaring that they were free to employ non-union men. "No interference by the National Society in the internal management by an employer of his factory," proclaimed the employers, "can be recognised."[144] The case then went to arbitration where a minimum rate was awarded but the proposal calling for a bonus to be paid only to Society members was rejected. The result was a drop in membership and a reduction in wages below the arbitrator's award.[145]

The following years witnessed a depression in trade leading to an increase in out-of-work pay by the Brassworkers' Society of over 50 percent.[146] Increasingly machinery was replacing skilled labor while, stated the *Annual Report* for 1905:

> To make matters worse, women are employed in increasing numbers, not because of a desire to find them work, but because, and only because, they are to be had for half the wages paid to men.[147]

"Nature's Ornament," the report lamented, was being robbed of her "charms and graces" as women were employed "in the hardest branches of trade where the dirt unfits them for domestic duties."[148]

Here in a couple of sentences were succinctly laid out the interrelated characteristics and problems of women's work that were found to be unacceptable. When such work was low-paid and competed with men's, and at the same time difficult and dirty, making it unfeminine, it was considered to have transgressed the boundaries, particularly as it interfered with the role women were expected to play in the household. Over the following years, such conditions of labor, suffered by women, were to gain increasing attention.

The *Women's Industrial News* in particular turned its attention to fines and deductions from women's wages in the Birmingham metal trades. Noting the low wages that women and girls received, the paper pointed out that they were reduced further by employers who issued a "Fine Tariff" to every employee, apparently spelling out the fines and deductions imposed for such offenses as being "late in [the] morning," "loitering in [the] yard or lavatory," and "spoiling work or tools through neglect."[149] While noting that there could be some justification for such reductions, the article pointed out that they were clearly "open to a great deal of abuse." For instance, female workers were fined for spoiled work "according to the value of the material, plus the cost of the processes it has passed through up to the stage when it is returned as 'scrap,'" despite the fact that a single laborer would not have the responsibility for all those stages of production.[150] The fact that girls worked under a foreman and were not allowed to test their own machines also provided an opportunity for abuse.[151]

In the fall of 1908, the Special Commissioner of the *Sunday Chronicle* reported that thousands of women between the ages of 16 and 40 were employed in the Birmingham brass trade while hundreds of male brassworkers were unable to find work. Moreover, the rate of pay for women averaged 10s. to 20s. per week compared to male earnings of 32s. to 45s.[152] Referring to the work of polishing at an emery wheel or "bob," the commissioner graphically described the conditions under which the women worked, as their arms were "bared from the shoulder and the grime and grit eat their way into the skin, fly into the eyes, and are drawn in into the lungs."[153]

Interviewed by the *Chronicle* correspondent, W. J. Davis, although he had long been an opponent of such labor for women, voiced little concern for young girls so employed, indicating that they:

> still retained the advantages and characteristics of their sex. In spite of the dirt, the coarse clothing, and the hard, mis-shaped hands, they possessed the airs, graces, and attractions of the eternal feminine. The work had not [Davis eloquently concluded] had time to disfigure their bodies, the brass had not entered into their souls.[154]

About the older women, however, he stated, "there was nothing feminine but their clothes" as they retained "pride only in their strength and endurance."[155]

To address the issue of female labor in such unfeminine pursuits, Davis returned to the exclusionary policy he had followed consistently over the previous decades. Seeing unionizing among women as "hopelessly ineffective,"[156] he instead turned to possible governmental solutions aimed at a prohibition on some female labor. At its meeting in 1908, the TUC took under consideration a resolution calling for measures to assure the general safe placement of machinery, as well as a healthy atmosphere in such areas as carding rooms in the textile trade.[157] The resolution further specifically stated that "stringent regulations should be made in all cases where women are employed in laborious, dusty and unhealthy trades." Davis then proposed an additional phrase stating "that women should not be permitted to work at metal polishing, turning, or screwing."[158]

To Davis' biographer, his support for the exclusion of women from certain trades reflected his adherence to the "old-fashioned" belief "that there are certain physical limitations in women beyond which, not only [in] the interests of the sex, but also of the race, they should not be permitted to go."[159] As earlier, this issue was thoroughly intertwined with the question of the effects of female competition on wages and the employment of male skilled labor. The question then became the extent to which this entire issue of female labor, in all its dimensions, could be effectively addressed through the implementation of exclusionary strategies. In taking this approach, Davis came to be opposed not only by women trade unionists but by the majority of the TUC as well.

Arguing that there were many trades that were "equally bad" for women, J. W. Clarke of the Scientific Instrument Makers presented a motion to strike the phrase injected by Davis. If they were to address the issue of female employment in this manner, he argued, they should really call for a prohibition on women's work in the metal trades generally.[160] Davis responded, indicating that the Brassworkers were not so "unreasonable" as to support the exclusion of women and girls from the metal trades altogether. "The women in the pen trade have always had that branch of the industry, and we have never competed with them," Davis declared.[161] As in the past, then, no objection was raised to female employment *per se.* Such labor was considered suitable in certain instances. The issue was the combination of its unfeminine nature and the fact that employers were able to hire women at 8s. instead of 38s.[162]

Over this issue, and the proper strategy to employ in addressing it, Davis came into sharp conflict with Mary Macarthur of the National Federation of Women Workers. Macarthur minced no words in expressing her amazement at the presentation of such a recommendation as Davis put forward, although she admitted that she was not surprised that "so impudent a proposal" emanated from the Brassworkers.[163] In a response similar to Clarke's, she asked:

> If the competition of women was to be got rid of in that way, why did they not go further and propose the entire abolition of female labour? Nay, why not propose the abolition of woman altogether?[164]

In reply to her own questions, Macarthur continued:

> The problem of female competition was not to be solved by a resolution of this kind. The only way was for the men to assist them in organising the women as the cotton operatives had done. They should receive the same money as the men for the same class of work.[165]

Davis responded by stating that he was "surprised and disgusted that there should be any woman in this country defending the practice of allowing women working at a trade that unfitted them as sweethearts and mothers." Then he clearly suggested how the issues of "fitness," femininity, and compensation were intertwined, as he pointed to the case of a girl who, he pointedly remarked, received wages of 4s. per week, and had recently been scalped in a workplace accident. "And if the beautiful headgear of the hair of a woman was not her crowning glory and stock-in-trade," he asked, "what was?" At this, there were reportedly "peals of laughter and great applause."[166] Nevertheless, the TUC defeated Davis' motion by a margin of 791,000 to 685,000.[167]

The battle, however, did not end there. The *Sunday Chronicle* severely criticized Macarthur for complaining only that the women were not paid the same rate as the men and being "indifferent to the physical limitations of her own sex."[168] In response, Macarthur reiterated her view, and that of the WTUL since the late 1880s, that the issue was not the protection of women from laboring in unhealthy trades but "the protection by law of men in one trade from women's admittedly unfair competition." By its vote, she indicated, the Congress had recognized that the protection of one group could only come at the expense of both men and women in other trades, which would then be overcrowded by women seeking work, resulting in increased competition and lower wages. While deploring "unhealthy and dangerous conditions in whatever trade they are found," Macarthur expressed her "wish to see men and women alike protected from their injurious effect." "It is the bad conditions, not the women," she declared, "that ought to be abolished."[169] With such comments, Macarthur was apparently not successful in persuading the Brassworkers, at least some of whom put out a flyer calling attention to female employment in polishing in a cycle factory in Coventry. In bold letters, it sarcastically proclaimed, "**FEMALES!** If you agree with Miss McARTHUR that females SHOULD do men's work – chimney sweeping, etc., **DO IT!**" but only at the same wages as men's.[170]

The following year Davis persisted with his campaign, again presenting a motion at the TUC instructing the Parliamentary Committee:

> to endeavour to obtain an amendment of the Factory and Workshops Act to prevent the employment of female workers in metal polishing, turning, and screwing. And that in such trades where the occupations are fitted for women workers [the motion continued] they shall receive the same rate of wages as are paid by men.[171]

In presenting the resolution, Davis indicated that it was being proposed "because we know that the work in question unfits women for performing the duties of life." He declared that polishing was a trade that could not be made clean simply by introducing appliances to carry dust away. The three processes should be considered dangerous trades, he concluded, while registering surprise that women's representatives would advocate women being engaged in such work. Davis then suggested that perhaps the previous year, when a similar motion had been defeated, there had been some mis-understanding.[172]

Mary Macarthur responded to the proposal, stating that indeed there had been "a good deal of misunderstanding, some misconception, and a good deal of misrepresentation." In particular, she referred to the article appearing in the *Sunday Chronicle* in which the reporter charged that, by taking the position she did, "she practically returns to the savage theory that woman is admirably fitted for a beast of burden."[173] To that charge, Macarthur indi-cated that the work of the WTUL over the previous twenty-five years pro-vided "sufficient refutation." She then went on to spell out the position of the League which advocated, "where there is special danger to the women, where there is proof of the injurious effects to the children," that women should not work in such trades until they were determined to provide a healthy environment. She further added that the League was not concerned only with the interests of women. In the Potteries for instance, she stated, "it will not satisfy us to protect the women; we want to protect the men as well." But if you pass this resolution, she declared, "you will not abolish the women; but you will put a weapon in the hands of those who are fighting us in our attempts to improve the women's conditions."[174]

Her remarks met with a mixed response, perhaps the most provocative being that of Ben Turner of the Batley Weavers who viewed Davis' proposal as "a very sound one, because it desired to substitute men's labour for incom-petent female labour." Others, from districts where women were engaged in "dangerous trades," also warned against rejection of the resolution, while the representative of the Scottish miners claimed that the men engaged in any trade were "the best judges as to their suitability for women." Julia Varley, in contrast, chastised some male delegates, declaring that "they had no right to come to Congress and say what trades the women should be excluded from" when they themselves allowed their children "to work for pocket money."[175] But it was not only women who took issue with Davis.

Macarthur proposed an amendment to Davis' resolution re-affirming the Congress's "belief in the principle of equal wage for equal work" and called upon women workers to organize into trade unions "in order to put a stop to a competition which is as unfair as it is detrimental to the interests of men and women alike." With regard to the issue of employment in dangerous trades and unhealthy work environments, the amendment instructed the Parliamentary Committee to pursue policies that were basically sex-blind, calling for legislation (1) prohibiting the employment of young persons "of both sexes in all trades at present scheduled as dangerous or unhealthy" and (2) "safeguarding the health of the men and women employed in such trades." Speaking to this amendment, Pete Curran of the Gasworkers stated that "he wanted to make it clear that Congress stood for women having the right to work, provided they received the same wages as men." He then called upon Davis to accept the amendment as an addendum to the resolution, to which the latter gave a positive response. Davis further indicated that he would withdraw the resolution with the understanding that the amendment would be adopted and that the Parliamentary Committee would be instructed to bring about a government inquiry. Here the Brassworkers would be given the opportunity to demonstrate that the specified trades were dangerous and that women should be prohibited from working in them. The amendment was then passed by a show of hands.[176]

This debate is of particular interest for its disentangling of the issues involved with regard to "women's work." While Davis attempted to maintain the focus, as had traditionally been the case, on both womanhood and wages, Macarthur and her male allies appealed solely to the issues of competition and conditions of work. Issues of womanhood and femininity, they strongly implied, were irrelevant. Only by addressing working conditions themselves, from a gender-neutral perspective, would the interests of all be served. And in making this argument, they succeeded.

The approach that Davis had taken toward women workers for over thirty years, attempting to exclude them from certain trades, was in jeopardy. His attempt to respond to employers' refusal to come to an agreement with the Brassworkers' Society by seeking to eliminate female competition had failed. Now he was forced to take on the organization of the brass trade itself. As in the Black Country metal industries, a re-working of understandings of both class and gender proved necessary.

The brass crusade

In the fall of 1909, the Brassworkers determined on a crusade, rejected previously by Davis, "to *give urgency* to *obtaining a rise of wages* to those in the trade known as the semi-skilled who, through *no fault of their own* are put on section work or on automatic machines."[177] The Executive proposed that all men earning less than 28s. per week be advanced one halfpenny per hour.[178] In initiating the crusade, Davis appealed to employers who had claimed they would "always be prepared to lift up those who earned the least wages." Now they were to be given such an "opportunity." "The age is against sweating," Davis declared. Town Councils had refused to contract with employers who paid below the standard rate. Now all workers had to combine to combat the "curse" of low wages.[179]

Early on in the series of meetings held in Birmingham, the issue of female employment was raised. In opening the first meeting, W. C. McStocker of the Brassworkers indicated that "the introduction of machinery has played havoc with our trade," resulting in highly skilled mechanics being "forced on to the streets" while women, girls, and boys filled their places.[180] Further, if they did find employment, he declared, "the brassworkers are being sweated to an alarming extent." "But is it right," he asked, "that we should have men sweated in such a skilled trade as ours?"[181]

The question was clearly framed in terms of the interrelated issues of skill and female competition. As Davis stated at this meeting, "it is the introduction of machinery, and the employment of women and girls that is all against the working-man."[182] The reputation of Birmingham was suffering as customers were beginning to go elsewhere seeking quality goods.[183] The status of the male skilled worker was clearly threatened, and the extent of his loss was demonstrated by the inability of the sweated laborer, which many brassworkers had become, to provide for his family. Lamented Davis, "we have men Sweated to such an extent, men who have a wife and five or six children to support, going away, after a full week's work, with 18s., 19s., and 20s. per week to maintain the household."[184] "For your better conditions, for your wives and children," a member called upon those earning so little "to join the Society, and organize yourselves into one solid body."[185] The aim of the movement was, Davis pointed out, not only to improve wages but for the men to realize their "manly independence." He then called upon the brassworkers to be "missioners to our sweated brothers; missioners to clear out of the trade those who have not [sic] business in it – wives,

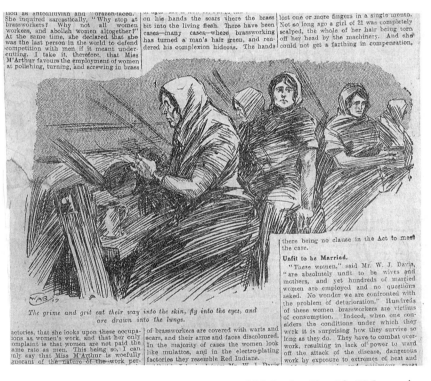

The grime and grit eat their way into the skin, fly into the eyes, and are drawn into the lungs.

Figure 7 "Working men! Unite to end this scandal." *Sunday Chronicle*, 20 September 1908, Gertrude Tuckwell Collection, 504a/2.

Source: TUC Library Collection, University of North London.

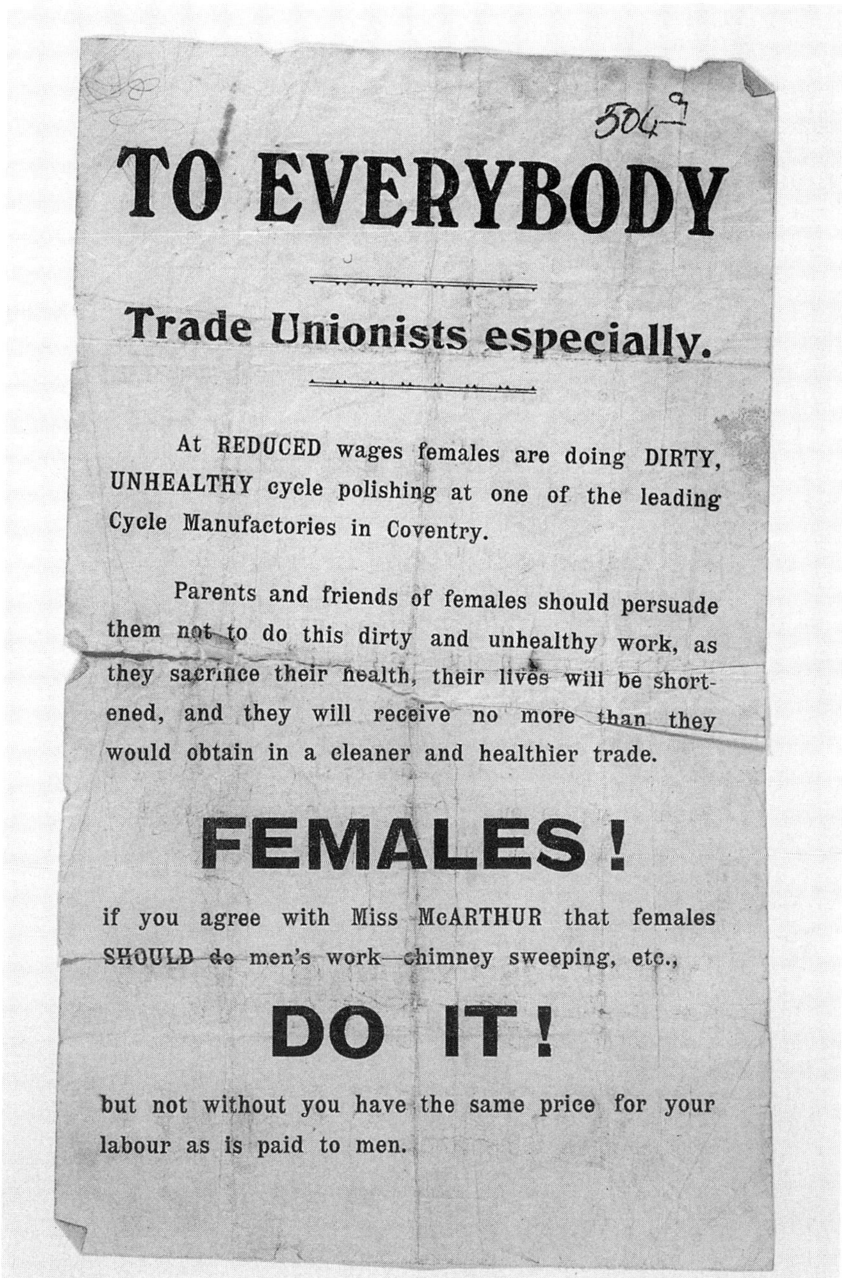

TO EVERYBODY

Trade Unionists especially.

At REDUCED wages females are doing DIRTY, UNHEALTHY cycle polishing at one of the leading Cycle Manufactories in Coventry.

Parents and friends of females should persuade them not to do this dirty and unhealthy work, as they sacrifice their health, their lives will be shortened, and they will receive no more than they would obtain in a cleaner and healthier trade.

FEMALES!

if you agree with Miss McARTHUR that females SHOULD do men's work—chimney sweeping, etc.,

DO IT!

but not without you have the same price for your labour as is paid to men.

Figure 8 Leaflet produced by the National Federation of Women Workers, Gertrude Tuckwell Collection, 504a/29. © GMB Union.

Source: TUC Library Collection, University of North London.

National Society of Amalgamated Brassworkers and Metal Mechanics.

Head Office:
70 LIONEL ST., BIRMINGHAM.

BRASS & METALWORKERS CRUSADE AGAINST SWEATING.

THE 3RD CRUSADE MEETING of BRASS AND METAL WORKERS was held at the Moseley Road Council Schools, Birmingham, on Tuesday evening, November 2nd, 1909, in support of the movement.

MR. W. J. DAVIS ON THE
CRUSADE AGAINST SWEATING.

Mr. W. C. McSTOCKER presided over a large gathering of all sections of the Brass and Metal Trades, and the proceedings were again enthusiastic.

THE CHAIRMAN said:—This is our third meeting in connection with the Brass-workers' Crusade. Our first meeting was held in the Bristol Hall, where we had a thoroughly representative meeting, and a unanimous vote. (Applause.) Our second meeting was held in the Hospital St. Council Schools and was an excellent meeting. A large number rushed for entrance forms, one of the most pleasing things in connection with that meeting. (Cheers.) It seemed to cheer us, and encourage us to go on. (Applause.) What are our proposals? We ask for one halfpenny per hour for all brass-workers who are getting less than 28s. per week. The Officers, Executive Council, and delegates are unanimous in asking for it, and at each of the meetings there was not a complaint raised against this proposal, and I hope to-night we shall be in that happy position of having to record a unanimous vote in favour of the proposal. (Applause.) Our demand is reasonable, and it is just. It is thirteen years since the brassworkers had a general rise of wages, but now we are not asking for a general rise, but for a halfpenny per hour for all those who are getting less than 28s. per week. The brassworkers are getting poorer, there is no mistake about

that. What with long holidays and short time, even those who get above 28s. it is less than scavengers' wages. (Applause.) The men who get the low rate of wages, 18s., 20s., 22s., and 24s. per week, what have they to say? If they have got any pluck to say; but the pluck and grit is taken out of them. We are here to-night to protest against this thing going on in our trade. It is a highly skilled trade. We make beautiful chandeliers and electroliers that hang in palaces and mansions. (Hear, hear.) Fancy receiving sweated wages on that class of work. (Shame.) Then there is the cabinet trade, beautiful work, and most of it done under sweated conditions. Steam and water fittings just the same. I say the pluck and the grit is taken out of the men, and it is almost impossible for us to put it back again. I am glad to see the Rev. G. H. Moore. (Loud applause.) We thank you, sir, for coming here to-night. Your presence will do us a great deal of good. (Hear, hear.)

Mr. W. J. DAVIS said:—Mr. Chairman and Gentlemen,—You have already said, sir, that this is the third meeting of the Crusade. The ramifications of the brass trade are so extensive in Birmingham that it will take at any rate another four weeks to get round

Figure 9 Banner of the "Crusade Against Sweating".

Source: Bishopsgate Library, Bishopsgate Institute.

Figure 10 National Society of Amalgamated Brassworkers and Metal Mechanics, "The 4th Crusade Meeting of Brass and Metal Workers," 4 November 1909.

Source: Bishopsgate Library, Bishopsgate Institute.

daughters, and sisters."[186] He further reiterated his basic outlook, stating, "We don't object to women working, but when we see women slimy, grimy, and in a position worse than a sweep in the street, we say it ought to be stopped in the interest of womankind."[187]

The twin threats of mechanization and female competition, resulting in the inability of the sweated laborer to provide for his family, were the evils to be countered. Moreover, for Davis, despite his encounter with Mary Macarthur described above, the issues of competition and understandings of womanhood remained joined. He thus called on "wives, daughters, and sisters" to "clear out of the trade" due to the unfeminine nature of the work. Yet the focus of the campaign was clearly on the plight of the sweated male laborers and the need to organize among them rather than the exclusion of women from specific trades. As with the chainmakers, how masculinity was defined became increasingly central, suggesting an expanded view of class. For women, some limited implications were apparent as well.

At the mass meetings organized by the Brassworkers, some speakers attempted to create a tone of conciliation toward the employers, indicating that they expected "the best" among them to join the crusade.[188] And Davis himself indicated that not all employers were alike, that some manufacturers at least wrote to him welcoming the brassworkers' efforts against sweating.[189] Yet he generally set an oppositional tone from the beginning. At the

Figure 11 *Cartoon* by Will Dyson, from the *Daily Herald*, 1914.

Source: Working Class Movement Library, Salford.

first meeting, he indicated his desire to make it "known to the world" that there were 50,000 men engaged in "the swindle of sweating" in Birmingham and district and, he asked, "for what? To make employers richer and you poorer" was his straightforward reply.[190] In a more humorous vein, he stated of the modern manufacturer, "he wants to pay low wages on the Saturday, go to church on the Sunday, collect his rents on the Monday, and put the bailiffs in on the Tuesday."[191]

Davis pointed specifically to the "tricks" played by the employers, naming them the "company," "competition," and "high wage" tricks. "Competition is so severe," the employer would cry, "We want you to help us on this occasion." Or to make the condition of the company look worse than it was, they would "cook the accounts" by raising the salaries of the executives.[192] Claiming to pay high wages, employers would hire a piece-worker for perhaps 50s. or £3 per week. That piece-worker in turn then actually hired perhaps thirteen men under him, the average wage coming to approximately £1 2s.[193] Most significant, however, was Davis' charge against the employers, that not one had come forward actually to assist in eradicating the sweating system since, with few exceptions known to him, they were "all guilty of the offense."[194] Further, Davis pointed out, the practice was not limited to the brass trade but extended to such trades as furniture, silversmithing, and jewelry as well.[195]

Yet it was the brassworkers that Davis called upon "to be men," to "dominate and influence this district" in the anti-sweating campaign.[196] They were not applying to be scheduled under the Board of Trades Act because, Davis stated, "we did not want that indignity."[197] Rather, they would take the responsibility upon themselves to improve their conditions through trade unionism. To that end, Davis and the other leaders called particularly on those who were suffering the most, the low-waged, sweated male laborers themselves, to support the trade union cause.

In taking this approach, these workers were severely chastised for not standing firm in the past. Referring to attempts by the Brassworkers to gain an advance on two previous occasions, McStocker indicated that those attempts had failed due to lack of unity within the trade.[198] "We want you men to be worthy of your hire," declared T. C. Headley, "and not sell yourselves so cheaply."[199] Stated J. Turton at the fourth crusade meeting:

> If they know that we have got the whole of the Brassworkers at our back we shall win. It is in your hands. Are you going to be with us? [he asked] You are fighting not for the Association only, you are fighting for yourselves, your wives and families.[200]

Whereas a decade previously Davis had determined against even raising the issue of sweated labor upon reaching an agreement with the employers, he now recognized that, "whether they were unskilled or not," those men earning the wages of the sweated laborer:

were married men, with the responsibility of a household, and they had children. The man who turns a handle or pulls a lever [he continued] was doing something which cheapened the cost of production. The public ought to pay him a living wage.[201]

J. Hughes of the Brassworkers appealed to the self-interest of the journey-men who were engaged in sweating themselves, indicating that they were "jeopardising their own positions." "It would be to the advantage of every journeyman in the trade," he declared, "as it would be the means of keeping their job more secure, if they keep up their underhands' wages."[202] Appeal-ing to the brassworkers in general, Davis cried, "You are the men who have the power to stop" sweating, and challenged them, "Why don't you do it? Why don't you be men?"[203]

Through the unity of the men, journeymen and underhands, those who were skilled and those who pulled a lever, but above all those who were manly enough to exercise their power to end sweating, the crusade would be won. Somewhat ironically, such an appeal, and the expanded concept of class it represented, served to open up the subject of organizing women workers. Thus, Julia Varley, who had moved from Yorkshire to Birmingham for that purpose, addressed the fifth meeting of the crusade. Referring to the fact that women workers in Yorkshire were, in places, well organized and, as a result, earning decent wages, she chastised the men of Birmingham for having been "rather slack as regards trade unionism." She then called upon them "to let charity begin at home, and to organize your own women-folk."[204] The "swindle of sweating" was now to be confronted straight on, not by conciliating the employers but by challenging them by organizing all workers, skilled and unskilled, male and female. New understandings of class, as well as womanhood and manhood, were suggested.

The most immediate result of the crusade, however, was the establishment of a new Conciliation Board consisting of representatives of the Brassmasters' Association and the National Society of Brassworkers by the end of 1909.[205] With its establishment, and under the impact of the crusade, employers admitted to the presence of sweating in the trade. For their part, the Brass-workers conceded to the possibility of governmental interference, which Davis had opposed during the course of the crusade, preferring that the Society attain its objectives on its own. Now, the two parties joined in seeking the inclusion of the brass trade among sweated industries under the recently passed Board of Trades Act. Under the provisions of this Act, to be discussed further in relation to chainmaking, one of Davis' long-cherished principles for the trade would be put in place, that of the minimum wage.[206] And, women's position in the trade would also apparently be recognized. The *Metal Worker* summed up the Society's apparently inclusive demand as follows:

that a man or a woman shall live by their work; that wages paid shall provide food in quantity and quality equal to the maintainence [*sic*] of physical fitness, and equal also to the maintainence [*sic*] of home and family in respectability and comfort; that the conditions of employment, whether the same applies to a man or a woman, shall be healthful and consonant with human dignity, and in no way degrading.[207]

The Board of Trade, however, rejected bringing the brass trade under the provisions of the newly enacted law. Instead, the Conciliation Board came to an agreement on a grading system that established minimum rates without any reduction in wages. In warning a meeting of Brassworkers considering the scheme that sweated employers would oppose it, W. J. Davis encouraged them to support it nevertheless, reminding them, "They had a society which could reasonably support every manly effort to bring in a new and improved state of things." The meeting, held in October 1910, voted to accept the scheme[208] and, in the following months, trade revived, wage advances were won, and the Society gained in membership, leading Davis to declare in the May following that the Brassworkers had enjoyed a "remarkable year."[209]

The implications for women were, however, limited, as Davis continued to emphasize the need for the Brassworkers to exert every "manly effort" in their defense while women's work in brass polishing remained an issue. Upon visiting two factories disguised as a laborer, a correspondent for the *Watch Dog* concluded that:

> half a day in each was ample to satisfy me that of all the industries in which women take part, that of brass-polishing and stamping is beyond all question the very worst that even a man can adopt, but to put a woman at it is to place her beyond the pale of humanity altogether.[210]

She reported women working at lathes with their breasts flattened against them as particles of brass ate their way into their skin and filled their eyes and lungs.[211] They often suffered from consumption and experienced other ailments due to exposure to extremes of hot and cold temperatures, poisonous gas, and insanitary conditions.[212] A majority of the women so employed were reportedly married and mothers often had their babies brought to them for their nourishment.[213] The girls and women reportedly earned 8s. to 14s. for a week's work, while the wages of men for the same labor ranged from 23s. to 45s. Some employers claimed, according to the *Watch Dog* correspondent, that they were compelled to employ women in this capacity due to competition. But the reporter readily recognized this fallacy, indicating that many firms refused to employ women in such work.[214]

Such conditions led the Special Commissioner of the *Sunday Chronicle* to declare Birmingham "the chosen home of the sweater of woman's labour." To "a very large extent," he claimed, cheap female labor had displaced skilled male artisans, leading to a lowered standard of living, neglected children, dirty homes, and "semi-starvation."[215] Interviewed by the *Chronicle* correspondent, W. J. Davis complained of the difficulty in organizing the brassworkers because of men being idled by the employment of women at lower wages, unlike in the north of England. And he continued to argue, as previously, that the women "are absolutely unfit to be wives and mothers. The deterioration of the race, which we hear so much of, is seen at its worst," he proclaimed, "among these wretched people."[216]

In response to such conditions, the metal polishers organized a movement with the aim of scheduling the trade under the "unhealthy" clause of the Factories and Workshops Act.[217] In February of 1912, the Brassworkers took up the cause at a meeting called to urge the Home Secretary to grant a public inquiry "with a view to preventing women continuing to be employed" in brass polishing. Reiterating his well-established position, Davis declared that "they were not against women working in fair competition with men," but asked why, with "plenty of occupations" available to women, they were employed at polishing. Of course he had a ready answer, that employers gave women work "at half the price paid to men," thereby giving "backward Birmingham" an advantage over other towns. And he further added the comment that the Brassworkers:

> did not disguise the fact that while they did not want women to be employed in such an industry they also wanted the women out of the trade in order that the men's wages might be increased, that they might be rid of unfair competition, and that employment might be more regular.[218]

In a context in which organizing among women was difficult and limited, the focus of Davis and the Brassworkers remained on the conjoined issues of the unfeminine nature of the work and the "unfair competition" that women workers represented. And of course, as the women's trade union movement itself had increasingly recognized, that competition remained, unarguably, a threat to the well-being of working people and their families as long as women remained unorganized. To Davis, the issues were not distinct but intermingled and legitimate, and he accordingly continued to pursue his time-honored policy.

Yet it was also becoming increasingly clear that exclusionary strategies, pursued by the Brassworkers in particular, did not represent a solution. The trade union movement itself had largely come to recognize this fact and, even among the women workers of the Black Country and Birmingham, some steps began to be taken toward a different approach. The place of women in the workforce was beginning to be recognized and to gain legitimacy as strides were made toward their organization. It is then left for us to assess the impact on the meanings of "women's work" and gender understandings in general.

Gender and strikes in metal

Our last look at the chainmakers suggested that some progress was being made in the organization of female workers, accompanied by some improvements in the condition of their work in the mid-1890s. In general, the trade was continuing to expand, with the number of female outworkers increasing by approximately 20 percent over the decade, to an estimated 1,883, by 1901. By 1911, R. H. Tawney estimated their numbers at 2,000 while male outworkers numbered 800 to 1,000.[219] Unionizing efforts were most successful among the male factory workers who were organized under the leadership of Thomas Sitch into the United Chain-makers' Association of Saltney, Pontypridd, and Staffordshire in 1889.

From an early date, Sitch took the view that "no permanent good could be done in the trade until the whole of the forces of the operatives were linked together." Apparently in 1903 a new effort was launched to organize women into the Cradley Heath Association of Women Working in the Chain, Nail and Spike Making Trades, which initially was reported to have 400 members. However, a year later that number had dwindled to 100 and the association ceased to exist.[220]

With the establishment of the National Federation of Women Workers in 1906 and the holding of contemporaneous exhibitions on sweated industries in London and Birmingham, which served to raise public awareness of the plight of the sweated laborer, the situation altered. At the Birmingham exhibition, a woman aged 20 hammering out links of chain attracted a "constant stream of curious visitors."[221] Wrote George Shann in the handbook on sweated industries, accompanying the *Daily News* exhibition in London:

> As one looks in the shop lit up with glare of the fire and hot irons and sees the women bare-armed, bare-chested, perspiring, and working with feverish eagerness, the vision suggests the nether regions, and the shock to the sensibilities of the visitor is almost overpowering.[222]

The public thus learned of the conditions under which the girls and women of the chainmaking district continued to labor, often working from 6 a.m. to past 8 p.m., despite the provisions of the factory laws, and earning only 6s. to 8s. per week, a wage not even equal to one-third of men's earnings.[223] As *The Women's Industrial News* reported, families were often only "kept afloat" by the cooperation of all its members in undertaking work if able to do so. Such a situation was all "the more inexcusable," commented the reporter, due to the lack of foreign competition in the trade.[224]

Alongside the growing awareness of these conditions, an organizing drive among the outworkers began to gain momentum. Reporting to a meeting of the Midland Counties Trades Federation in April of 1907, Thomas Sitch spoke of the demoralization among that section of workers which had existed a few months previously. Now, however, he announced that not only were the men thoroughly organized but, for the first time in the history of the trade, some employers had signed an agreement with the operatives' representatives which included a standard list of prices. As a result, a 10 to 30 percent increase in wages had been realized.[225]

The women as well were reported to be rapidly organizing following a visit to the region by Mary Macarthur of the newly formed National Federation of Women Workers. At a meeting of women chainmakers presided over by Sitch, and attended by Macarthur, he indicated that the women's branch of the trade had been in a state of disorganization, despite an apparent attempt to form a society in 1905. Now, however, a nucleus of a society had been formed, called the Cradley Heath Women Chainmakers' Union, which soon became the Hammered Chain Branch of the NFWW.[226] By June of 1907, it had enrolled nearly 1,100 women, with 700 to 800 paying contributions of 2d. per week. Sitch and Macarthur apparently worked closely together during this organizing drive as they joined forces in canvassing employers for an advance in wages.[227]

Unfortunately, within six months of these efforts which appeared to be meeting with considerable success, "the chain trade was plunged into its worst depression for over thirty years."[228] Demand for chains had fallen as the Admiralty had determined that shorter cables were sufficient and the larger ships now being built required fewer of them.[229] As a result, in the spring of 1909 the factory branch of the trade was forced to accept a 10 percent reduction.[230] Interest among women in their Society apparently remained strong as 250 to 300 attended a meeting at which both Macarthur and Julia Varley of Birmingham were present. However, the news they received was undoubtedly disheartening as Sitch, the honorable secretary, indicated that, while they had hoped for an advance, due to the depression their funds were low and could not support a turnout. Membership in the Society was also reported to have fallen nearly 50 percent, to 600 women.[231]

An alternative route to some improvement in their conditions, however, emerged with passage of the Trade Boards Act of 1909. Under this Act, which was a direct result of the sweated industries exhibitions and pressure exerted by the newly founded National Anti-Sweating League, minimum wages were to be established in selected industries where sweating was prominent. Immediately the League and the men's unions attempted to bring the chainmaking trade under the provisions of the Act. Generally "narrow minded and preoccupied with their own parochial trade interests," the employers soon joined the campaign as well, recognizing for the moment at least, as Sheila Blackburn has demonstrated, that it was in their interest to do so.[232]

The chain trade was basically organized in such a way that the factory and sweated sections did not compete. However, factory owners were now turning to the production of small chain, due to the decreased demand for large, and, as they did, their product came into competition with chain produced in the sweated section of the trade where small chains predominated and wages were naturally lower. A legally enforced minimum wage, members of the Chain Manufacturers' Association surmised, would go far in preventing the resulting underselling. The employers also concluded that bringing the chain trade under the Trade Boards Act would serve to raise the quality of chain being produced, thereby, Blackburn indicates, "redeeming its reputation in the eyes of overseas customers." Leading employers then came to support scheduling of the trade under the Act.[233]

When the Chain Trade Board was actually put in place, however, with three appointed members and six representatives each from among the workers and employers, the five factory owners took a position that proved disruptive of its efforts, leading to a dramatic confrontation with the female chainmakers. Rather than addressing the issue of the minimum wage in such a way that would serve to alleviate the conditions of the operatives and undermine the whole system of sweating, they were instead determined that the new rates should not reduce their profits significantly or lead to a loss of business.[234] Such an attitude led Sitch, serving as a workers' representative, to conclude that "we were living in a fool's paradise when we entertained a thought that our employers were anxious to see the trade free from the evils of sweating."[235] On the contrary, he charged:

> The minimum rate suggested by the employers is nothing less than an attempt to perpetuate the abominable system of sweating, and to make this measure an instrument of legalising sweating, instead of using it as a means to stamp out an evil which has blighted the district throughout its whole history.[236]

Only after a number of meetings was the Board able to determine on a minimum time rate for women of $2\frac{1}{2}$d. per hour which, although "regrettably low," amounted to an increase on the most common quality of chain of 80 percent or more.[237] But this agreement failed to settle things between the women and their employers.

Under the provisions of the Trade Boards Act, a period of three months was allowed for representatives of the interested parties to object to the minimum wage agreement. When this period was up, in August 1910, a number of employers issued agreements, which they asked the women to sign, contracting out of the minimum wage for another six months. Such an action was allowed under the provisions of the Act, and hundreds of women, undoubtedly under considerable pressure, signed. However, it was clear that employers had taken advantage of the first waiting period to stockpile chain worked at the old rates. Recognizing that this practice was likely to continue, resulting in considerable unemployment when the minimum wage came into effect, union leaders called a mass meeting of women workers. Here many were reluctant to admit they had signed such an agreement, but it was not surprising that many were manipulated into doing so since they often could not read or understand the legal forms.[238] The *Daily News* reported that when they learned of the significance of their action, the women "were appalled at realising that they had signed away for six months the boons won for them by the Trade Boards Act and very eager to sign themselves into repossession of their rights."[239] Within days the *Wolverhampton Chronicle* reported that all women had now indicated their refusal to sign such agreements. Employers then refused to give out work to those who would not sign, and perhaps 1,000 women, about half of whom belonged to the union and "stood loyally" by the others, were effectively locked out by the end of the month.[240]

The scene in Cradley Heath encountered by the many reporters who were now drawn to the area by events was not unlike that described in inspectors' reports and pamphlets appearing in the 1870s. A writer from the *Daily Express,* who was in the area just before the strike, visited a woman making plough chains with her baby hung from a cradle while two other "sickly, stunted" children were seated on cinders. As she did her work, she kept her eye on the children while answering the reporter's questions without stopping, indicating that she worked ten to eleven hours per day, her net earnings per week amounting to 5s. 6d. Evidently not lacking a sense of humor, when asked why she did it, she responded, "'To pass the time and keep mysel' warm.' She [then] laughed bitterly, and added more seriously, pointing to the children, 'I've 'em to keep and feed somehow, ye know.'"[241]

The special correspondent of the *Birmingham Dispatch* wrote of "the most pathetic figure in the strike of women chain-makers," Mrs. Patience Round, who was 79 years of age and whose figure was bent and hands indented with marks of chains from a career spanning sixty-nine years. She told the reporter:

> In the whole of my life I have never stopped working in the shop for more than two days. I started when I was a little girl of ten – it seems long, long years ago now – and ever since then I have made chains – hundreds and hundreds of miles of them. Once I used to count, and counted up to 3,000 miles, but that was long ago.
>
> I have learned to love the forge, [she continued] for in the winter the glowing fire keeps me warm, and the bright sparks keep me cheerful; [and then on reflection added] I'm getting just a little old now. My husband is a cripple, and it is hard work to keep our little home together.[242]

The reporter seemed to be convinced that it was the work at the forge that kept her going as he concluded, "Her life is wrapped up in the making of chains, and she will talk for hours of the sparks and the wonderful chains she has made during her career." Her children, too, were all chainmakers as were their children as well.[243]

To Mrs. Round, the period of the strike represented "wonderful times. I never thought that I should live to assert the rights of us women," she proclaimed. "It has been the week of my life – three meetings, and such beautiful talking."[244] The women generally quickly became known for their fortitude and determination. As a man with life-long experience in chainmaking declared, "I have never seen anything like it before." "Though they were in an appalling state of destitution," wrote *Votes for Women*, "there was no begging, no whining, only a keen desire for work, so that they might provide food for their children and themselves."[245] Stated this reporter:

> The apathy of sweated women regarding their own condition has always been held to be the stumbling-block in the way of any improvement, but the example of the women chain-makers shows that, given a ray of hope and a sign of encouragement, they are ready to face incredible hardship in order to obtain better conditions of life for themselves and their families.[246]

It was apparently clear as well that, while the women desired improvement in their conditions, they continued to identify with their work at the forge. Reported Mary Mortimer Maxwell of the *Daily Express*, "Women who have been chainmakers and become charwomen or washerwomen or domestic servants almost invariably go back to chainmaking, even at the miserably low wages." Asked why they would not prefer to work as housemaids in London, Mortimer declared, "The answer was always the same: 'I'd rather be a chainmaker!'"[247] When questioned by the BBC in the 1970s in reference to the strike, Christine Coates reports that the workers "were more interested in describing the skills involved in their trade than in recalling what may appear to them to be an exciting but perhaps less important episode."[248] Wrote the *Weekly Dispatch* at the time, "All they desire is a more adequate payment for the work they perform."[249]

This end appeared to be gained by the end of October when every employer had been forced to sign a list of those complying with the new rates under the Act.[250] "The effect of the lock-out," claimed the *Women's Industrial News*, "was to arouse the women, as nothing had hitherto done," as nearly all now enrolled in the union. And the men benefitted as well in their dispute with the employers. Assisted by the surplus of funds from the women's dispute, they were also able to gain immediate payment of the new rates.[251] The spring of 1912 thus found the Midland Counties Trades Federation heralding the gains made by the chainmakers. Not only had the workers gained from the increase in wages but, it was claimed, "tyranny and oppression had been put down."[252] Further, reported Thomas Sitch at a conference of the NFWW held in Cradley Heath in July of that year:

> There was a very warm feeling between the men and women trade unionists. What was good for women, as far as labour was concerned, was good for men, and if the improvement took place among the women workers some good would follow for the male workers.[253]

"The thought swept through the working class," states the Birmingham Trades Council historian John Corbett, "that if these unorganised, depressed women could rise, organise and win, then almost every other section, however poor and subservient, could do the same."[254]

Following upon the strike among the chainmakers, the NFWW, with the aid of Sitch's son, Charles, took on the organization of holloware workers. Approximately 1,800 women were employed in this trade in shops in Birmingham, Bilston, Wolverhampton, Dudley, Walsall, and the Lye district, embracing Cradley Heath and Old Hill.[255] Here women, half of whom were wives and mothers, were employed in making kitchen-ware, which involved such processes as galvanizing, enamelling, dipping, or tinning items in chemical solutions, and removing and wiping them, all of which exposed them to dangerous chemical fumes. Under a code of regulations resulting from a Home Office inquiry in 1907, no lead was to be used in the tinning of metal holloware and no female was to be employed in dipping or wiping. However, these regulations continued to be flagrantly violated in the Lye district, where employers took advantage of the sweated labor system already existing in the nail trade. As a result the women suffered from loss of hair, loss of their voices and teeth, lead poisoning, and poor digestion.[256] A correspondent from the *Daily Citizen* reported a conversation with:

> a little middle-aged mother with her face tied up. She pressed her fingers on her cheek bones or held her hand on the top of her head all the while she talked. She is a galvanizer [the reporter indicated]. The effect of chemical fumes has been to give her incessant faceache, but she did not speak of it until I asked why she wore the bandage.[257]

While the woman indicated she could "stand it," she added, "My girl here couldn't; it stopped her breathing."[258] For such labor, the women earned 4s. 6d. to 9s. for a fifty-four-hour week.[259]

By November 1912, the NFWW had reportedly organized 1,600 of the 1,800 women employed in the trade and began to press for a minimum wage of 10s. per week. While many employers agreed to this rate, those in the Lye district where the lowest rates were paid generally did not and a strike ensued. The men, particularly in Birmingham, were often working at list rates, but when the women went out, hundreds of men joined them.[260] "Masters denying to women and girls the wretched minimum wage would have found it impossible to set on boys to do their work," reported the *Daily Citizen*.[261] As a result, the major demands of the workers were conceded. Nevertheless, the *Citizen* concluded:

> From common tinning [women and girls] should be immediately withdrawn, or debarred from galvanising. . . . It is commonly said among them [the paper added] that such work is not fit work for women to do. . . . They do it because the men have been hitherto paid too badly

to keep wives and families. There is no idea hereabouts that women have something to gain by being independent of men.[262]

The women themselves will abandon the work, the reporter predicted, "as opportunity offers, and as the standard of life in this Inferno rises."[263]

In Birmingham as well, where an expanding economy was met with a militant spirit among the workers, a new-found unity between men and women was a striking feature of what George Barnsby has called the "Big Bang" of 1910–14.[264] At the Birmingham Small Arms plant in the fall of 1911, piece-work rates were falling, while girls and women, paid 11s. to 15s. per week, were replacing male capstan-lathe operators earning 23s. to 28s.[265] Rather than the men meeting this threat with a call for the exclusion of female labor, however, "women struck with the men, the skilled with the labourers, the unorganised with the organised."[266] In all, approximately 600 to 700 organized men were on strike with 2,000 other workpeople including 600 girls and women.[267] At a demonstration in the Bull Ring, 8,000 demonstrated their support, while a member of the Birmingham Trades Council declared "the loyalty of the women" to be "beyond praise."[268] A notable feature of the settlement reached after the month-long strike, Barnsby points out, was the support given to the unskilled by the skilled workers. Although the latter gained little beyond that offered at the beginning of the struggle, they approved the settlement which contained improved wages for the unskilled and a minimum weekly rate for piece-work.[269] The Trades Council responded by spearheading a movement for a minimum wage for unskilled workers of 23s. per week for men and 15s. for women. Under pressure from a number of strikes, by July of 1913 employers had largely conceded these rates.[270]

The Black Country as well witnessed an extraordinary workers' revolt, from April through July of 1913, in which women played an incomparable role, alongside men, under the leadership of the Workers' Union and Julia Varley. At Bayliss, Jones, and Bayliss, nuts and bolts manufacturers of Wolverhampton, women and girls went on strike over a wages agreement that they claimed the employers had not honored. When the company put forward an offer with which they were generally satisfied, however, the employers then closed the bolt department, throwing 700 people out of work. The women then "decided to stand by the men and not resume work until all the discontented sections have been satisfied," leading to a strike of 1,200 workpeople. A settlement was reached, with the men earning a minimum weekly rate of 21s. and women 10s.[271] By the end of May 30,000 hardware workers were on strike in the Black Country for a 23s. weekly minimum for men and 12s. for women which was agreed to in July,[272] prompting the *Daily Citizen* to write:

We congratulate the men and women of the Black Country on the steadfastness with which they have fought their fight. They have been loyal to each other and to the union, and disciplined class-loyalty is a force which the employers find it hard, and often impossible, to break.[273]

The women and men were indeed "steadfast" and "loyal" but the settlements that were reached among the chainmakers and the Black Country and Birmingham workers generally were gendered, with the agreed wages of women equaling barely half those of men. Only the Workers' Union stood in opposition to such an approach as women trade union leaders generally, and the women workers themselves, often proved willing to accept such inequity. Thus Mary Mortimer Maxwell reported on her visit to the chainmakers of Cradley Heath that she noticed that men were employed using the dollie and thereby were able to produce "a better class of work." When the men defended their monopoly on such labor, they were defended by women, one of whom said to Maxwell that, if a woman were to take up such work, she would "be taking the bread out of ... men's mouths. . . . The women haven't any business with 'dollies.'" she declared.[274]

With reference to the chainmakers, Christine Coates concluded:

> The campaign had been based totally on the sex of the workers and therefore strengthened the view that women workers were a special case. It was accepted that their biology did and should limit the range of occupations to which they might have access, and that their image as helpless victims of the industrial system, emphasised by the use of chains as the dominant symbol of the agitation, demanded a condescending chivalry rather than comradely mutual support.[275]

The lesson that was learned, Coates continued, was that women were best served by protective means, such as government Boards, which institutionalized the gender division of labor while confirming the connection between low wages and women's work.[276]

On the surface, it appears difficult to quarrel with such a conclusion. By means of the Trade Boards Act, as well as labor agreements, "women's work" was inscribed with certain meanings, being secondary and low-paid, unskilled and generally apart from men's. Yet such a conclusion, suggesting that such an outcome was the singular result of the events described, requires us to tear from their original context the legislation passed and the agreements reached and ignore the process by which they were attained. The construction of women as secondary laborers had been solidified. It was expressed in the discourse as well as through legislation and in the course of labor disputes. But the events and experiences described here transcended the images on which such a construction was based in important respects.

The artisanal tradition that associated some work of women with immorality and proclaimed it illegitimate, pervasive a quarter-century previously, had been largely undermined. And it had been undermined by a process of negotiating gender difference. From the 1880s, the exclusionary strategies pursued by leaders such as Juggins and Davis came under pressure from a multitude of forces, including women's continued and growing presence in the small metal trades, mechanization, the organized women's trade union movement, and diverging community interests. As a result, ideas of womanhood and the labor in which women were engaged had to be reconciled.

This process of reconciliation was varied and often tentative. In chain-making it apparently ultimately involved an increasing distinction between women's and men's work in the outwork portion of the trade, involving the hand-hammered and dollied sections respectively. The dolly, operated by a foot treadle, was brought down upon a link of chain after it was welded by hand, giving the light chain upon which it was employed a smoother finish. Apparently, R. H. Tawney suggests, it was used only by men because the worker had to keep it in repair.[277] This separation of workers along gender lines was accompanied by the establishment of separate trade union organizations. At the same time, however, considerable cooperation among union leaders and workers, male and female, existed, as all were struggling for the same ends.

In Birmingham, strong opposition to female labor in certain instances remained in place. But given the conditions under which such labor was carried out and the advantage taken by employers, such opposition was understandable, and accompanied by attempts, sometimes tentative and not always successful, to organize women workers and improve conditions for women and men alike. Further, the trade union movement itself, in responding to the Birmingham Brassworkers, now took the position that removing women from one trade was not a solution to the problems presented by female labor.

The continuing significance of gender difference, of ideas of womanhood and manhood, is apparent in relation to the small metal industries into the twentieth century. But that difference must be examined in the larger context, in terms of the apparent contradictions and ambiguities involved in the continued opposition to some women's employment, particularly in unfeminine settings, and their continued presence. Through an ongoing process of negotiating gender difference, the work of women was recognized and legitimated, women increasingly organized in their own interests, and a mutuality between male and female trade unionists emerged.

Conclusion

As the chainmakers' struggle to uphold the minimum wage got under way in the fall of 1910, the reporter for *Votes for Women* found herself in a quandary, stating of her experience:

> I came away from Cradley Heath distressed in mind by the terrible scenes of poverty and privation I had witnessed, and yet, at the same time, inexpressibly cheered by the knowledge that even these down-trodden women were proving strong enough to protect their own interests, and to take a way of escape from their miserable lot when it was pointed out to them.[1]

Perhaps this statement, made by an observer of the events that marked the end of our story, represents a fitting way of concluding our tale of negotiating gender in English working-class culture from the mid-nineteenth to the early twentieth century. For this statement effectively expresses the ambiguities, tensions, and contradictions that the woman worker embodied, and which we have foregrounded throughout this work.

From their entry into the factory in the earliest stage of the industrializing era, women workers represented a challenge to what Anna Clark argues was an emerging separate spheres ideology adopted by working-class men. Increasingly women were constructed as wives and mothers, dependent on male support and state legislation, while men emerged as independent citizens, holding property in skill and recognized as family providers. Despite their continuing role in the workforce, women workers were thus effectively marginalized, Sonya Rose has argued. Ideas of femininity and masculinity, and thus "women's work" and "men's work," became increasingly hardened categories, leading to attempts to exclude or restrict female labor from settings considered unfeminine or areas of work not traditionally identified as suitable for women. Jane Long argues that women so employed represented a challenge to the gender order and the progress it served to uphold. Critics of female labor saw the women themselves in negative terms, seemingly taking on characteristics identified with the negative aspects of the work in which they were engaged.[2]

In a culture "convinced of the centrality of women's domestic work," women were thus constructed as secondary laborers, and governmental policy, at the end of our period, was formulated on the basis of such an understanding. As Susan Pedersen has indicated, state health insurance and even policies covering maternity benefits targeted working men as the breadwinners in an effort to enhance their ability to maintain themselves and their families during difficult periods. When feminists and women's labor organizations supported granting entitlements, including maternity benefits, directly to women as citizens, such an approach was considered controversial within the organized trade union movement as it was perceived to undercut the place of working men as providers.[3] Women were not yet citizens and as workers they were often considered out of place.

By placing gender difference at the center of analysis and bringing these issues to the fore, scholars have enriched our understanding of English working-class culture and the place women were often understood to occupy within it. At the same time, they have at times been cognizant of the ambiguities brought out by the comment made by the reporter for *Votes for Women*. Women have not only been victims of extreme exploitation at the workplace and a predominant discourse, expressing definite ideas of what constituted womanhood and manhood, but have been agents as well. In particular, scholars have noted that women have often constructed their own feminine identity. Clark suggests that women redefined their political identities through their own participation in political movements and points to the "tension between women's militant activism and the rhetoric of radical domesticity" as "an important dynamic of the working-class movement."[4] States Long:

> While middle-class conceptions of progress may have manifested themselves as a drive to fix female identity, the variety of material conditions and the individual responses of women illustrated that idealised visions of how women should behave and what their priorities should be, were subject to constant processes of negotiation.

"The construction of women's identity," Long concludes, "occurred within working-class culture" itself.[5]

This work has intended to build upon these analyses, and particularly to put flesh on the bones of the latter points, by bringing to greater prominence the tensions, ambiguities, and shifting interrelationships, suggested by these quotes, upon which gender identities were constructed. There was an ongoing process of negotiating gender which simultaneously incorporated and transcended dominant discourses and, as such, contained within it implications for class as well. This may be readily seen by returning briefly to our three predominant male figures who appeared to embody and sanctify the meanings of femininity and masculinity.

In the 1830s and 1840s, Rev. Joseph Rayner Stephens waxed eloquently about the sanctity of the cottage, and women's protection within it. Seeing him as a champion of the dignity of working-class life, despite the gender hierarchy implicit in his paternalistic outlook, women of the cotton district were responsive to his message. They in turn, alongside the men of their families and communities, participated in the agitations for the Charter and the Ten Hours Act as well as union organizing. Working-class respectability thus came to be based not only on women's subordination, but on a gaining of some measure of control over work time and family time, wages and working conditions. Beyond the factory gates, the working-class family was increasingly able to exercise control over fertility, as women, as expected of them, took primary responsibility for the household. The gender order on which working-class respectability thus came to rest was founded upon independence and control as well as subordination, collectivity as well as division.

Outside the cotton district, gender identities, particularly in relation to work, appeared more sharply defined, as the male artisan, and the discourse of femininity and masculinity that he embraced, appeared to emerge predominant. Ideas of manhood and womanhood, morality and legitimacy, personified by Richard Juggins and W. J. Davis, often led to a sharply sex-segregated workforce and attempts to exclude or restrict female labor to those areas deemed appropriate. Technology itself was not fully determining of workforce composition.

Yet neither the discourse nor the gender order it espoused could remain static, determining, and unchallenged in the ever-changing industrial world in which it resided. Regional identities, multiple masculinities, community interests, and feminist viewpoints all worked to place pressure on and subvert apparently established gender understandings. Increased attempts, despite difficulties, were made by union leaders to organize women workers and defend their interests, in concert with the women themselves, as the male-led trade union movement moved to reject exclusionary strategies. Ideas of gender difference were not abandoned, however, as women continued to labor under wretched conditions, and their presence in the workforce, due to their construction as cheap laborers, undermined the interests of men as well. W. J. Davis thus remained adamant in his views opposing female labor in certain instances, where it was both considered unsuitable and, by any measure, underpaid. The minimum wage agreements further served to maintain a gender hierarchy while reducing competition. Economic interests and understandings of gender were never fully disentangled. Rather, improved conditions of work as well as pay, accompanied by organization, often represented the means by which ideas of womanhood and women's work were reconciled. Further, the process of attaining these objectives suggested an increase in class unity across gender lines.

As Michael Savage has argued, diverse processes have constantly threatened class unity and stability, among them ties of community and gender difference, considered extensively here. Yet there is a "fluid and dynamic" process of class formation, or unifying of class interests, that continues on the basis of re-working and negotiating those bonds and understandings as well.[6] The privileging of discourse analysis fails fully to capture this process as it tends to privilege the discourse of the dominant group as it ascribed meanings, for instance, to "women's work." From such analyses, one too easily gains a sense of fully gender identities. Through examining the interplay of discourse and the material, however, which themselves are intertwined, we are able to grasp more fully not only the ambiguities inherent in gender identities but the process of class, its fragmentation and processes of unification, as well.

Notes

1 Introductory essay – gender in labor history

1 E. P. Thompson, *The Making of the English Working Class*, New York, Random House, 1963, p. 12.
2 Ibid., p. 9.
3 I employ the term "understandings of gender" as opposed to "constructions of gender," used by many scholars, not to suggest a different meaning. Both terms refer to a culture's understanding at a particular time of what constitutes womanhood and manhood, of what attributes are associated with women and men, serving to define their gender identities. I find "understandings of gender" more satisfactory since it is less jargonistic and suggests an ongoing process of shaping such understandings rather than the solidity and static quality suggested, although perhaps not always intended, by the term "construction."
4 Louise A. Tilly and Joan W. Scott, *Women, Work, and Family*, New York, Holt, Rinehart and Winston, 1978, p. 64.
5 Ibid.
6 Ibid., p. 68.
7 Ibid., p. 87.
8 Ibid., pp. 124–31.
9 Ibid., pp. 68–9.
10 Ibid., p. 64.
11 Michael Anderson, *Family Structure in Nineteenth Century Lancashire*, Cambridge, Cambridge University Press, 1971.
12 Heidi I. Hartmann and Ann R. Markusen, "Contemporary Marxist theory and practice: a feminist critique," *Review of Radical Political Economics*, Summer 1980, vol. 12, p. 89.
13 Joan Kelly, *Women, History and Theory: The Essays of Joan Kelly*, Chicago, University of Chicago Press, 1984, p. 12.
14 Ibid., p. 57.
15 Annette Kuhn and Ann Marie Wolpe, "Feminism and materialism," in Annette Kuhn and Ann Marie Wolpe (eds.) *Feminism and Materialism: Women and Modes of Production*, London, Routledge and Kegan Paul, 1978, pp. 8–9.
16 Ibid., p. 9.
17 Roisin McDonough and Rachel Harrison, "Patriarchy and relations of production," in Kuhn and Wolpe (eds.) *Feminism and Materialism*, p. 11.
18 Ibid., p. 35; Jackie West, "Women, sex, and class," in ibid., p. 249.
19 Juliet Mitchell, *Woman's Estate*, Baltimore, Penguin Books, 1971, pp. 100–1.
20 Ibid., pp. 103–20.
21 Ibid., pp. 120–2.

22 Sylvia Walby, *Patriarchy at Work: Patriarchal and Capitalist Relations in Employment*, Minneapolis, University of Minnesota Press, 1986; see my review: "Industrialization and women's labor," *Nature, Society, and Thought*, 1989, vol. 2, pp. 252–7.

23 Gerda Lerner, "New approaches to the study of women in American history," *Journal of Social History*, Fall 1969, vol. 3, pp. 56–7.

24 Ann D. Gordon, Mari Jo Buhle, and Nancy Schrom Dye, "The problem of women's history," in Berenice A. Carroll (ed.) *Liberating Women's History: Theoretical and Critical Essays*, Urbana, University of Illinois Press, 1976, p. 86.

25 Gerda Lerner, "Placing women in history: definitions and challenges," *Feminist Studies*, Fall 1975, vol. 3, p. 6.

26 Nancy Cott, "Feminist theory and feminist movements: the past before us," in Juliet Mitchell and Ann Oakley (eds.) *What is Feminism?* New York, Pantheon Books, 1986, p. 49.

27 Jane Lewis, "Feminism and welfare," in ibid., p. 86.

28 Jane Humphries, "Class struggle and the persistence of the working-class family," *Cambridge Journal of Economics*, 1977, vol. 1, pp. 241–58.

29 Sheila Rowbotham, "The trouble with 'patriarchy,'" in Raphael Samuel (ed.) *People's History and Socialist Theory*, London, Routledge and Kegan Paul, 1981, pp. 364–9.

30 Joan Wallach Scott, "Gender: a useful category of historical analysis," in *Gender and the Politics of History*, New York, Columbia University Press, 1988, p. 34.

31 See, for example, Judith M. Bennett, "Feminism and history," *Gender and History*, Autumn 1989, vol. 1, pp. 251–72.

32 Rowbotham, "Trouble with 'patriarchy,'" in Samuel, *People's History*, p. 365.

33 See in particular Denise Riley, *Am I That Name? Feminism and the Category of 'Women' in History*, London, Macmillan, 1988.

34 Juliet Mitchell, "Reflections on twenty years of feminism," in Mitchell and Oakley, *What is Feminism?*, p. 47.

35 Linda J. Nicholson, "Introduction," in Linda J. Nicholson (ed.) *Feminism/Postmodernism*, New York and London, Routledge, 1990, pp. 1–2.

36 Nancy Fraser and Linda J. Nicholson, "Social criticism without philosophy: an encounter between feminism and postmodernism," in ibid., pp. 26–9.

37 Ibid., p. 33.

38 Scott, "Gender: a useful category," in *Gender and Politics*, pp. 40–1.

39 Ibid., pp. 28–9.

40 Ibid., pp. 42–4.

41 Leonore Davidoff and Catherine Hall, *Family Fortunes: Men and Women of the English Middle Class, 1780–1850*, Chicago, University of Chicago Press, 1987, p. 29.

42 Scott, "Gender: a useful category," in *Gender and Politics*, p. 50.

43 Joan W. Scott, "On language, gender, and working-class history," *International Labor and Working-Class History*, Spring 1987, no. 31, p. 3.

44 Ibid.

45 Ibid., p. 5.

46 Ibid., pp. 5–6.

47 Joan Wallach Scott, "On language, gender, and working-class history," in *Gender and Politics*, p. 60.

48 Bryan D. Palmer, "Response to Joan Scott," *International Labor and Working-Class History*, Spring 1987, no. 31, p. 15.

49 Christine Stansell, "A response to Joan Scott," *International Labor and Working-Class History*, Spring 1987, no. 31, p. 25.

50 Ibid., p. 26.

51 Ava Baron, "Gender and labor history: learning from the past, looking to the future," in Ava Baron (ed.) *Work Engendered: Toward a New History of American Labor*, Ithaca and London, Cornell University Press, 1991, p. 7.

52 Sonya Rose, "Gender and labor history: the nineteenth-century legacy," *International Review of Social History*, 1993, no. 38, Supplement, p. 161.

53 Ibid., p. 159.

54 Ibid., pp. 152–6.

55 Ibid., pp. 157–8.

56 Mari Jo Buhle, "Gender and labor history," in J. Carroll Moody and Alice Kessler-Harris (eds.) *Perspectives on American Labor History: The Problems of Synthesis*, DeKalb, Northern Illinois University Press, 1989; Sonya O. Rose, *Limited Livelihoods: Gender and Class in Nineteenth-century England*, Berkeley, University of California Press, 1992, pp. 10–11.

57 Rose, *Limited Livelihoods,* pp. 7–13.

58 Baron, "Gender and labor history," p. 8.

59 Ibid., p. 31.

60 Ibid., pp. 6 and 21.

61 Neville Kirk, "Class and the 'linguistic turn' in Chartist and post-Chartist historiography," in Neville Kirk (ed.) *Social Class and Marxism: Defences and Challenges*, Aldershot, Scolar Press, 1996, p. 96. Kirk, it should be noted, is a leading critic of post-structuralism and post-modernism. I have relied extensively on his analysis in a series of essays on language, post-modernism, and class.

62 Barbara Taylor, *Eve and the New Jerusalem. Socialism and Feminism in the Nineteenth Century*, London, Virago, 1983.

63 Catherine Hall, "The tale of Samuel and Jemima: gender and working-class culture in nineteenth-century England," in Harvey J. Kaye and Keith McClelland (eds.) *E. P. Thompson: Critical Perspectives*, Philadelphia, Temple University Press, 1990, pp. 81–2.

64 Deborah Valenze, *The First Industrial Woman*, New York and Oxford, Oxford University Press, 1995, p. 9.

65 Ibid., chapters 1, 3, and 7. Ruth L. Smith and Deborah M. Valenze, "Mutuality and marginality: liberal moral theory and working-class women in nineteenth-century England," *Signs*, Winter 1988, vol. 13, p. 295.

66 Joan W. Scott, "The woman worker," in Genevieve Fraisse and Michelle Perrot (eds.) *A History of Women in the West: Emerging Feminism from Revolution to World War*, vol. iv, Cambridge, Mass., Harvard University Press, 1993, p. 402; see also Valenze, *First Industrial Woman*.

67 Deborah Simonton, *A History of European Women's Work, 1750 to the Present*, London and New York, Routledge, 1998, p. 2.

68 Anne Phillips and Barbara Taylor, "Sex and skill: notes towards a feminist economics," *Feminist Review*, 1980, vol. 6, p. 86.

69 Simonton, *A History of European Women's Work*, pp. 46–7.

70 Eleanor Gordon, *Women and the Labour Movement in Scotland, 1850–1914*, Oxford, Clarendon Press, 1991, p. 10.

71 R. W. Connell, *Gender and Power: Society, the Person and Sexual Politics*, Stanford, Calif., Stanford University Press, 1987, p. 100.

72 For examples of hosiery and pottery see Harriet Bradley, "Frames of reference: skill, gender and new technology in the hosiery industry," in Gertjan de Groot and Marlou Schrover (eds.) *Women Workers and Technological Change in Europe in the Nineteenth and Twentieth Centuries*, London, Taylor and Francis, 1995, pp. 25–6; Jacqueline Sarsby, "Gender and technological change in the North Staffordshire pottery industry," in ibid., pp. 130–1; and Ulla Wikander, "Periodization and the engendering of technology: the pottery of Gustavsberg, Sweden, 1880–1980," pp. 138–9.

73 Jane Long, *Conversations in Cold Rooms: Women, Work and Poverty in Nineteenth-century Northumberland*, Rochester, NY, Boydell Press, 1999, pp. 78–99.
74 Bradley, "Frames of reference," pp. 23–4.
75 John Rule, "The property of skill in the period of manufacture," in Patrick Joyce (ed.) *The Historical Meanings of Work*, Cambridge, Cambridge University Press, 1987, pp. 108–12.
76 Bradley, "Frames of reference," pp. 23–4.
77 Rule, "Property of skill," p. 108.
78 Gertjan de Groot and Marlou Schrover, "General introduction," in de Groot and Schrover (eds.) *Women Workers and Technological Change*, p. 8. See also Phillips and Taylor, "Sex and skill," pp. 79–88.
79 Ibid., p. 6; see Sarsby, "Gender and technological change," pp. 130–1.
80 De Groot and Schrover, "General introduction," p. 10.
81 Gordon, *Women and the Labour Movement*, p. 35.
82 Long, *Conversations*, p. 19.
83 Meta Zimmeck, "'The mysteries of the typewriter': technology and gender in the British civil service, 1870–1914," in de Groot and Schrover (eds.) *Women Workers and Technological Change*, pp. 67–96.
84 Wikander, "Periodization and engendering of technology," pp. 141–5.
85 Long, *Conversations*, p. 21.
86 Gordon, *Women and the Labour Movement*, pp. 99–100.
87 Ibid., pp. 30–6.
88 Valenze, *First Industrial Woman*, chapter 5.
89 Gordon, *Women and the Labour Movement*, p. 10.
90 Simonton, *European Women's Work*, p. 1.
91 Long, *Conversations*, pp. 5–22.
92 Anna Clark, *The Struggle for the Breeches: Gender and the Making of the British Working Class*, Berkeley, University of California Press, 1995, p. 4. States Clark, "What people do is as important as what they say." Further, she points out that political rhetoric only has power if it incites people to action. Political issues are also broader than constitutional and parliamentary concerns, extending to issues involving food and families. Anna Clark, "Manhood, womanhood, and the politics of class in Britain, 1790–1845," in Laura L. Frader and Sonya O. Rose (eds.), *Gender and Class in Modern Europe*, Ithaca and London, Cornell University Press, 1996, pp. 264–5.
93 Nancy Fraser, "The uses and abuses of French discourse theories for feminist politics," in Nancy Fraser and Sandra Lee Bartky (eds.) *Critical Essays on Difference, Agency, and Culture*, Bloomington, Indiana University Press, 1992, p. 185; Kathleen Canning, "Feminist history after the linguistic turn: historicizing discourse and experience," in Barbara Laslett, Ruth-Ellen B. Joeres, Mary Jo Maynes, Evelyn Brooks Higginbotham, and Jeanne Barker-Nunn (eds.) *History and Theory: Feminist Research, Debates, Contestations*, Chicago, University of Chicago Press, 1997, pp. 418–19.
94 Ibid., pp. 430–1.
95 M. M. Bakhtin, "Discourse in the novel," in Michael Holquist (ed.) and Caryl Emerson and Michael Holquist (trans.) *The Dialogic Imagination: Four Essays by M. M. Bakhtin*, Austin and London, University of Texas Press, 1981, pp. 276–7.
96 Fraser, "Uses and abuses," in Fraser and Bartky, *Critical Essays*, p. 178.
97 Laura Lee Downs, "If 'woman' is just an empty category, then why am I afraid to walk alone at night? Identity politics meets the postmodern subject," *Comparative Studies in Society and History*, April 1993, vol. 35, p. 419.
98 Neville Kirk, "History, language, ideas and post-modernism: a materialist view," *Social History*, 1994, vol. 19, p. 227.

99   Joan W. Scott, "The evidence of experience," *Critical Inquiry*, Summer, 1991, vol. 17, pp. 792 and 779. The question for historians, according to Scott, is "how to analyze language" in order "to understand the operations of the complex and changing discursive processes by which identities are ascribed," not to capture reality itself.

100 Palmer, "Response to Joan Scott," p. 21.

101 Marc W. Steinberg, "Culturally speaking: finding a commons between post-structuralism and the Thompsonian perspective," *Social History*, May 1996, vol. 21, pp. 197–9.

102 Downs, "If 'woman' is just an empty category," p. 423.

103 Ibid.

104 Bakhtin, "Discourse," pp. 263–77.

105 Ibid., p. 270.

106 Ibid., p. 272.

107 Fraser, "Uses and abuses," p. 185.

108 Ibid., p. 179.

109 Canning, "Feminist history," p. 421; Steinberg, "Culturally speaking," p. 207.

110 Canning, "Feminist history," pp. 424–32.

111 Carole Anne Taylor, "Positioning subjects and objects: agency, narration, relationality," *Hypatia*, Winter 1993, vol. 8, p. 57.

112 Steinberg, "Culturally speaking," p. 205.

113 See discussion in William H. Sewell, Jr., "A theory of structure: duality, agency, and transformation," *American Journal of Sociology*, July 1992, vol. 98, pp. 1–29.

114 Steinberg, "Culturally speaking," pp. 208–9.

115 Ibid., pp. 203–4.

116 Kirk, "Class and the 'linguistic turn,'" pp. 110–11.

117 Steinberg, "Culturally speaking," pp. 202–3.

118 Robert Gray, *The Factory Question and Industrial England, 1830–1860*, Cambridge, Cambridge University Press, 1996, p. 29.

119 Ibid., pp. 22–6.

120 Neville Kirk, *Change, Continuity and Class: Labour in British Society, 1850–1920*, Manchester, Manchester University Press, 1998. Gray argues that while there may have been more settlement and less "cultural uncertainty" with regard to "discursive hierarchies" at mid-century, that should not be "taken to imply the disappearance of social tensions, or their containment within some dominant discourse. In so far as there was wider acceptance of an authoritative language of debate, it simply altered the terms of conflict." Gray, *Factory Question*, pp. 11–12. Chapters 2 and 3 attempt to flesh out this point.

121 Kirk, "History, language, ideas and post-modernism," p. 230.

122 Alice Kessler-Harris, "A new agenda for American labor history: a gendered analysis and the question of class," in Moody and Kessler-Harris (eds.) *Perspectives on American Labor History*, p. 226. As Laura Frader states, the categories of gender, race, class, and ethnicity are all inflected and shaped by the others as individuals occupy those multiple positions. Insights of feminist theory and post-structuralism may then be used to revitalize class. "Bringing political economy back in: gender, culture, race, and class in labor history," *Social Science History*, Spring 1998, vol. 22, pp. 11–15. Declaring that "class matters," Sonya Rose, in an article appearing in the same roundtable discussion, adds that "we need a way of thinking about class that captures . . . linkages . . . that recognizes . . . the diversity of possible working-class subjects and their multiple identities." "Resuscitating class," p. 22.

2 Cooperation, conflict, and community

1 Anna Clark, *The Struggle for the Breeches: Gender and the Making of the British Working Class*, Berkeley, University of California Press, 1995, pp. 1–9.
2 Catherine Hall, "The tale of Samuel and Jemima: gender and working-class culture in nineteenth-century England," in Harvey Kaye and Keith McClelland (eds.) *E. P. Thompson: Critical Perspectives*, Philadelphia, Temple University Press, 1990, p. 82.
3 Ibid.
4 Ibid., pp. 84–7.
5 Clark, *Struggle for the Breeches*, p. 2.
6 Sonya O. Rose, "Protective labor legislation in nineteenth-century Britain: gender, class, and the liberal state," in Laura L. Frader and Sonya O. Rose (eds.) *Gender and Class in Modern Europe*, Ithaca and London, Cornell University Press, 1996, p. 194.
7 Friedrich Engels, *The Condition of the Working Class in England*, W. O. Henderson and W. H. Chaloner (eds. and trans.) Stanford, Calif., Stanford University Press, 1968, pp. 12–13.
8 W. English, *The Textile Industry*, London, Longmans, Green, and Co., 1969, p. 48; Neil J. Smelser, *Social Change in the Industrial Revolution: An Application of Theory to the British Cotton Industry*, Chicago, University of Chicago Press, 1959, p. 184.
9 English, *Textile Industry*, pp. 56–74; Edward Baines, Jr., *History of the Cotton Manufacture in Great Britain*, London, H. Fisher, R. Fisher, and P. Jackson, 1835, pp. 15–199.
10 Engels, *Condition of the Working Class*, p. 14.
11 Ivy Pinchbeck, *Women Workers and the Industrial Revolution, 1750–1850*, London, George Routledge and Sons, 1930, p. 148.
12 Ibid.
13 Frances Collier, 'An early factory community', *Economic History*, 1930, vol. 2, Supplement, p. 119.
14 Ralph Turner, 'The cultural significance of the early English industrial town,' *Studies in British History*, 1941, vol. 11, p. 33; Arthur Redford, *Labour Migration in England, 1800–1850*, 2nd edn., W. H. Chaloner (ed.) Manchester, Manchester University Press, 1964; *Report of the Select Committee on the State of the Children Employed in the Manufactories of the United Kingdom*, 1816, iii, pp. 158–61.
15 Peter Gaskell, *Artisans and Machinery*, London, John W. Parker, 1836, p. 142; C. H. Lee, *A Cotton Enterprise, 1795–1840: A History of M'Connel and Kennedy, Fine Cotton Spinners*, Manchester, Manchester University Press, 1972, p. 114.
16 Frances Collier, *The Family Economy of the Working Classes in the Cotton Industry, 1784–1833*, R. S. Fitton (ed.) Manchester, The Chetham Society, 1965, pp. 16–18.
17 Ibid., Appendix, p. 60.
18 Duncan Bythell, *The Handloom Weavers: A Study in the English Cotton Industry during the Industrial Revolution*, Cambridge, Cambridge University Press, 1969, pp. 44–8; Pinchbeck, *Women Workers*, pp. 162–3.
19 Bythell, *Handloom Weavers*, pp. 60–1.
20 Pinchbeck, *Women Workers*, pp. 173–4.
21 Ibid., p. 179; Bythell, *Handloom Weavers*, pp. 50, 60–1, and 107.
22 Ibid.
23 Baines, *History*, p. 231; William Radcliffe, *Origin of the New System of Manufacture*, Stockport, James Lomax, 1828, pp. 12–28; English, *Textile Industry*, pp. 101–3.
24 Bythell, *Handloom Weavers*, pp. 74–5; Baines, *History*, pp. 234–7; Thomas

Ellison, *The Cotton Trade of Great Britain*, London, E. Wilson, 1886; reprint edn., New York, Augustus M. Kelley, 1968, pp. 35–7.

25 London, London School of Economics, Webb Trade Union Collection, section A, vol. 37, p. 18.

26 Clark, *Struggle for the Breeches*, pp. 1–9.

27 Ibid., p. 6 and pp. 20–4.

28 H. A. Turner, *Trade Union Growth, Structure, and Policy: A Comparative Study of the Cotton Unions in England,* Toronto, University of Toronto Press, 1962, p. 62; "John Singleton to ? John King, Wigan, 27 May 1799," in A. Aspinall (ed.) *The Early English Trade Unions: Documents from the Home Office Papers in the Public Record Office*, London, The Batchworth Press, 1949, pp. 20–4; Bythell, *Handloom Weavers*, p. 149.

29 "John Singleton," in Aspinall, *Early English Trade Unions*, p. 21.

30 Ibid., pp. 21–4.

31 Turner, *Trade Union Growth*, p. 62.

32 G. D. H. Cole and Raymond Postgate, *The Common People, 1746–1946*, 2nd edn., London, Methuen and Co., 1946, pp. 172–3; J. L. Hammond and Barbara Hammond, *The Town Labourer, 1760–1832*, London, Longmans, Green, and Co., 1920, pp. 115–17; Bythell, *Handloom Weavers*, p. 149.

33 Bythell, *Handloom Weavers*, pp. 153–4.

34 Ibid., p. 189.

35 Turner, *Trade Union Growth*, pp. 64–5.

36 *Times*, 24 June 1808; *Times*, 25 June 1808; "Thomas Drake, D. D., and J. Entwistle to Lord Hawkesbury, Rochdale, 4 June 1808," in Aspinall, *Early English Trade Unions*, pp. 99–100; Bythell, *Handloom Weavers*, p. 191.

37 Bythell, *Handloom Weavers*, pp. 190–1.

38 *Times*, 25 June 1808.

39 Turner, *Trade Union Growth*, pp. 64–6.

40 G. D. H. Cole, *Attempts at General Union: A Study in British Trade Union History, 1818–1834,* London, Macmillan and Co., 1953, pp. 555–7; Turner, *Trade Union Growth*, pp. 66–7.

41 Turner, *Trade Union Growth*, pp. 67–8; Cole, *Attempts at General Union*, p. 7; *Times*, 22 August 1818.

42 Cole, *Attempts at General Union*, pp. 7–12; Bythell, *Handloom Weavers*, pp. 193–4; Turner, *Trade Union Growth*, pp. 69–70; "Handbill dated 19 August 1818, Manchester," and "James Norris to Viscount Sidmouth, Manchester, 11 October 1818," in Aspinall, *Early English Trade Unions*, pp. 272–4 and 304–5.

43 *Wheeler's Manchester Chronicle*, 5 September 1818, cited in *Times*, 8 September 1818.

44 Bythell, *Handloom Weavers*, pp. 195–6.

45 Archibald Prentice, *Historical Sketches and Personal Recollections of Manchester*, 3rd edn., with intro. by Donald Read, London, Frank Cass and Co., 1970, pp. 86–90.

46 Ibid., p. 114.

47 Donald Read, *Peterloo: The 'Massacre' and its Background*, Manchester, Manchester University Press, 1958, pp. 16–18.

48 Ibid., pp. 47–8; Robert F. Wearmouth, *Some Working-class Movements of the Nineteenth Century*, London, The Epworth Press, 1948, pp. 36–7.

49 Read, *Peterloo*, pp. 40–1.

50 Samuel Bamford, *Passages in the Life of a Radical*, 2 vols., London, Simpkin, Marshall, and Co., 1844, p. 165; E. P. Thompson claims that the role of the female reform societies was confined to giving moral support to the men, making banners and caps of liberty which were presented with ceremony at reform demonstrations, passing resolutions and addresses, and swelling the

numbers at meetings. *The Making of the English Working Class*, New York, Random House, 1963, p. 417. See Ruth and Edmund Frow (eds.) *Political Women, 1800–1850*, London, Pluto Press, 1989.

51 *The Annual Register*, London, Baldwin, Cradock, and Jay, 1820, p. 104.

52 *Times*, 1 July 1819.

53 "Address to a Blackburn Public Meeting by the members of the Female Reform Society, in the town and neighbourhood of Blackburn," *Manchester Observer*, 10 July 1819; *Times*, 13 July 1819. William Cobbett characterized this Address as "Unaffected, clear, strong, eloquent and pathetic; the heart that dictated it is worthy of the fairest and most tender bosom, and the heart that remains unwarmed by it is unworthy of the breast of a human being." "To the Female Reform Society of Blackburn in Lancashire," *Cobbett's Weekly Political Register*, 23 October 1819, p. 262.

54 "Female reformers," *Leeds Mercury*, 31 July 1819; "Female Union Society established at Stockport," *Wooler's British Gazette*, 25 July 1819.

55 "Declaration and Rules of the Female Union Society of Stockport," *Manchester Observer*, 17 July 1819.

56 *Leeds Mercury*, 31 July 1819; *Times*, 21 July 1819.

57 "The Manchester Female Reformers' Address to the Wives, Mothers, Sisters, and Daughters of the Higher and Middling Classes of Society," *Manchester Observer*, 31 July 1819. All further references to this Address are taken from this source.

58 Clark, *Struggle for the Breeches*, p. 163.

59 *Newcastle Courant*, 24 July 1819.

60 Marian Ramelson, *The Petticoat Rebellion: A Century of Struggle for Women's Rights*, London, Lawrence and Wishart, 1967, pp. 66–7.

61 *Manchester Observer*, cited in *Times*, 26 July 1819.

62 Banford, *Passages in Life of Radical*, p. 200.

63 Read, *Peterloo*, pp. 129–30; Edmund Frow and Ruth Frow, "Women in the early radical and labour movement," *Marxism Today*, April 1968, vol. 12, p. 106.

64 Prentice, *Historical Sketches*, pp. 167–8; Frow and Frow, "Women in radical movement," p. 106.

65 Bamford, *Passages in Life of Radical*, pp. 265 6.

66 Clark, *Struggle for the Breeches*, pp. 171–2.

67 Ibid., pp. 171–3.

68 Dorothy Thompson, *The Chartists: Popular Politics in the Industrial Revolution*, New York, Pantheon Books, 1984, p. 120.

69 Clark, *Struggle for the Breeches*, pp. 228–9.

70 Thompson, *The Chartists*, p. 131.

71 Ibid., p. 132.

72 Clark, *Struggle for the Breeches*, p. 226.

73 Anna Clark, "The rhetoric of Chartist domesticity: gender, language, and class in the 1830s and 1840s," *Journal of British Studies*, 1992, vol. 31, p. 74.

74 Thompson, *The Chartists*, pp. 122–7.

75 For discussions of spinning and the issue of skill, see William Lazonick, "Industrial relations and technical change: the case of the self-acting mule," *Cambridge Journal of Economics*, 1979, vol. 3, pp. 231–62; Michael Huberman, "The economic origins of paternalism: Lancashire cotton spinning in the first half of the nineteenth century," *Social History*, May 1987, vol. 12, pp. 177–92; John Foster, *Class Struggle and the Industrial Revolution: Early Industrial Capitalism in Three English Towns*, with foreword by E. J. Hobsbawm, London, 1974.

76 R. G. Kirby and A. E. Musson, *The Voice of the People: John Doherty, 1798–1854, Trade Unionist, Radical, and Factory Reformer*, Manchester, Manchester University Press, 1975, pp. 29–43 and 73–8.

77   Mary Freifeld, "Technological change and the 'self-acting mule': a study of skill and the sexual division of labour," 1986, vol. 11, p. 334.
78   Baines, *History of Cotton Manufacture*, pp. 235–7.
79   Ibid., pp. 373–9; B.P.P., *Supplementary Report of the Factories Inquiry Commission*, part I, 1834, xix, pp. 124–38.
80   Richard Marsden, *Cotton Weaving: Its Development, Principles, and Practice*, London, 1895.
81   *A Report of the Proceedings of a Delegate Meeting, of the Operative Spinners of England, Ireland and Scotland, Assembled at Ramsey, Isle of Man, on Saturday, December 5, 1829, and Three Following Days*, Manchester, 1829, pp. 50–1.
82   Ernst von Plener, *The English Factory Legislation, from 1802 till the Present Time*, Frederick L. Weinmann (trans.) London, Chapman and Hall, 1873, pp. 1–3; J. T. Ward, "The factory movement," in J. T., Ward (ed.) *Popular Movements, c. 1830–1850*, London, Macmillan and Co., 1970, p. 65.
83   Von Plener, *English Factory Legislation*, p. 4; Ward, "Factory movement," p. 65.
84   Von Plener, *English Factory Legislation*, pp. 5–6; J. T. Ward, *The Factory Movement, 1830–1850*, London, Macmillan and Co., 1962, pp. 41–3.
85   B.P.P., *First Report of the Factories Inquiry Commission with Minutes of Evidence*, 1833, xx, pp. 7–32.
86   Ibid., pp. 4–6; Philip Grant, *The Ten Hours Bill: The History of Factory Legislation*, Manchester, Johy Heywood, 1866, p. 15; Ward, "Factory movement," p. 65.
87   "Yorkshire Slavery," *Leeds Mercury*, 16 October 1830, quoted in Cecil Driver, *Tory Radical: The Life of Richard Oastler*, New York, Oxford University Press, 1946, pp. 42–3.
88   Ibid., pp. 81–3; von Plener, *English Factory Legislation*, pp. 8–9; Ward, *Factory Movement*, pp. 45–56.
89   Ibid, pp. 52–3; Driver, *Tory Radical*, pp. 147–9.
90   *Report of Public Meeting on Restriction of Children's Wages, 14 March 1832*, London, London University Library, White Slavery Collection, vol. 2, no. 3, pp. 93–4 and 98, Goldsmiths' Collection.
91   Grant, *Ten Hours Bill*, pp. 52–3; Samuel Kydd [Alfred], *The History of the Factory Movement*, London, Simpkin, Marshall, and Co., 1857, vol. 2, p. 57.
92   *Report of the Proceedings of the Great Leeds Meeting, 9 January 1831*, Leeds, Hernaman and Perring, n.d., London, London University Library, White Slavery Collection, vol. 4, no. 6, p. 29, Goldsmiths' Collection; see also in the same place *Report of the Proceedings of a Public Meeting, Held in the Piece Hall, Halifax, 6 March 1832*, Leeds, Hernaman and Perring, n.d., p. 11.
93   Kirby and Musson, *Voice of the People*, p. 109.
94   *The Report and Resolutions of a Meeting of Deputies from the Hand Loom Worsted Weavers Residing in and Near Bradford, Leeds, Halifax, etc., Yorkshire*, Bradford, n.d., p. 12.
95   William Rathbone Greg, *An Enquiry into the State of the Manufacturing Population and the Causes and Cures of the Evils Therein Existing*, London, 1831; James Phillips Kay, *The Moral and Physical Condition of the Working Classes Employed in the Cotton Manufacture in Manchester*, London, 1832.
96   B.P.P., *Report from the Select Committee on the Bill to Regulate the Labour of Children in the Mills and Factories of the United Kingdom with Minutes of Evidence, Appendix and Index*, 1831–2, xv, pp. 318–20.
97   "The ten hours' factory question," *Manchester and Salford Advertiser*, 8 January 1842.
98   Kydd, *History of Factory Movement*, vol. 1, p. 235.
99   B.P.P., *First Report of Factories Inquiry Commission*, pp. 35–112. Further references to women testifying before this Commission refer to these pages.

100 B.P.P., *Report from Select Committee on Bill to Regulate Labour of Children*, pp. 282–3.

101 Ibid., pp. 314–18; Driver, *Tory Radical*, pp. 175–6; Ward, *Factory Movement*, pp. 59–62.

102 B.P.P., *First Report of Factories Inquiry Commission*, p. 77.

103 Ibid., pp. 83–5.

104 Von Plener, *English Factory Legislation,* pp. 15–16.

105 Ward, *Factory Movement,* pp. 146–73; Driver, *Tory Radical*, pp. 331–77.

106 For the implications and operation of the New Poor Law, see Derek Fraser (ed.) *The New Poor Law in the Nineteenth Century*, New York, 1976. For its introduction and opposition to it in the North, see Nicholas C. Edsall, *The Anti-Poor Law Movement, 1834–44*, Manchester, 1971.

107 Driver, *Tory Radical*, p. 313.

108 George Jacob Holyoake, *Life of Joseph Rayner Stephens, Preacher and Political Orator*, with an introductory chapter by John Stephens Storr, London, 1881, p. 9.

109 Driver, *Tory Radical*, p. 314.

110 "Anti-Poor Law meeting, Rochdale," *Northern Star*, 3 February 1838.

111 Ibid.

112 *The Political Pulpit*, no. 6: "A sermon by the Rev. J. R. Stephens, May 12th 1839," p. 46.

113 *The Political Pulpit*, no. 8: "A sermon by the Rev. J. R. Stephens, delivered on Kennington Common, on Sunday afternoon, May 12th, 1839," p. 59.

114 *The Political Pulpit*, no. 9: "A sermon by the Rev. J. R. Stephens, delivered at Ashton-under-Lyne, on Sunday afternoon, May 26th, 1839," p. 72.

115 "Great radical demonstration at Wigan," *Northern Star*, 17 November 1838.

116 *The Political Pulpit*, no. 8: "A sermon by the Rev. J. R. Stephens, delivered on Kennington Common, on Sunday afternoon, May 12th, 1839," p. 63.

117 *The Political Pulpit*, no. 2: "A sermon by the Rev. J. R. Stephens, delivered at Hyde, in Lancashire, on Sunday evening, February 17th, 1839," p. 11.

118 *The Political Pulpit*, no. 1: "A sermon by the Rev. J. R. Stephens, delivered at Staley-Bridge, on Sunday evening, February 10th, 1839," p. 5.

119 *The Political Pulpit*, no. 2, p. 12; *The Political Pulpit*, no. 9, "A sermon by the Rev. J. R. Stephens, delivered at Ashton-under-Lyne, on Sunday afternoon, May 26th, 1839," p. 72.

120 *The Political Pulpit*, no. 3: "A sermon by the Rev. J. R. Stephens, delivered at Staley-Bridge, on Sunday evening, February 24th, 1839," p. 21.

121 Ibid.

122 Eileen Yeo, "Chartist religious belief and the theology of liberation," in Jim Obelkevich, Lyndal Roper, and Raphael Samuel (eds.) *Disciplines of Faith: Studies in Religion, Politics and Patriarchy*, London, 1987, p. 420.

123 Regarding the significance of this outlook, see Neville Kirk, "In defence of class: a critique of recent revisionist writing upon the nineteenth-century English working class," *International Review of Social History*, 1987, no. 32, p. 23; Patrick Joyce, *Visions of the People: Industrial England and the Question of Class, 1848–1914*, Cambridge, Cambridge University Press, 1991, p. 34.

124 In her article, Clark recognizes but does not emphasize the breadth of meaning that was embedded in the term "domesticity." "Rhetoric of Chartist domesticity," pp. 64–5.

125 Gareth Stedman Jones, "Rethinking Chartism," in his *Languages of Class: Studies in English Working Class History, 1832–1982*, Cambridge, Cambridge University Press, 1983, p. 96.

126 Clark, "Rhetoric of Chartist domesticity," p. 78.

127 "Radical Association," *Northern Star*, 27 January 1838.

128 "The men's petition," *Northern Star*, 3 February 1838.
129 "Anti-Poor Law proceedings at Manchester," *Northern Star*, 3 February 1838.
130 *The Political Pulpit*: "Rev. J. R. Stephens, Sermon IV. Delivered at Ashton-under-Lyne, on Sunday afternoon, March 3, 1839, in the market-place," p. 17.
131 Thompson, *The Chartists*; *Copies of the True Bills Found Against the Rev. J. R. Stephens, at Liverpool and Chester, with Comments Thereon* (published with *The Political Pulpit*, no place or date); see also "Arrest of Mr. Stephens," *Northern Star*, 5 January 1839.
132 Ibid.
133 Thompson, *The Chartists*, p. 133.
134 Ibid., p. 150.
135 Ibid., p. 126.
136 Ibid., p. 149.
137 Ibid., p. 126.
138 "Meeting at Ashton: Glasgow cotton spinners," *Northern Star*, 17 February 1838.
139 Reprinted from *Sun* and *Observer* in *Northern Star*, 5 January 1839. Responding to charges against Stephens, the *Champion* stated, "The people will understand all this. They will read in it that the Government believe Mr. Stephens to be a true, sincere, and resolute friend of the oppressed millions; that they deem him, from his sincerity and zeal, formidable to the oppressors; that, on that account, a deep conspiracy has been formed to destroy him in the Irish manner, by the circulation . . . of false but alarming charges."
140 "Female radicals," *Northern Star*, 9 March 1839.
141 "State of political feeling," *Northern Star*, 9 March 1839.
142 "Female Radical Association," *Northern Star*, 30 March 1839.
143 "Female Association," *Northern Star*, 20 April 1839.
144 As James Epstein has pointed out, men and women of the factory district realized an "identity of interests" through the vehicle of the mass platform. "Rethinking the categories of working-class history," *Labour/Le Travail*, 1986, vol. 18, p. 199.

3 Shaping women's identities

 1 B.P.P., *Report of Leonard Horner for the Quarter Ended 31 December 1841*, 1842, xxii, p. 29; B.P.P., *Report of Robert Baker for the Six Months Ended 31 October 1862*, 1863, xviii, p. 69.
 2 Ibid., p. 29.
 3 B.P.P., *1841 Census of Great Britain: Age Abstract with Appendices*, 1843, xxii, pp. 28–9 and 140–1; B.P.P., *1841 Census of Great Britain: Occupation Abstract with Preface*, 1844, xxvii, pp. 10 and 72; B.P.P., *1851 Census of Great Britain: Ages, Civil Condition, Occupations, and Birthplaces*, part 2, 1852–3, pp. 611 and 626–35.
 4 B.P.P., *1851 Census of Great Britain: Ages, Civil Condition, Occupations, and Birthplaces*, part 2, pp. 626–35; B.P.P., *1871 Census of England and Wales: Ages, Civil Condition, Occupations, and Birthplaces*, part 1, 1873, lxxi, p. 420.
 5 See Richard Marsden, *Cotton Weaving: Its Development, Principles, and Practice*, London, 1895; William Alexander Abram, *Blackburn Characters of Past Generation*, Blackburn, 1894, pp. 366–7; P. A. Whittle, *Blackburn As It Is: A Topographical, Statistical, and Historical Account*, Preston, 1852, p. 393; D. A. Farnie, *The English Cotton Industry and the World Market, 1815–1896*, Oxford, 1970, pp. 102 and 282.
 6 Ibid., pp. 115 and 286–317; B.P.P., *Reports of Leonard Horner, Factory Inspector*: "Half year ended 31 October 1852," 1852–3, xl, p. 22; "Half year ended 31

October 1853," 1854, xix, p. 15; "Half year ended 30 April 1854," 1854, xix, pp. 9–10; "Half year ended 31 October 1854," 1854–5, xv, pp. 9–10; "Half year ended 31 October 1855," 1856, xviii, pp. 24–5; "Half year ended 31 October 1856," 1857, iii, p. 42. *Half-yearly Joint Reports of the Inspectors of Factories*: "Half year ended 31 October 1852," 1852–3, xl, pp. 65–8; "Half year ended 31 October 1853," 1854, xix, pp. 106–7; "Half year ended 31 October 1856," 1857, iii, p. 27.

7 B.P.P., *Returns of the Number of Cotton, Woollen, Worsted, Flax and Silk Factories Subject to the Factories Acts*, 1850, xlii, pp. 456–7; B.P.P., *Returns of the Number of Cotton, Woollen, Worsted, Flax, Hemp, Jute, Hosiery, and Silk Factories Subject to the Factories Act*, 1862, lv, pp. 630–1.

8 Ibid., pp. 456–7; B.P.P., *Returns of the Number of Cotton, Woollen, Worsted, Flax and Silk Factories*, 1857, xiv, pp. 176–7; *Returns of the Number of Cotton . . .*, 1862, pp. 630–1. The *Returns* refer to Lancashire and Cheshire.

9 Ibid.

10 Farnie, *English Cotton Industry*, p. 301; Arthur Redford, *Labour Migration in England, 1800–1850*, 2nd edn, W. H. Chaloner (ed.) Manchester, Manchester University Press, 1964, pp. 63–5; Michael Anderson, *Family Structure in Nineteenth Century Lancashire*, Cambridge, Cambridge University Press, 1971, pp. 34–9; Neville Kirk, *The Growth of Working Class Reformism in Mid-Victorian England*, Urbana and Chicago, University of Illinois Press, 1985, p. 143; John K. Walton, *Lancashire: A Social History, 1558–1939*, Manchester, Manchester University Press, 1987, p. 202.

11 Thomas Ellison, *The Cotton Trade of Great Britain*, London, 1886, pp. 66–7; David Chadwick, "On the rate of wages in Manchester and Salford, and the manufacturing districts of Lancashire, 1839–1859," *Journal of the Royal Statistical Society*, series A, March 1860, Appendix, pp. 23–4; George Henry Wood, *The History of Wages in the Cotton Trade during the Past Hundred Years*, London, 1910, pp. 16–37.

12 Louise A. Tilly and Joan W. Scott, *Women, Work, and Family*, New York, Holt, Rinehart and Winston, 1978, p. 131; Kirk, *Growth of Working Class Reformism*, p. 94.

13 B.P.P., *First Report from the Select Committee on the Act for the Regulation of Mills and Factories*, 1840, x, pp. 87–8.

14 J. T. Ward, *The Factory Movement, 1830–1850*, London, Macmillan and Co., 1962, pp. 220–6; B. L. Hutchins and B. Harrison, *A History of Factory Legislation*, 2nd edn., rev., London, P. S. King and Son, 1911, p. 64.

15 "The Ten Hours factory question," *Manchester and Salford Advertiser*, 8 January 1842.

16 Hutchins and Harrison, *History of Factory Legislation*, p. 65.

17 B.P.P., *Report of Leonard Horner for the Quarter Ended 30 September 1843*, 1844, xxviii, p. 4.

18 B.P.P., *Report of Leonard Horner for the Quarter Ended 31 December 1843*, 1844, xxviii, p. 13.

19 B.P.P., *Report of Leonard Horner for the Quarter Ended 31 December 1842*, 1843, xxvii, pp. 23–4.

20 B.P.P., *Report of Leonard Horner for the Quarter Ended 30 September 1843*, pp. 3–4.

21 Ibid., p. 4.

22 Ward, *Factory Movement*, pp. 283–8.

23 "The Ten Hours Factory Bill: meeting at the Corn Exchange," *Manchester and Salford Advertiser*, 16 March 1844; "The Ten Hours Factory Bill," *Manchester and Salford Advertiser*, 20 April 1844, p. 2.

24 *The Trial of Feargus O'Connor and 58 Others*, London, 1843, p. 249.

25　Ward, *Factory Movement*, p. 298; Ernst von Plener, *The English Factory Legislation, from 1802 till the Present Time*, Frederick L. Weinmann (trans.) London, Chapman and Hall, 1873, pp. 27–8.

26　Letter to editor, *Ten Hours' Advocate*, 26 September 1846.

27　"Female factory operatives," *Ten Hours' Advocate*, 3 October 1846.

28　"Condition of female factory operatives," *Ten Hours' Advocate*, 24 October 1846.

29　"The Ten Hours Factory Bill: meeting at the Corn Exchange," *Manchester and Salford Advertiser*, 16 March 1844.

30　Ibid., p. 26.

31　Ibid., pp. 36–7.

32　Ibid., p. 48.

33　Sara Horrell and Jane Humphries, "Women's labour force participation and the transition to the male-breadwinner family, 1790–1865," *Economic History Review*, February 1995, vol. 48, pp. 105–6.

34　Mick Jenkins, *The General Strike of 1842*, London, Lawrence and Wishart, 1980, pp. 64 and 214.

35　Op. cit., p. 253.

36　B.P.P., *Report of Leonard Horner for the Half-year Ended 31 October 1848*, 1849, xxii.

37　B.P.P., *Report of Leonard Horner from 1 October 1844, to 30 April 1845*, 1845, xxv, p. 19; "The Ten Hours' Bill: great meeting of power-loom weavers in Carpenters Hall," *Manchester and Salford Advertiser*, 13 September 1845.

38　"The Short-Time Bill," *Manchester Guardian*, 13 September 1845.

39　Ibid.; "The Ten Hours' Bill," *Manchester and Salford Advertiser*, 13 September 1845.

40　Ibid.

41　Letter to editor, *Ten Hours' Advocate*, 24 October 1846; "The progress of the Ten Hours' Bill in the districts," *Ten Hours' Advocate*, 12 December 1846; "Letter from committee of the card-room operatives of Manchester to secretary of Lancashire Short Time Committee," *Ten Hours' Advocate*, 1 May 1847.

42　"The Ten Hours' Bill," *Manchester and Salford Advertiser*, 20 February 1847.

43　"The progress of the Ten Hours' Bill in the districts," *Ten Hours' Advocate*, 12 December 1846.

44　"Petitions to Parliament–legislative interference," *Ten Hours' Advocate*, 9 January 1847.

45　"To the factory operatives of Lancashire," *Ten Hours' Advocate*, 26 December 1846.

46　Ibid.

47　Letter to editor, *Ten Hours' Advocate*, 9 January 1847.

48　B.P.P., *Report of Leonard Horner from 1 October 1844, to 30 April 1845*, p. 15.

49　Ward, *Factory Movement*, p. 346; von Plener, *English Factory Legislation*, pp. 35–6.

50　"Turn-outs," *Manchester Guardian*, 6 May 1848.

51　"Amendment of the Ten Hours Bill," *Manchester Guardian*, 20 May 1848.

52　Ibid.

53　"Turn-outs," *Manchester Guardian*, 24 May 1848.

54　B.P.P., *Report of Leonard Horner for the Half-year Ended 31 October 1848*, 1849, xxii, p. 14. Factories visited were located in Accrington and neighborhood, Ashton-under-Lyne and neighborhood, Bacup, Blackburn, Bolton and neighborhood, Burnley, Glossop, Heywood, Manchester and Salford, Middleton, Oldham, Preston and neighborhood, Ramsbottom, Radcliffe, Royton, Rochdale and neighborhood, Saddlesworth, Shaw, and Stalybridge.

55　Ibid., p. 15. The following discussion is based on this report.

56 Ibid., pp. 3–8; Cecil Driver, *Tory Radical: The Life of Richard Oastler*, New York, Oxford University Press, 1946, p. 480.

57 "The Ten Hours Act. Important meeting of delegation from the manufacturing districts," *Morning Post*, 17 April 1849.

58 B.P.P., *Report of Leonard Horner for the Half-year Ended 30 April 1849*, 1849, xxii, pp. 4–5.

59 "More ways of working in Leech's mill," *Ashton Chronicle*, 20 January 1849.

60 "Turn-out," *Manchester Guardian*, 14 February 1849.

61 "Termination of the strike at Sir William Feilden, Son, and Co.'s mill," *Manchester Guardian*, 24 March 1849.

62 "Conspiracy of masters at Stalybridge," *Ashton Chronicle*, 21 April 1849; "Record of the 'lock-out' at Stalybridge," *Ashton Chronicle*, 21 April 1849.

63 "Refusal to work by relays at Stalybridge," *Morning Post*, 9 April 1849.

64 "Record of the 'lock-out' at Stalybridge," *Ashton Chronicle*, 21 April 1849.

65 Ibid.

66 "Record of the lockout at Stalybridge," *Ashton Chronicle*, 28 April 1849.

67 "Critical condition of the factory district," *Morning Post*, 17 April 1849; "Record of the 'lock-out' at Stalybridge," *Ashton Chronicle*, 21 April 1849.

68 "Record of the lockout at Stalybridge," *Ashton Chronicle*, 28 April 1849.

69 B.P.P., *Report of Leonard Horner for the Half-year Ended 31 October 1848*, pp. 8–9; *Report of Leonard Horner for the Half-year Ended 30 April 1849*, appendix 4, pp. 17–18 and pp. 4–5; *Report of Leonard Horner for the Half-year Ended 31 October 1848*, pp. 12–13; Ward, *Factory Movement*, pp. 354–5; See *Manchester Guardian*, 19 May 1848, 16 December 1848, 6 and 10 January 1849, 10 February 1849, 14 February 1849; 14, 18, 21, 25, and 28 July 1849; 1, 4, and 8 August 1849; Ward, *Factory Movement*, pp. 358–9 and 371–3.

70 Von Plener, *English Factory Legislation*, pp. 40–4.

71 Kirk, *Growth of Working Class Reformism*, pp. 38 and 185.

72 Patrick Joyce, *Work, Society and Politics: The Culture of the Factory in Later Victorian England*, New Brunswick, Rutgers University Press, 1980, pp. 148–9.

73 Richard Price, "Conflict and co-operation: a reply to Patrick Joyce," *Social History*, May 1984, vol. 9, pp. 219–20; Michael Huberman, "The economic origins of paternalism: Lancashire cotton spinning in the first half of the nineteenth century," *Social History*, May 1987, vol. 12, pp. 177–9; H. I. Dutton and J. E. King, "The limits of paternalism: the cotton tyrants of North Lancashire, 1836–54," *Social History*, January 1982, vol. 7, pp. 59–74.

74 B.P.P., *Report of Leonard Horner for the Half-year Ended 31 October 1848*, 1849, xxii, p. 28. Apparently many married women were employed at this particular mill. Similar comments were made by other operatives at other mills. See, for instance, p. 31.

75 Ibid., p. 29.

76 Ibid., p. 32. See also p. 33.

77 Ibid., pp. 57–8.

78 "Ten Hours' Bill—Over Darwen," *Blackburn Standard*, 14 November 1849.

79 "Attempt to Defeat the Ten Hours' Bill," *Blackburn Standard*, 24 May 1848.

80 B.P.P., *Report of Leonard Horner for the Half-year Ended 31 October 1848*, pp. 31–5 and 58.

81 Ibid., p. 56.

82 Ibid., p. 60.

83 Ibid., p. 55.

84 Angus Bethune Reach, *Manchester and the Textile Districts in 1849*, C. Aspin (ed.) Helmshore, 1972, p. 34.

85 Ibid., pp. 36–7.

86 Ibid., pp. 43–6; Thomas Walter Laqueur, *Religion and Respectability: Sunday*

Schools and Working Class Culture, 1780–1850, New Haven, Yale University Press, 1976, pp. 90–1.

87 June Purvis, *Hard Lessons: The Lives and Education of Working-class Women in Nineteenth-century England,* Minneapolis, University of Minnesota Press, 1989, pp. 101–41.

88 Quoted in ibid., p. 144.

89 Clare Evans, "Unemployment and the making of the feminine during the Lancashire cotton famine," in Pat Hudson and W. R. Lee (eds.) *Women's Work and the Family Economy in Historical Perspective,* Manchester, Manchester University Press, 1990, pp. 248–70.

90 Reach, *Manchester and the Textile Districts,* p. 7.

91 Ibid., p. 8.

92 Pat Hudson and W. R. Lee, "Women's work and the family economy in historical perspective," in their *Women's Work,* p. 18.

93 Reach, *Manchester and the Textile Districts,* pp. 10–11.

94 B.P.P., *Report of Leonard Horner for the Half-year Ended October 1848,* p. 33.

95 Ibid., p. 49.

96 Ibid., p. 28. See also pp. 31–2.

97 Ibid., p. 72.

98 Elizabeth Roberts, *A Woman's Place: An Oral History of Working-class Women, 1890–1940,* Oxford, Basil Blackwell, 1984, p. 128.

99 Jane Lewis, "Working-class wife and mother and state intervention, 1870–1918," in Jane Lewis (ed.) *Labour and Love: Women's Experience of Home and Family, 1850–1940,* Oxford, Basil Blackwell, 1985, p. 108.

100 See Dorothy Thompson, "Women, work and politics in nineteenth-century England: the problem of authority," in Jane Rendall (ed.) *Equal or Different: Women's Politics 1800–1914,* Oxford, 1987, pp. 70–1.

101 Joanna Bourke, "Housewifery in working-class England 1860–1914," *Past and Present,* May 1994, no. 143, pp. 171–9.

102 Roberts, *A Woman's Place,* p. 137.

103 "The labour crisis," *Preston Pilot and County Advertiser,* 12 November 1853.

104 Ibid.

105 Farnie, *English Cotton Industry,* pp. 296–7.

106 "Weavers' meeting," *Burnley Advertiser,* 30 April 1859; "The wages agitation," *Preston Guardian,* 16 February 1861.

107 "The crisis in the cotton trade," *Blackburn Times,* 13 April 1878.

108 Sonya Rose, *Limited Livelihoods: Gender and Class in Nineteenth-century England,* Berkeley, University of California Press, 1992, p. 173.

109 Neville Kirk, *Change, Continuity and Class: Labour in British Society, 1850–1920,* Manchester, Manchester University Press, 1998, p. 116.

110 The notion of the collective nature of working-class respectability is central to Kirk's account. Ibid., pp. 115–37; See Jane Humphries, "Class struggle and the persistence of the working-class family," *Cambridge Journal of Economics,* 1977, vol. 1, pp. 241–58.

111 Hudson and Lee, "Women's work," in their *Women's Work,* p. 33.

112 Neville Kirk, however, argues: "Notwithstanding the accelerated feminisation of domestic service and the continued employment of large numbers of women, including married women, in textiles, in a range of largely depressed crafts and trades . . . and in a variety of low-paid tasks . . . in the home, and the partial involvement of women workers in trade unionism, notions of a 'woman's place', firmly situated in the domestic sphere, and of the 'family wage', based *solely* rather than, as often in the past, *mainly* upon the income of the male breadwinner, took strong root in organised and wider working-class circles." Kirk, *Change, Continuity and Class,* p. 116.

113 Michael Savage, *The Dynamics of Working-class Politics: The Labour Movement in Preston, 1880–1940,* Cambridge, Cambridge University Press, 1987, p. 68.
114 Anna Clark, "The New Poor Law and the breadwinner wage: contrasting assumptions," *Journal of Social History*, December 2000. I wish to thank Anna Clark for sharing this article with me prior to its publication.
115 Kirk, *Change, Continuity, and Class,* p. 122.
116 *Stockport Advertiser*, 29 May 1840, 12 June 1840, 10 July 1840.
117 Mick Jenkins, *The General Strike of 1842*, with Introduction by John Foster, London, Lawrence and Wishart, 1980, p. 214.
118 *Manchester Guardian*, 25, 29 November, 2, 9 December 1843.
119 Henry Ashworth, *The Preston Strike: An Enquiry into its Causes and Consequences*, Manchester, 1854, p. 14.
120 J. Lowe, "An account of the strike in the cotton trade at Preston in 1853," in *Trades' Societies and Strikes: Report of the Committee on Trades' Societies Appointed by the National Association for the Promotion of Social Science*, London, 1860, pp. 219–20.
121 In addition to those strikes cited in the text, women's participation was also noted in strikes occurring in Chorley, Clitheroe, and Great Harwood. *Blackburn Weekly Times*, 15 May 1858; *Preston Guardian*, 16, 30 March 1861.
122 "Weavers' meeting," *Preston Guardian*, 30 April 1859; "Weavers' meeting," *Burnley Advertiser*, 30 April 1859; "Meetings in the market place," *Burnley Advertiser*, 6 August 1859.
123 "The strike," *Preston Guardian*, 11 May 1861.
124 Andrew Bullen, *The Lancashire Weavers Union: A Commemorative History*, Manchester, Amalgamated Textile Workers Union, 1984, p. 6.
125 London, Library of Political and Economic Science, Webb Trade Union Collection, section A, vols. 37 and 47.
126 Mike Savage, "Capitalist and patriarchal relations at work: Preston cotton weaving, 1890–1914," in Linda Murgatroyd, Mike Savage, Dan Shapiro, John Urry, Sylvia Walby, Alan Warde, with Jane Mark-Lawson (eds.) *Localities, Class, and Gender*, London, Pion Press, 1985, pp. 177–94.
127 Savage, *Dynamics of Working-class Politics*, pp. 66–79.
128 Cited in ibid., p. 152.
129 Roberts, *A Woman's Place*, pp. 22–38.
130 Diana Gittins, *Fair Sex: Family Size and Structure in Britain, 1900–39*, New York, St. Martin's Press, 1982, p. 63.
131 Webb Trade Union Collection, section A, vol. 47, p. 218.
132 Roberts, *A Woman's Place*, p. 137; Harold Benenson, "The 'family wage' and working women's consciousness in Britain, 1880–1914," *Politics and Society*, 1991, vol. 19, pp. 73–9.
133 Webb Trade Union Collection, section A, vols. 37 and 47; Jill Liddington and Jill Norris, *One Hand Tied Behind Us*, London, Virago, 1978, chapter 9; Roberts, *A Woman's Place*, p. 2.
134 Webb Trade Union Collection, section A, vol. 47, p. 231.
135 Ibid., p. 189.

4 Gender at work

1 Maxine Berg and Pat Hudson, "Rehabilitating the Industrial Revolution," *Economic History Review*, February 1992, vol. 45, pp. 27–35.
2 Deborah Simonton, *A History of European Women's Work, 1700 to the Present*, London and New York, Routledge, 1998, pp. 42–4.

3   Maxine Berg, *The Age of Manufactures: Industry, Innovation and Work in Britain 1700–1820*, Totowa, NJ, Barnes and Noble, 1985, pp. 129–35; Katrina Honeyman and Jordan Goodman, "Women's work, gender conflict, and labour markets in Europe, 1500–1900," *Economic History Review*, 1991, vol. 44, pp. 614–18.

4   Judy Lown, *Women and Industrialization: Gender at Work in Nineteenth-century England*, Minneapolis, University of Minnesota Press, 1990, pp. 28–9.

5   Berg and Hudson, "Rehabilitating," p. 36.

6   Ibid., pp. 24–35.

7   Berg, *Age of Manufacturers*, p. 294.

8   Bill Kings and Margaret Cooper, *Glory Gone: The Story of Nailing in Bromsgrove*, Bromsgrove, Halfshire Books, 1989, pp. 59–62.

9   Noah Forrest, "The chain and tracemakers of Cradley Heath and its vicinity and their employers; or union and disunion, and their consequences," *Transactions of the National Association for the Promotion of Social Science*, 1859, p. 655.

10   B.P.P., *Report under the Laws Relating to Factories and Workshops by Robert Baker, Esq, for the Half Year ended April 30, 1875*," 1875, xx.

11   Berg, *Age of Manufactures*, pp. 311–12; G. C. Allen, *The Industrial Development of Birmingham and the Black Country 1860–1927*, London, George Allen and Unwin, 1929, p. 167.

12   Allen, *Industrial Development*, pp. 35–6.

13   "British industries. Messrs. Joseph Gillott & Sons," *Tinsley's Magazine*, October 1889, no. 5, pp. 576–7.

14   Ibid., p. 579.

15   Simonton, *European Women's Work*, chapters 3 and 7.

16   Lown, *Women and Industrialization*, pp. 45–9.

17   Pamela Sharpe, *Adapting to Capitalism: Working Women in the English Economy, 1700–1850*, New York, St. Martin's Press, 1996, pp. 38–69.

18   Ibid., p. 69.

19   Honeyman and Goodman, "Women's work," p. 613.

20   Ibid., pp. 613–15; Simonton, *European Women's Work*, pp. 46–7.

21   Deborah Valenze, *The First Industrial Woman*, New York and Oxford, Oxford University Press, 1995, chapters 1–3.

22   Ibid., chapter 3.

23   Ibid.; Lena Sommestad, "Creating gender: technology and femininity in the Swedish dairy industry," in Gertjan de Groot and Marlou Schrover (eds.) *Women Workers and Technological Change in Europe in the Nineteenth and Twentieth Centuries*, London, Taylor and Francis, 1995, pp. 151–9.

24   Sara Horrell and Jane Humphries, "Women's labour force participation and the transition to the male-breadwinner family, 1790–1865," *Economic History Review*, February 1995, vol. 48, p. 94.

25   Ibid., p. 105.

26   Honeyman and Goodman, "Women's work," pp. 618–19.

27   Harriet Bradley, "Frames of reference: skill, gender and new technology in the hosiery industry," in de Groot and Schrover (eds.) *Women Workers*, pp. 19–24.

28   Marianne Rostgard, "The creation of a gendered division of labour in the Danish textile industry," in de Groot and Schrover (eds.) *Women Workers*, pp. 35–51.

29   Horrell and Humphries, "Women's labour force participation," p. 112.

30   Bradley, "Frames of reference," pp. 29–30.

31   Keith McClelland, "Rational and respectable men: gender, the working class, and citizenship in Britain, 1850–1867," in Laura L. Frader and Sonya O. Rose (eds.) *Gender and Class in Modern Europe*, Ithaca, Cornell University Press, 1996, p. 285.

32 See articles appearing in de Groot and Schrover (eds.) *Women Workers*; Jane Long, *Conversations in Cold Rooms: Women, Work and Poverty in Nineteenth-century Northumberland*, Rochester, NY, Boydell Press, 1999, pp. 78–99; Simonton, *European Women's Work*, pp. 83 and 163; R. W. Connell, *Gender and Power: Society, the Person and Sexual Politics*, Stanford, Calif., Stanford University Press, 1987, pp. 99–111 and 131.

33 Long, *Conversations,* pp. 52–3 and 78–99; Jane Humphries, "'. . . The most free from objection . . .' the sexual division of labour and women's work in nineteenth-century England," *Journal of Economic History*, December 1987, vol. 47, pp. 929–49.

34 Miriam Glucksmann, *Women Assemble: Women Workers and the New Industries in Inter-war Britain*, London and New York, Routledge, 1990, p. 277.

35 Lown, *Women and Industrialization*, pp. 8 and 19.

36 Ibid., p. 62.

37 Ibid., pp. 110–16.

38 Connell, *Gender and Power,* pp. 102–3.

39 McClelland, "Rational and respectable men," pp. 180–8; Connell, *Gender and Power*, p. 109.

40 Long, *Conversations,* p. 61.

41 Angela V. John, *By the Sweat of their Brow: Women Workers at Victorian Coal Mines*, London, Routledge & Kegan Paul, 1984, p. 71.

42 Ibid., pp. 70–3.

43 Ibid.; "Pit brow women," *Labour Tribune*, 24 April 1886.

44 John, *Sweat of their Brow*, pp. 77–89.

45 Ibid., pp. 81–90.

46 Ibid., p. 137.

47 *The Times*, 20 October 1885; quoted in ibid., p. 139.

48 *Labour Tribune*, 6 March 1886.

49 "Pit-bank Girls," *Labour Tribune*, 27 March 1886.

50 Ibid.

51 *Labour Tribune*, 6 March 1886.

52 "Pitwomen's right of labour," *Englishwoman's Review* (new series) 15 February 1886, no. 154, pp. 49–51; see also discussion of opinion in John, *Sweat of their Brow*, pp. 166–203.

53 John, *Sweat of their Brow*, pp. 111–12.

54 Ibid., pp. 138–45.

55 Long, *Conversations*, pp. 57–65.

56 Ibid., pp. 66–71.

57 Ibid., pp. 218–19.

58 Ibid., p. 219.

59 Ibid., p. 220.

60 "Pitwomen's right of labour," *Englishwoman's Review*, p. 50.

61 Ibid.

62 "Pit brow women and their work. Meeting at Pemberton," *Women's Union Journal*, April 1886, no. 123, p. 44.

63 "Proposed legislation against pit brow women," *The Englishwoman's Review* (new series) 15 May 1886, no. 157, p. 226.

64 Ibid., pp. 226–7.

65 John, *Sweat of their Brow*, p. 140.

66 "The employment of women at Lancashire collieries," *Labour Tribune,* 27 March 1886.

67 John, *Sweat of their Brow*, pp. 139–40.

68 Ibid., pp. 119–27.

69 Ibid., p. 115.

70 "Pit brow women and their work," *Women's Union Journal*, April 1886, no. 123, p. 44. In Whitehaven, 125 of the 140 girls and women employed in the three pits of the area attended the meeting addressed by Lydia Becker, while the meeting supported by Rev. Fox and the vicar of Ashton "was got up at the request of the women themselves," 200 of whom were in attendance. "Proposed legislation," *The Englishwoman's Review* (new series) 15 February 1886, pp. 225–7.
71 John, *Sweat of their Brow*, pp. 145–8.
72 "Pit brow women," *The Englishwoman's Review* (new series) 15 June 1887, no. 169, p. 272.
73 John, *Sweat of their Brow*, p. 204.
74 Ibid., pp. 204–5.
75 "The employment of women at Lancashire collieries," *Labour Tribune*, 27 March 1886.
76 Ibid.
77 "Pit-bank girls," *Labour Tribune*, 27 March 1886.
78 Ibid.
79 "Pit brow women," *Labour Tribune*, 24 April 1886.
80 *Labour Tribune*, 17 April 1886.
81 "More opinions as to pit-brow girls," *Labour Tribune*, 8 May 1886.
82 Ibid.
83 Ibid.
84 Ibid.
85 Ibid.
86 "Deputation of pit-brow women to the Home-secretary," *Labour Tribune*, 21 May 1887.
87 "'The Womens' [*sic*] Suffrage Journal' and Parliamentary proceedings," *Labour Tribune*, 16 July 1887.
88 M. M. Bakhtin, "Discourse in the novel," in Michael Holquist (trans.) and Caryl Emerson and Michael Holquist (eds.) *The Dialogic Imagination: Four Essays by M. M. Bakhtin*, Austin and London, University of Texas Press, 1981, p. 271.
89 Ibid., p. 272.
90 Horrell and Humphries, "Women's labour force participation," pp. 105–6.
91 Ulla Wikander, "Periodization and the engendering of technology: the pottery of Gustavsberg, Sweden, 1880–1980," in de Groot and Schrover (eds.), *Women Workers*, pp. 137 and 145.
92 Glucksmann, *Women Assemble*, pp. 198–9.
93 See Connell, *Gender and Power*, pp. 109 and 131. State Michael Roper and John Tosh, "Understanding gender in relational terms is also important because ... dominant or 'hegemonic' masculinities function by asserting their superiority over the 'other', whether that be gay men, younger men, women, or subordinated ethnic groups." "Introduction," Roper and Tosh (eds.) *Manful Assertions: Masculinities in Britain since 1800*, London and New York, Routledge, 1991. Added to this list in the present context should be unskilled male laborers.

5 Gender divisions and class relations

1 G. C. Allen, *The Industrial Development of Birmingham and the Black Country 1860–1927*, London, George Allen and Unwin, 1929, pp. 13–17.
2 Clive Behagg, *Politics and Production in the Early Nineteenth Century*, London and New York, Routledge, 1990, p. 143.
3 Ibid., pp. 2–50.
4 Ibid., pp. 46–7.

5 J. S. Wright, "On the employment of women in factories in Birmingham," *Transactions of the National Association for the Promotion of Social Science*, 1857, p. 538.
6 Ibid., p. 540.
7 Ibid, pp. 539–40.
8 Ibid.
9 Samuel Timmins (ed.) *Birmingham and the Midland Hardware District*, London, Robert Hardwicke, 1866, pp. 222, 308, 361.
10 "British industries. Brassfounding: Messrs. Tonks, Limited," *Tinsley's Magazine*, November 1889, no. 6, p. 685.
11 Wright, "Employment of women," p. 543.
12 P. E. Razzell and R. W. Wainwright (eds.) *The Victorian Working Class: Selections from Letters to the 'Morning Chronicle,'* London, Frank Cass, 1973, pp. 295–6.
13 Ibid.
14 Ibid.
15 Wright, "Employment of women," p. 542.
16 Dennis Smith, *Conflict and Compromise: Class Formation in English Society 1830–1914: A Comparative Study of Birmingham and Sheffield*, London, Routledge & Kegan Paul, 1982, p. 70.
17 "The manufacture of steel-pens," in Razzell and Wainwright, *Victorian Working Class*, pp. 297–9.
18 Ibid., p. 297.
19 Wright, "Employment of women," p. 542.
20 Smith, *Conflict and Compromise,* pp. 70 and 43.
21 W. J. Davis, *A Short History of the Brass Trade*, Birmingham, Hudson and Son, 1892, p. 6.
22 Ibid., pp. 26–7.
23 Ibid., pp. 27–42.
24 Martin J. Wiener, "The sad story of George Hall: adultery, murder and the politics of mercy in mid-Victorian England," *Social History*, May 1999, Vol. 24, pp. 174–95.
25 William A. Dalley, *The Life Story of W. J. Davis, J.P.*, Birmingham, Birmingham Printers Limited, 1914, p. 66.
26 See Smith, *Conflict and Compromise*, pp. 238–40.
27 Amalgamated Society of Brassworkers, *Second Annual Report and Financial Statements, April 26th, 1873, to April 25th, 1874*, Birmingham, 1874, p. 6.
28 Ibid.
29 *Dictionary of Labour Biography*, vol. vi, Macmillan, 1982, p. 92.
30 Webb Trade Union Collection, section A, vol. 19, p. 32.
31 Ibid., p. 44.
32 Ibid., p. 4.
33 Rosemary Feurer, "The meaning of 'sisterhood': the British women's movement and protective labor legislation, 1870–1900," *Victorian Studies*, Winter 1988, vol. 31, p. 233.
34 "Restrictions on women's labour," *Englishwoman's Review* (new series), April 1874, no. 18, pp. 127–9. The Vigilance Association for the Defence of Personal Rights was originally founded in 1871 to oppose the Contagious Diseases Act. States Rosemary Feurer regarding the position of the VA, "Like state regulation of prostitution, the factory acts were regarded as laws which victimized poor women." "Meaning of 'sisterhood,'" p. 236.
35 Ibid., pp. 129–30.
36 Feurer, "Meaning of 'sisterhood,'" pp. 238–9.
37 Trades Union Congress, *Report of the Tenth Annual Trades Union Congress*, 1877, p. 18.

38 Ibid., p. 17.
39 "Trades' unions.—Leicester," *Englishwoman's Review* (new series) 15 October 1877, no. 54, p. 465.
40 Ibid., p. 466.
41 Ibid.
42 B.P.P., *Report of the Commissioners Appointed to Inquire into the Working of the Factory and Workshops Acts, with Minutes of Evidence*, 1876, xxx, p. 254.
43 Ibid., p. 253.
44 Ibid., p. 250.
45 Ibid., p. 254.
46 Amalgamated Society of Brassworkers, *Fourteenth Annual Report and Financial Statements, February 14th, 1885, to February 13th, 1886*, Birmingham, 1886, pp. 7–8; Amalgamated Society of Brassworkers, *Fifteenth Annual Report and Financial Statements, February 13th, 1886, to February 12th, 1887*, Birmingham, 1887, p. 6; Amalgamated Society of Brassworkers, *Sixteenth Annual Report and Financial Statements, February 12, 1887, to February 11, 1888*, Birmingham, 1888, p. 6.
47 Amalgamated Society of Brassworkers, *Sixteenth Annual Report and Financial Statements, February 12, 1887, to February 11, 1888*, Birmingham, 1888, p. 8; Amalgamated Society of Brassworkers, *Twenty-first Annual Report and Financial Statements. Year Ending February 4, 1893*, Birmingham, 1893, pp. 12–13.
48 Dalley, *Life Story*, p. 116.
49 Amalgamated Society of Brassworkers, *Fifth Annual Report and Financial Statements, April 23rd, 1876, to February 24th, 1877,* Birmingham, 1877, p. 5.
50 Amalgamated Society of Brassworkers, *Seventh Annual Report and Financial Statements, Feb. 28th, 1878, to Feb. 22nd, 1879*, Birmingham, 1879, pp. 4–5; Amalgamated Society of Brassworkers, *Eighth Annual Report and Financial Statements, Feb. 25th, 1879, to Feb. 25th, 1880*, Birmingham, 1880, pp. 6–7.
51 Amalgamated Society of Brassworkers, *Third Annual Report and Financial Statements, April 26th, 1874, to April 25th, 1875*, p. 6.
52 Webb Trade Union Collection, section A, vol. 19, p. 30.
53 Dalley, *Life Story*, p. 98.
54 Ibid., p. 163.
55 Ibid., p. 164. Quote from Davis at Brassworkers' Annual Meeting, 1890.
56 Ibid., pp. 167–8.
57 Ibid., pp. 171–4.
58 Amalgamated Society of Brassworkers, *Sixteenth Annual Report and Financial Statements, February 12, 1887, to February 11, 1888*, Birmingham, 1888, pp. 7–8; Society of Brassworkers, *Nineteenth Annual Report*, p. 3.
59 Dalley, *Life Story*, pp. 140–6; Webb Trade Union Collection, section A, vol. 19, p. 47.
60 *Birmingham Daily Post*, 30 October 1891; cited in Dalley, *Life Story*, pp. 170–1.
61 Webb Trade Union Collection, section A, vol. 20, p. 15.
62 Ibid., p. 89.
63 Ibid., pp. 103–4.
64 Ibid., p. 75.
65 Ibid., p. 303.
66 Ibid., pp. 296–7.
67 "Female labour organisation in Birmingham," *Daily Gazette*, 10 September 1890.
68 Ibid.
69 Ibid.
70 Ibid.

71 Amalgamated Society of Brassworkers, *Twenty-first Annual Report and Financial Statements. Year Ending February 4, 1893*, Birmingham, 1893, pp. 13–14.
72 Amalgamated Society of Brassworkers, *Sixteenth Annual Report and Financial Statements, February 12, 1887, to February 11, 1888*, Birmingham, 1888, p. 7.
73 Ibid.
74 B.P.P., *Report from the Departmental Committee on the Conditions of Labour in the Manufacture of Brass and of Kindred Amalgams*, 1896, xxv, pp. 64–6.
75 Ibid., p. 68.
76 Dalley, *Life Story*, pp. 182–4.
77 Ibid., pp. 184–6.
78 Ibid., pp. 187–8.
79 Quoted in ibid., pp. 186–7.
80 Keith McClelland, "Some thoughts on masculinity and the 'representative artisan' in Britain, 1850–1880," *Gender and History*, Summer 1989, vol. 1, p. 166.

6 Gender, class, and community in the Black Country

1 Marie B. Rowlands, *Masters and Men in the West Midland Metalware Trades before the Industrial Revolution*, Manchester, Manchester University Press, 1975, p. 13.
2 Ibid., pp. 5–6.
3 Ibid.; Marie Rowlands, "Continuity and change in an industrialising society: the case of the West Midlands Industries," in Pat Hudson (ed.) *Regions and Industries: A Perspective on the Industrial Revolution in Britain*, Cambridge, Cambridge University Press, 1989, p. 109.
4 Rowlands, "Continuity and change," pp. 103–16.
5 Rowlands, *Masters and Men*, pp. 40–4.
6 Ibid., p. 40.
7 Ibid., pp. 126–7.
8 Maxine Berg, *The Age of Manufactures: Industry, Innovation and Work in Britain 1700–1820*, Totowa, NJ, Barnes and Noble, 1985, pp. 36–8 and 267; Rowlands, "Continuity and change," pp. 124–5.
9 G. C. Allen, *The Industrial Development of Birmingham and the Black Country 1860–1927*, London, George Allen and Unwin, 1929, pp. 89–90.
10 Ibid., p. 94.
11 Rowlands, *Masters and Men*, p. 166.
12 David Philips, *Crime and Authority in Victorian England: The Black Country 1835–1860*, London, Croom Helm, 1977, pp. 32–3.
13 "The collieries and the truck system," in P. E. Razzell and R. W. Wainwright (eds.) *The Victorian Working Class: Selections from Letters to the 'Morning Chronicle,'* London, Frank Cass, 1973, pp. 245–6; Philips, *Crime and Authority*, pp. 32–3; David Charles Woods, "Crime and society in the Black Country 1860–1900," Ph.D. dissertation, University of Aston, 1979, pp. 33 and 41–52.
14 "Birmingham: parochial and moral statistics," in Razzell and Wainwright, *Victorian Working Class*, pp. 285–6.
15 Philips, *Crime and Authority*, p. 160.
16 Ibid., pp. 125–6.
17 Ibid., pp. 182–4.
18 Ibid., p. 149.
19 Ibid., p. 128.
20 R. G. Hobbs, "A Midland tour," *The Leisure Hour*, 1872.
21 Woods, "Crime and society," pp. 53–9.

22 Ibid., p. 20.
23 Bill Kings and Margaret Cooper, *Glory Gone: The Story of Nailing in Bromsgrove*, Bromsgrove, Halfshire Books, 1989, p. 58.
24 Ibid., pp. 58–9; B.P.P., *Report as to the Condition of Nail Makers and Small Chain Makers in South Staffordshire and East Worcestershire, by the Labour Correspondent of the Board of Trade*, 1888, xci, p.11.
25 B.P.P., *Report as to Condition of Nail Makers*, p. 4; Kings and Cooper, *Glory Gone*, p. 61.
26 Kings and Cooper, *Glory Gone*, pp. 62–4.
27 Eric Hopkins, "Working conditions in Victorian Stourbridge," *International Review of Social History*, xix, part 3 (1974): 417; B.P.P., *Report as to Condition of Nail Makers*, p. 11.
28 Kings and Cooper, *Glory Gone*, p. 58.
29 J. W. Billingham, "The decline of the nail trade!" *Bugle Annual*, December 1974, p. 10.
30 Rev. Harold Rylett, "Nails and chains," *The English Illustrated Magazine*, 1890, p. 163.
31 Ibid., p. 164.
32 Ibid.
33 Ibid., p. 168.
34 Ibid.
35 Ibid.
36 B.P.P., *Report as to Condition of Nail Makers*, p. 4.
37 Rylett, "Nails and chains," pp. 164–5.
38 Ibid., p. 165.
39 Kings and Cooper, *Glory Gone*, p. 60.
40 B.P.P., *Report of Robert Baker, Inspector of Factories, for the six months ended the 31st of October 1868*, 1868–9, xiv, p. 301. The Dudley Wood or Old Hill district included Dudley Wood, Netherton, Cradley Heath, Cradley, Lye Waste, and Old Hill. B.P.P., *Report of the Commissioners Appointed to Inquire into the Working of the Factory and Workshops Acts, with Minutes of Evidence*, 1876, xxx, p. 293.
41 *Women at Work: Chainmaking in the Black Country*, Gateshead, H. Kelly, 1877, p. 4. London, Library of Political and Economic Science, Webb Trade Union Collection, section B, vol. II.
42 Ibid., p. 12.
43 "'Chains and slavery.' A visit to the strikers at Cradley-Heath," *Sunday Chronicle*, 7 November 1886.
44 "The chain-makers' strike," *Sunday Chronicle*, 21 November 1886.
45 "The small chain makers of Cradley Heath," *Labour Tribune*, 1 September 1888.
46 "Chains and slavery," *Sunday Chronicle*, 7 November 1886.
47 *Women at Work*, pp. 6–17.
48 Sheila Blackburn, "Working-class attitudes to social reform: Black Country chainmakers and anti-sweating legislation, 1880–1930," *International Review of Social History*, 1988, pp. 47–8, vol. 33. I wish to acknowledge the work of Sheila Blackburn whose path-breaking discussion of chainmaking in relation to social legislation served to bring my attention to this industry.
49 Ibid. The role of middlemen in the industry is described by Thomas Harrison and Samuel Stringer of the Walsall Chainmakers Association in B.P.P., *Report of the Commissioners Appointed to Inquire into the Factory and Workshops Acts*, pp. 292–3. According to Stringer, when workers would present themselves at the warehouse to get work, a master often "deputes some subordinate, who, with a dismal countenance, tells the men that trade is bad, the master is out, and that he is afraid that there will be no more orders until there is a general reduc-

tion." Those most in need finally take work and "they, with their wives and children, go to work day and night, as far as they dare, to make up for lost time." The system thus, Stringer concluded, "compels men to work at the same low rate as women and children."

50 Ibid.; *Women at Work*, pp. 6–12.
51 H.O. 41/1, 2, and 3 (?), Public Record Office; cited in George Barnsby, *The Working Class Movement in the Black Country 1750 to 1867*, Wolverhampton, Integrated Publishing Services, 1977.
52 Kings and Cooper, *Glory Gone*, p. 91.
53 Ibid.
54 Barnsby, *Working Class Movement*, pp. 103–10.
55 Ibid, p. 103.
56 Kings and Cooper, *Glory Gone*, p. 91.
57 Barnsby, *Working Class Movement*, p. 146.
58 Kings and Cooper, *Glory Gone*, p. 92.
59 Barnsby, *Working Class Movement*, pp. 173–4; "Account of the Chain Makers' Strike, in 1859–60," *National Association for the Promotion of Social Science*, 1860, pp. 149–58.
60 Barnsby, *Working Class Movement*, p. 174.
61 Ibid., p. 175.
62 Philips, *Crime and Authority*, pp. 188–9.
63 Ibid., p. 168.
64 Kings and Cooper, *Glory Gone*, pp. 93–5.
65 Ibid., pp. 96–7.
66 Barnsby, *Working Class Movement*, p. 176.
67 Ibid., p. 98.
68 B.P.P., *Report as to Condition of Nail Makers*, pp. 10–11.
69 Billingham, "Decline of nail trade!" p. 10.
70 Ibid.; B.P.P., *Report as to Condition of Nail Makers*, pp. 4–23.
71 B.P.P., *Report under the Laws relating to Factories and Workshops by Robert Baker, Esq, for the Half Year ended April 30, 1875*, 1875, xx.
72 Ibid.
73 *Women at Work*, pp. 15–16.
74 Philips, *Crime and Authority*, pp. 29–30.
75 W. H. Robinson, *Guide to Walsall*, pp. 54–66; quoted in Woods, "Crime and society," p. 29.
76 Ibid.; *Saddlers', Harness Makers' and Carriage Builders' Gazette*, December 1871, vol. 1, pp. 5–6. I wish to thank Marc Steinberg for calling my attention to this source.
77 B.P.P., *Report of the Commissioners Appointed to Inquire into the Factory and Workshops Acts,* pp. 292–3.
78 "The labour question," *Walsall Free Press*, 29 June 1872.
79 Ibid.
80 Woods, "Crime and society," pp. 59 and 66.
81 *Women at Work*, pp. 7–8.
82 Ibid., pp. 4–8.
83 B.P.P., *Report of the Commissioners Appointed to Inquire into the Factory and Workshops Acts*, p. 293.
84 Ibid., p. 294.
85 Trades Union Congress, "Parliamentary Committee Report," 1877, p. 8.
86 Trades Union Congress, *Report of the Eleventh Annual Trades Union Congress*, 1878.
87 *Women at Work*, p. 14.
88 Woods, "Crime and society," pp. 58–9.

89   Eric Taylor, "Richard Juggins," in Joyce M. Bellamy and John Saville (eds.) *Dictionary of Labour Biography*, vol. I, London, Macmillan, 1972, p. 207.
90   J. A. C. Baker, "Richard Juggins and Black Country unionism in the late nineteenth century," *Transactions of the Lichfield and South Staffordshire Archaeological and Historical Society*, 1968, vol. 9, p. 68; Eric Taylor, "The Midland Counties Trades Federation 1886–1914," *Midland History,* Spring 1972, vol. 1, pp. 29–32.
91   Trades Union Congress, "Parliamentary Committee Report," 1883, pp. 1–2.
92   Letter to editor, *Birmingham Daily Gazette*, 5 March 1883.
93   "The Sedgley nailers and the female labour question," *Birmingham Daily Gazette*, 1 March 1883.
94   Letter to editor, *Birmingham Daily Gazette*, 5 March 1883.
95   "Female labour in the district," *Advertiser*, 27 January 1883.
96   "The South Staffordshire and East Worcestershire Trades Council," *Advertiser*, 10 February 1883.
97   "Trades' Union Congress," *Women's Union Journal*, 8 October 1883, no. 93, pp. 88–9.
98   Letter to editor, *Sunday Chronicle*, 5 December 1886.
99   Ibid.
100 Letter to editor, *Birmingham Daily Gazette*, 5 March 1883.
101 B.P.P., *Report of the Commissioners Appointed to Inquire into the Factory and Workshops Acts,* p. 293.
102 Blackburn, "Working-class attitudes," p. 62.
103 "The female labour question," *Advertiser*, 24 March 1883.
104 "Non-unionism and the nailmakers," *Sunday Chronicle*, 25 October 1891.
105 Ibid.
106 "The small chain makers of Cradley Heath," *Labour Tribune*, 1 September 1888.
107 "Chains and slavery," *Sunday Chronicle*, 7 November 1886.
108 Janet Horowitz Murray, "Class vs. gender identification in the *Englishwoman's Review* of the 1880s," *Victorian Periodicals Review*, Winter 1985, vol. 18, p. 138.
109 "Proposed extension of the Factory Acts," *Englishwoman's Review* (new series) March 1875, no. 23, p. 102.
110 Ibid.
111 "Trades' unions.—Leicester," *Englishwoman's Review* (new series) 15 October 1877, no. 54, p. 465.
112 Trades Union Congress, *Report of the Tenth Annual Trades Union Congress*, 1877, p. 17.
113 Letter to editor, *Advertiser*, 24 March 1883.
114 "Women and nailmaking," *Women's Union Journal*, May 1883, no. 88, p. 37.
115 "Chain-making," *Englishwoman's Review* (new series) 15 March 1883, no. 99, pp. 110–11.
116 "Mr. Broadhurst, M.P., and female labour in the Black Country," *Advertiser*, 21 April 1883.
117 "Female labour in the nail and chain trades. Great meeting at Old Hill," *Advertiser*, 17 March 1883.
118 "The female labour question," *Advertiser*, 12 May 1883.
119 Ibid.
120 "Trades' Union Congress," *Women's Union Journal*, October 1883, no. 93, p. 86. See below for further discussion of women's views on legislative restrictions.
121 "Women and nailmaking," *Women's Union Journal*, May 1883, no. 88, p. 37.
122 Women's Protective and Provident League, *Ninth Annual Report*, 1883, p. 8;

"Factory and Workshops Act (1878) Amendment Bill," *Women's Union Journal*, May 1883, no. 88, pp. 36–7.

123 Ibid.; "Trades' Union Congress," *Women's Union Journal*, October 1883, no. 93, p. 85.

124 "Trades' Union Congress," *Women's Union Journal*, October 1884, no. 105, p. 90.

125 "Women as nail makers," *Women's Union Journal*, November 1884, no. 106, pp. 99–100.

126 Ibid.

127 Ada Heather Bigg, "Female labour in the nail trade," *Fortnightly Review*, 1886, vol. 45, p. 829.

128 Ibid.

129 Ibid., p. 831.

130 Ibid., pp. 831–2.

131 Ibid., p. 832.

132 Ibid., pp. 832–3.

133 "The Trades' Union Congress," *Women's Union Journal*, October 1887, no. 141, p. 76.

134 Ibid., pp. 76–7.

135 "Female labour in the Black Country," *Birmingham Daily Post*, 2 April 1891.

136 Ibid.

137 Ibid.; "Female labour in the nail and chain trades," *Birmingham Daily Gazette*, 6 April 1891.

138 "Deputation of chain and nail makers to the Home Secretary," *Birmingham Daily Post*, 18 April 1891.

139 "Female chainmakers in London," *Labour Tribune*, 25 April 1891.

140 The local vicar sent greetings to the meeting at which the JP, W. Bassano, spoke, indicating that work in the chain trade was no worse than in factories and workshops. It did not affect the workers' health, he argued, since the "females were, as a rule, strong and healthy." Abolishing female labor without putting anything in its place, he concluded, "would be productive of great mischief, as the women and girls thus employed were from their occupation unfitted for domestic service." At the meeting, "The reading of this letter was received with much applause." "Female labour in the nail and chain trades. Great meeting at Old Hill," *Advertiser*, 17 March 1883.

141 "Female labour in the district," *Advertiser*, 24 February 1883; "Female labour in the district," *Advertiser*, 6 January 1883.

142 "Female labour," *Advertiser*, 6 January 1883.

143 "Female labour," *Advertiser*, 17 March 1883.

144 Ibid.

145 "Female labour in the district," *Advertiser*, 27 January 1883.

146 B.P.P., *Report of the Commissioners Appointed to Inquire into the Factory and Workshops Acts,* p. 298.

147 "Female labour," *Advertiser*, 6 January 1883.

148 Letter to editor signed by Benjamin Billingham, *Advertiser*, 10 March 1883.

149 "Female labour in the chain trade.—Deputation to M. H. B. Sheridan," *Advertiser*, 17 February 1883.

150 Ibid.

151 Letter to editor, *Advertiser*, 24 February 1883.

152 Although Green denied using middlemen, or foggers as they were called, Thomas Harrison of Walsall claimed that, out of 3,000 women employed in the nail and chain trades, 1,000 were employed by Green through foggers. Letter to editor, *Advertiser*, 10 March 1883.

153 "South Staffordshire and East Worcestershire Trades Council," *Advertiser*, 10 March 1883.

154 Letter to editor, *Advertiser*, 3 March 1883.
155 Ibid.; "South Staffordshire and East Worcestershire Trades Council," *Advertiser*, 10 March 1883.
156 Letter to editor, *Advertiser*, 24 February 1883.
157 "The South Staffordshire and East Worcestershire Trades Council," *Advertiser*, 10 February 1883.
158 "South Staffordshire and East Worcestershire Trades Council," *Advertiser*, 10 March 1883.
159 Ibid.
160 Letter to editor, *Advertiser*, 3 March 1883; "Female labour in the nail and chain trades," *Birmingham Daily Gazette*, 26 February 1883.
161 "The Sedgley nailers and the female labour question," *Birmingham Daily Gazette*, 1 March 1883.
162 Letter to editor by Richard Juggins, *Advertiser*, 3 March 1883.
163 "South Staffordshire and East Worcestershire Trades Council," *Advertiser*, 10 March 1883.
164 B.P.P., *Report of the Commissioners Appointed to Inquire into the Factory and Workshops Acts*, p. 294.
165 Ibid., 293.
166 Allen, *Industrial Development*, p. 132.
167 "Female labour in the nail and chain trades," *Birmingham Daily Gazette*, 23 March 1883. At the meeting where the deputation from Newcastle spoke, a resolution was put forward based on this approach: "That the time has not arrived when female labour in the chain trade can be wholly abolished; but we advocate the further restriction of the hours of labour and call the attention of the members of Parliament to the matter." "Female labour in the district," *Advertiser*, 27 January 1883.
168 Berg, *Age of Manufactures*, pp. 159–60.
169 Ibid., p. 173.
170 Angela V. John, *By the Sweat of their Brow: Women Workers at Victorian Coal Mines*, London, Routledge & Kegan Paul, 1984, p. 137.
171 Laura Lee Downs, "If 'woman' is just an empty category, then why am I afraid to walk alone at night? Identity politics meets the postmodern subject," *Comparative Studies in Society and History*, April 1993, vol. 35.

7 Negotiating gender difference in the small metal industries

1 "A piteous cry from Staffordshire," *Sunday Chronicle*, 7 November 1886.
2 "The English chain trade; or white slavery at Cradley," *Labour Tribune*, 4 December 1886; reprinted from West Bromwich *Free Press*.
3 Ibid.; "'Chains and slavery.' A visit to the strikers at Cradley-Heath," *Sunday Chronicle*, 7 November 1886.
4 Ibid.
5 "Chains and slavery."
6 Ibid.
7 Letter to editor, *Sunday Chronicle*, 5 December 1886.
8 "Chains and slavery."
9 "The English chain trade."
10 "Chains and slavery."
11 "The English chain trade."
12 "Chains and slavery."
13 "The chain-makers' strike," *Sunday Chronicle*, 21 November 1886; "The chain-makers' strike at Cradley," *Sunday Chronicle*, 5 December 1886.
14 "Latest from Cradley Heath," *Sunday Chronicle*, 17 April 1887.

15 Ibid.
16 Ibid.
17 Ibid.
18 "Female labour in the district," *Advertiser*, 6 January 1883; "Female labour in the district," *Advertiser*, 24 February 1883.
19 "The female labour question," *Advertiser*, 24 March 1883.
20 "The female labour question," *Advertiser*, 12 May 1883.
21 *Birmingham Daily Post*, 20 April 1891.
22 "Deputation of chain and nail makers to the Home Secretary," *Birmingham Daily Post*, 18 April 1891.
23 Rosemary Feurer, "The meaning of 'sisterhood': the British women's movement and protective labor legislation, 1870–1900," *Victorian Studies*, Winter 1988, vol. 31, p. 147.
24 Women's Protective and Provident League, *Eleventh Annual Report*, 1885, p. 3.
25 Ibid.
26 Women's Protective and Provident League, *Fourteenth Annual Report*, 1888, p. 4.
27 Ibid.
28 Clementina Black, "The organization of working women," *Fortnightly Review*, 1889, vol. 52, p. 697.
29 Emilia Dilke, "Trades unionism among women," *Fortnightly Review*, 1891, vol. 55, p. 743.
30 Ibid., pp. 743–4.
31 Emilia Dilke, "The industrial position of women," *Fortnightly Review*, 1893, vol. 60, pp. 500–1.
32 Ibid., p. 503.
33 Ibid., p. 504.
34 Ibid.
35 Ibid., pp. 504–5.
36 Ibid., p. 505.
37 Feurer, "Meaning of 'sisterhood,'" pp. 249–50.
38 Ibid., p. 252.
39 Ibid., p. 251.
40 "Proposed society of women working in the saddlery trade in Walsall," *Women's Union Journal*, 15 June 1888, no. 149, pp. 41–2.
41 Ibid.
42 Trades Union Congress, *Trades Union Congress Report*, 1888, p. 48.
43 "Notes on the Trades' Union Congress," *Women's Union Journal*, 15 September 1888, no. 151, p. 66.
44 "Midland Counties Trades Federation," *Labour Tribune*, 4 August 1888.
45 Trades Union Congress, "Parliamentary Committee Report," 1888, p. 4.
46 B.P.P., *Third Report from the Select Committee of the House of Lords on the Sweating System*, 1889, xiii, pp. 50–1.
47 Ibid., p. 69.
48 B.P.P., *Report as to the Condition of Nail Makers and Small Chain Makers in South Staffordshire and East Worcestershire, by the Labour Correspondent of the Board of Trade*, 1888, xci, p. 29.
49 B.P.P., *Third Report from Select Committee on Sweating System*, p. 69.
50 B.P.P., *Report as to Condition of Nail Makers*, p. 44.
51 Ibid.
52 Ibid., p. 11.
53 B.P.P., *Second Report of the Royal Commission on Labour, with Minutes of Evidence*, 1893–4, xxxii, pp. 436–9.
54 Ibid., p. 440.

55　B.P.P., *Third Report from Select Committee on Sweating System*, pp. 69–70.
56　B.P.P., *Second Report of Royal Commission on Labour*, p. 439.
57　B.P.P., *Third Report from Select Committee on Sweating System*, pp. 70 and 75–6.
58　Ibid., p. 70.
59　B.P.P., *Second Report of Royal Commission on Labour,* p. 443.
60　B.P.P., *Third Report from Select Committee on Sweating System*, p. 52.
61　Ibid., p. 49.
62　Ibid.
63　B.P.P., *Report as to Condition of Nail Makers*, p. 43.
64　Ibid.
65　Ibid.
66　"Lady Dilke at Cradley Heath," *Advertiser*, 19 October 1889, p. 3.
67　"Non-unionism and the nailmakers," *Sunday Chronicle*, 25 October 1891.
68　*Women's Trades Union Review*, 15 January 1892, no. 4, p. 14.
69　"The chainmakers and organisation: two parties in the trade," *Advertiser*, 11 March 1893; "Cradley Heath chainmakers and organisation," *Advertiser*, 18 March 1893.
70　"Wages in the chain trade," *Advertiser*, 22 April 1893; "Wages in the chain trade," *Advertiser*, 29 April 1893.
71　"The strike in the chain trade. Mr. Juggins and the chainmakers," *Advertiser*, 10 June 1893.
72　*Women's Trade Union Review*, October 1895, no. 19, p. 5.
73　"Strike in the chain trade at Cradley Heath," *Advertiser*, 21 September 1895.
74　"The chainmakers' strike at Cradley Heath," *Advertiser*, 28 September 1895.
75　"The strike in the chain trade," *Advertiser*, 5 October 1895; "Wages in the block chain trade," *Advertiser*, 2 November 1895.
76　"Chain trade conference," *Advertiser*, 11 January 1896; "Strike in the small chain trade," *Advertiser*, 8 February 1896; "The strike in the chain trade," *Advertiser*, 15 February 1896.
77　"The strike in the small chain trade at Cradley Heath," *Advertiser*, 29 February 1896.
78　"Cradley Heath and District Best Chainmakers' Association," *Advertiser*, 24 October 1896.
79　Ibid.
80　"Organisation in the chain trade. Tea and public meeting," *Advertiser*, 7 November 1896.
81　Ibid.
82　"Mass meeting of chain-makers at Cradley Heath," *Advertiser*, 23 October 1897.
83　Ibid.; "Cradley Heath chainmakers and the blast question," *Advertiser*, 6 February 1897.
84　"Mass meeting of chain-makers at Cradley Heath," *Advertiser*, 23 October 1897.
85　Ibid.
86　Ibid.
87　Edward Cadbury, M. Cecile Matheson, George Shann, *Women's Work and Wages*, London, T. Fisher Unwin, 1906, p. 47; Carl Chinn, *They Worked all their Lives: Women of the Urban Poor in England, 1880–1939*, Manchester, Manchester University Press, 1988, pp. 86–92; City of Birmingham Education Committee. Central Care Committee, *Birmingham Trades for Women and Girls*, 1914.
88　City of Birmingham. Health Department, *Report on Industrial Employment of Married Women and Infantile Mortality*, Birmingham, 1910, p. 5; Chinn, *They Worked*, p. 96.

89 London, Library of Political and Economic Science. British Association for the Advancement of Science Collection, Misc. 486, 2/5.
90 City of Birmingham, *Report on Industrial Employment*, p. 5.
91 Cadbury *et al.*, *Women's Work*, p. 50.
92 Ibid., pp. 51–2.
93 BAAS Collection, Misc. 486, 2/5.
94 Cadbury *et al.*, *Women's Work*, pp. 62–8.
95 Ibid., pp. 54–7.
96 Ibid., p. 56.
97 Ibid., pp. 52–3.
98 Ibid., p. 57.
99 Ibid., pp. 47–56.
100 City of Birmingham, *Birmingham Trades*.
101 Ibid.; Cadbury *et al.*, *Women's Work*, pp. 48–9.
102 BAAS Collection, Misc. 486, 2/5. The following discussion is based on this source.
103 "Birmingham Trades Council," *Birmingham and District Trades Journal*, 12 September 1896.
104 Ibid.
105 "The Birmingham penworkers," *Birmingham and District Trades Journal*, 12 November 1898; BAAS Collection, Misc. 486, 2/5.
106 "The League at Congress," *Women's Trades' Union Review*, October 1897, no. 27, p. 7.
107 Ibid.
108 "Messrs. Joseph Gillott & Sons' steel pen manufactory, Birmingham," *The British Mail*, 2 August 1880. BAAS Collection, Misc. 486.
109 "British Industries. Messrs. Joseph Gillott & Sons," *Tinsley's Magazine*, October 1889, no. 5, pp. 576–7.
110 "Messrs Gillott & Sons' pen manufactory," BAAS Collection, Misc. 486.
111 "The Birmingham penworkers," *Birmingham and District Trades Journal*, 12 November 1898.
112 Letter of Mr A. Keegan to Mrs Muirhead, 6 May 1900, BAAS Collection, Misc. 486, 2/5.
113 Ibid.
114 Ibid.
115 Discussion with Mrs M. T. Muirhead, Hon. Sec. of Industrial Subcommittee, Birmingham Branch of Women Workers, BAAS Collection, Misc. 486, 2/5.
116 Ibid.
117 Interview with Martin Smith of Perry's Pen's, BAAS Collection, Misc. 486, 2/6.
118 Interview with A. Keegan, Secretary of Penworkers' Union, BAAS Collection, Misc. 486, 2/6.
119 Ibid.
120 "Birmingham Trades Council," *Birmingham and District Trades Journal*, 13 May 1899.
121 Letter dated 15 June 1902 to Mrs Muirhead from Bertita Bayne, Hon. Sec., BAAS Collection, Misc. 486, 2/5; Interview with A. Keegan, Secretary of Penworkers' Union, BAAS Collection, Misc. 486, 2/6.
122 E. A. Pratt, *Trade Unionism and British Industry*, London, John Murray, 1904, p. 115.
123 Ibid.
124 Ibid., pp. 115–19.
125 Notes collected by B. L. Hutchins, 1902, BAAS Collection, Misc. 486, 2/6.
126 States Chinn: "Compared with upper-working-class and middle-class women,

those of the urban poor were more self-reliant and less dependent on men, whether husbands or fathers. . . . It can be argued that in this field the affluent followed in the furrow ploughed by the lower working class." Chinn, *They Worked*, pp. 84–5.

127 *Report of the Medical Officer of Health on the Unhealthy Conditions in the Floodgate Street Area and the Municipal Wards of St. Mary, St. Stephen, and St. Bartholomew*, October 1904, p. 16.

128 City of Birmingham, *Report on Industrial Employment*, p. 6.

129 *Report of the Medical Officer of Health on the Health of the City of Birmingham for the Year 1909*, pp. 21–2.

130 Chinn, *They Worked*, p. 107.

131 Ibid., p. 100.

132 City of Birmingham, *Report on Industrial Employment*, p. 19.

133 Chinn, *They Worked*, p. 100.

134 Ibid., p. 114.

135 Ibid., pp. 116–20.

136 Interview with W. J. Davis, BAAS Collection, Misc. 486, 2/6.

137 Ibid.

138 Letter from W. J. Davis to B. L. Hutchins, 5 March 1902, BAAS Collection, Misc. 486, 2/6.

139 Ibid.

140 Cited in William A. Dalley, *The Life Story of W. J. Davis*, Birmingham, Birmingham Printers Ltd, 1914, p. 191.

141 Ibid., p. 196; National Society of Amalgamated Brassworkers and Metal Mechanics, *Twenty-eighth Annual Report and Financial Statement, Year Ending January 27th, 1900*, p. 19.

142 Dalley, *Life Story of W. J. Davis*, p. 192; Amalgamated Brassworkers, *Twenty-eighth Annual Report*, p. 12.

143 Amalgamated Brassworkers, *Twenty-eighth Annual Report*, p. 31.

144 Dalley, *Life Story of W. J. Davis*, p. 202.

145 Ibid., pp. 214–55.

146 National Society of Amalgamated Brassworkers and Metal Mechanics, *Thirty-third Annual Report and Financial Statement. Year Ending January 21st, 1905*, p. 3.

147 Ibid.

148 Ibid.

149 "Some fines and deductions from women's wages in the metal trades of Birmingham and district," *Women's Industrial News*, July 1909, no. 47, p. 17.

150 Ibid., pp. 19–20.

151 Ibid., p. 20.

152 "In gyves of brass. The dangerous and laborious life of Birmingham's women metal workers," *Sunday Chronicle*, 20 September 1908.

153 Ibid.

154 Ibid.

155 Ibid.

156 Interview with Davis, BAAS Collection, Misc. 486, 2/6.

157 Trades Union Congress, *Report of Proceedings at the Forty-first Annual Trades Union Congress*, 1908, p. 190.

158 Ibid.

159 Dalley, *Life Story of W. J. Davis*, p. 105.

160 Trades Union Congress, *Report of Proceedings*, 1908, p. 189.

161 Ibid.

162 Ibid.

163 Ibid.

164 Ibid.

165 Ibid.

166 Ibid.; National Society of Amalgamated Brassworkers & Metal Mechanics, "Women polishers, turners & screwers." Flyer. 18 September 1908. Gertrude Tuckwell Collection 504a/22.

167 Trades Union Congress, *Report of Proceedings*, p. 190.

168 "In gyves of brass," *Sunday Chronicle*, 20 September 1908.

169 "Women brassworkers: Miss Macarthur replies to our special commissioner," *Sunday Chronicle*, 27 September 1908.

170 "To everybody." Flyer. n.d. Gertrude Tuckwell Collection 504a/29.

171 Trades Union Congress, *Report of Proceedings at the Forty-second Annual Trades Union Congress*, 1909, p. 167.

172 Ibid.

173 Ibid.; "The dangerous and labouring life," *Sunday Chronicle*, 20 September 1908.

174 Trades Union Congress, *Report of Proceedings*, 1909, pp. 167–8.

175 Ibid., p. 168.

176 Ibid., pp. 167–9.

177 National Society of Amalgamated Brassworkers & Metal Mechanics, "Brass & metalworkers crusade against sweating." London, Bishopsgate Institute Reference Library Collection, ref. no. 331.8.

178 Ibid.

179 Ibid.

180 National Society of Amalgamated Brassworkers & Metal Mechanics, "Brass & metalworkers crusade against sweating. Report of meeting of brass and metal workers, 19 October 1909," Bishopsgate Collection.

181 Ibid.

182 Ibid., p. 2.

183 National Society of Amalgamated Brassworkers & Metal Mechanics, "Meeting of brass and metalworkers crusade against sweating, 26 October 1909," p. 1, Bishopsgate Collection.

184 National Society of Amalgamated Brassworkers & Metal Mechanics, "Meeting of the brass and metalworkers crusade against sweating, 2 November 1909," p. 2, Bishopsgate Collection.

185 National Society of Amalgamated Brassworkers & Metal Mechanics, "Meeting of the brass & metalworkers crusade against sweating, 4 November 1909," p. 2, Bishopsgate Collection.

186 Amalgamated Brassworkers, "Meeting of brass and metalworkers crusade, 26 October 1909," p. 4. Sheila Blackburn has described the manner in which sweated labor became associated only over time with women and homework. "'No necessary connection with homework': gender and sweated labour, 1840–1909," *Social History*, October 1997, vol. 22, pp. 269–85.

187 National Society of Amalgamated Brassworkers & Metal Mechanics, "Meeting of brass & metalworkers crusade against sweating, 9 November 1909," p. 3, Bishopsgate Collection.

188 Amalgamated Brassworkers, "Meeting of crusade," 26 October 1909, p. 4.

189 Amalgamated Brassworkers, "Meeting of crusade," 9 November 1909, p. 3.

190 Amalgamated Brassworkers, "Meeting of crusade," 19 October 1909, p. 2.

191 Ibid., p. 3.

192 Ibid., p. 2.

193 Amalgamated Brassworkers, "Meeting of crusade," 2 November 1909, p. 2.

194 Amalgamated Brassworkers, "Meeting of crusade," 4 November 1909, p. 3.

195 Ibid.

196 Ibid.

197 Ibid.
198 Amalgamated Brassworkers, "Meeting of crusade," 4 November 1909, p. 1.
199 Ibid., p. 2.
200 Ibid., p. 4.
201 Amalgamated Brassworkers, "Meeting of brass & metalworkers crusade," 28 October 1909, p. 3.
202 Amalgamated Brassworkers, "Meeting of crusade," 2 November 1909, p. 3.
203 Amalgamated Brassworkers, "Meeting of brass & metalworkers crusade," 9 November 1909, p. 3
204 Ibid., p. 2.
205 Dalley, *Life story of W. J. Davis*, pp. 265–70.
206 "Birmingham brass trade," *Birmingham Daily Post*, 21 October 1910. Gertrude Tuckwell Collection 504a/8.
207 "Birmingham brass trade under the Trade Board Act of 1909," *The Metal Worker*, March 1910, p. 66.
208 "Brass trade," *Daily Post*, 21 October 1910.
209 "Mr. Davis's annual review," *Birmingham Daily Post*, 24 May 1911. Gertrude Tuckwell Collection 504a/11.
210 "The women slaves of Birmingham," *The Watch Dog*, 13 January 1912. Gertrude Tuckwell Collection 504a/12.
211 Ibid.
212 "Midland work-slaves. The lot of Birmingham women workers contrasted with that of Lancashire operatives," *Sunday Chronicle*, 26 November 1911, Webb Trade Union Collection, section B, vol. liii.
213 Ibid.; "Women slaves," *Watch Dog*, 13 January 1912.
214 Ibid.
215 "Midland work-slaves," *Sunday Chronicle*, 26 November 1911.
216 Ibid.
217 National Society of Brassworkers and Metal Mechanics, *Fortieth Annual Report and Financial Statement Year Ending January 13th, 1912*, p. 4.
218 "Women polishers. Metal workers' drastic proposals," *Birmingham Daily Post*, 10 February 1912. Gertrude Tuckwell Collection, 504a/13.
219 R. H. Tawney, *The Establishment of Minimum Rates in the Chain-making Industry under the Trade Boards Act of 1909*, London, G. Bell & Sons Ltd., 1914, pp. 2–4.
220 Arthur Marsh and Victoria Ryan, *Historical Directory of Trade Unions*, vol. 2. Aldershot, 1984.
221 "The 'white slaves' of the Black Country," *County Express*, 6 April 1907.
222 Ibid., p. 61.
223 George Shann, "Chain making: Cradley Heath and District," in Richard Mudie-Smith (ed.) *Handbook of the 'Daily News' Sweated Industries' Exhibition*, London, Burt & Sons, 1906, p. 59.
224 "Operations under the Trade Boards Act," *The Women's Industrial News*, April 1911, no. 54, p. 57.
225 "Midland Counties Trades' Federation," *County Express*, 6 April 1907.
226 "Miss Macarthur at Cradley Heath," *County Express*, 22 June 1907; "Record of registered and unregistered chainmakers' strikers' and anchorsmiths' trade unions," Trades Union Congress Library. According to R. H. Tawney, "The most important event in the history of the chain trade between 1890 and 1909 was the formation in 1905 of a society of women chainmakers under the title of 'the Cradley Heath and District Hammered and Country Chainmakers' Association." Tawney, *Establishment of Minimum Rates*, p. 25.
227 Ibid.
228 Sheila Blackburn, "Employers and social policy: Black Country chain-masters,

the minimum wage campaign and the Cradley Heath strike of 1910," *Midland History*, vol. 12, 1987, p. 91.
229 Ibid.
230 "Chain trade crisis," *County Express*, 1 May 1909; "Crisis averted," *County Express*, 8 May 1909.
231 "Mr. Churchill's promise," *County Express*, 19 June 1909.
232 Blackburn, "Employers and social policy," pp. 86–91; "Trade Boards," *The Women's Industrial News*, April 1910, no. 50, p. 9.
233 Blackburn, "Employers and social policy," pp. 91–2; letter from Thomas Sitch in "The chain trade and the Trades Boards Act, 1909," *The Metal Worker*, April 1910.
234 Blackburn, "Employers and social policy," p. 92.
235 "Alleged chain trade sweating," *Catholic Herald*, 30 July 1910. Gertrude Tuckwell Collection 200b/35. Cited in Blackburn, "Employers and social policy," p. 93.
236 "Alleged chain trade sweating," *Catholic Herald*, 30 July 1910. Gertrude Tuckwell Collection 200b/35.
237 Women's Trade Union League, *Annual Report*, 1910. Cited in Trades Union Congress, *Parliamentary Committee Report*, 19 September 1910. Gertrude Tuckwell Collection 405a/116; "Operations under the Trade Boards Act," *Women's Industrial News*, p. 57.
238 Ibid.; "Operations under the Trade Boards Act," *Women's Industrial News*, p. 58; "Cradley Heath chainmakers," *Northampton Echo*, 23 August 1910; "Chainmakers at bay," *Daily News*, 23 August 1910. Gertrude Tuckwell Collection 405a.
239 "Chainmakers at bay," *Daily News*.
240 "Women on strike," *Wolverhampton Chronicle*, 24 August 1910; "Chainmaking," *Express and Star*, 24 August 1910; Trades Union Congress, *Parliamentary Committee Report*. Gertrude Tuckwell Collection 405a.
241 "Women who work harder than men," *Daily Express*, 27 August 1910. Gertrude Tuckwell Collection 405a.
242 "Cradley Heath dispute," *Birmingham Dispatch*, 1 September 1910. Gertrude Tuckwell Collection 405b.
243 Ibid.
244 Ibid.
245 "The women chain-makers' strike," *Votes for Women*, 2 September 1910. Gertrude Tuckwell Collection 405b.
246 Ibid.
247 "Bound to the forge," *Daily Express*, 6 September 1910. Gertrude Tuckwell Collection 405b.
248 Christine Coates, "The Cradley Heath chainmakers' strike 1910," MA Dissertation, Birkbeck College, London, 1987, p. 37.
249 "The lot of the woman worker," *Weekly Dispatch*, 4 September 1910. Gertrude Tuckwell Collection 405c.
250 Coates, "Cradley Heath chainmakers' strike," p. 36.
251 "Operations under the Trade Boards Act," *Women's Industrial News*, pp. 58–9.
252 "Midland Counties' Trades Federation," *Advertiser*, 13 April 1912.
253 "Women workers' conference at Cradley Heath," *Advertiser*, 20 July 1912.
254 John Corbett, *The Birmingham Trades Council, 1866–1966*, Foreword by George Woodcock, London, Lawrence & Wishart, 1966, p. 95.
255 "Sweated women," *Daily Citizen*, 5 November 1912; "Broken women," *Daily Citizen*, 7 November 1912.
256 Ibid.; "Black Country horrors," *Daily Citizen*, 8 November 1912; "Broken women," *Daily Citizen*, 18 November 1912; "The broken women," *Daily Citizen*, 19 November 1912.

257 "Broken women," *Daily Citizen*, 7 November 1912.
258 Ibid.
259 "Sweated women," *Daily Citizen*, 5 November 1912.
260 Ibid.
261 "Victory for the broken women," *Daily Citizen*, 20 November 1912.
262 Ibid.
263 Ibid.
264 George Barnsby, *Birmingham Working People: A History of the Labour Movement in Birmingham 1650–1914*, Wolverhampton, Integrated Publishing Services, 1989, pp. 481–94.
265 Ibid., p. 484; Corbett, *Birmingham Trades Council*, p. 97
266 Barnsby, *Birmingham Working People*, p. 484.
267 *Amalgamated Engineers' Monthly Journal*, January 1912, p. 30.
268 Birmingham Trades Council, *Forty-sixth Annual Report and Balance Sheet for the Year ended December, 1911*, p. 7.
269 Barnsby, *Birmingham Working People*, p. 484.
270 Ibid., p. 491; Birmingham Trades Council, *Forty-seventh Annual Report of the Birmingham Trades and Labour Council for the Year ended December, 1912*, p. 9.
271 "Settlement at Aston," *Birmingham Daily Post*, 30 April 1913; "Demands of Black Country rivet makers," *Birmingham Daily Post*, 2 May 1913; "Settlement of Wolverhampton strike," *Birmingham Daily Post*, 19 May 1913.
272 "Black Country strike," *Daily Citizen*, 30 May 1913; "Black Country strike over," *Daily Citizen*, 8 July 1913; see *Daily Citizen* for entire period.
273 "The strike movement," *Daily Citizen*, 9 July 1913.
274 "Bound to the forge," *Daily Express*, 6 September 1910. Gertrude Tuckwell Collection 405b; also cited in Coates, "Cradley Heath chainmakers' strike," p. 22.
275 Coates, "Cradley Heath chainmakers' strike," p. 42.
276 Ibid.
277 Tawney, *Minimum Rates in the Chain-making Industry*, pp. 10–11.

Conclusion

1 *Votes for Women*, 2 September 1910. Gertrude Tuckwell Collection, 405b.
2 See Anna Clark, *The Struggle for the Breeches: Gender and the Making of the British Working Class*, Berkeley, University of California Press, 1995; Sonya Rose, *Limited Livelihoods: Gender and Class in Nineteenth-century England*, Berkeley, University of California Press, 1992; Jane Long, *Conversations in Cold Rooms: Women, Work and Poverty in Nineteenth-century Northumberland*, Rochester, NY, Boydell Press, 1999.
3 Susan Pedersen, *Family, Dependence, and the Origins of the Welfare State: Britain and France, 1914–1945*, Cambridge, Cambridge University Press, 1993, pp. 49–58.
4 Clark, *Struggle for the Breeches*, p. 4.
5 Long, *Conversations*, p. 220.
6 Michael Savage, "Space, networks and class formation," in Neville Kirk (ed.) *Social Class and Marxism: Defences and Challenges*, Aldershot, Scolar Press, 1996, pp. 58–86.

Bibliography

Newspapers

Advertiser for Brierley Hill, Stourbridge, Dudley, and Kidderminster, 1883, 1889, 1893, 1895–7, 1912
Ashton Chronicle, 1849
Birmingham Daily Gazette, 1883 and 1890
Birmingham Daily Post, 1891 and 1912–13
Blackburn Standard, 1849
Blackburn Times, 1878
Burnley Advertiser, 1859
County Express, 1907–9
Daily Citizen, 1912–13
Labour Tribune, 1886–91
Manchester and Salford Advertiser, 1842–5
Manchester Guardian, 1845 and 1848–9
Morning Post, 1849
Northern Star, 1838–9
Preston Guardian, 1861
Preston Pilot and County Advertiser, 1853–4
Saddlers', Harness Makers' and Carriage Builders' Gazette, 1871
Sunday Chronicle, 1886, 1891, 1908–9
Ten Hours' Advocate, 1846–7
Walsall Free Press, 1872

Monthly journals

Birmingham and District Trades' Journal, 1896–9
Bugle Annual, 1974
Englishwoman's Review, 1874–87
Metal Worker, 1908–10
Tinsley's Magazine, 1889
Women's Industrial News, 1909–11
Women's Trade Union Review, 1892–7
Women's Union Journal, 1883–9

Special collections

British Association for the Advancement of Science, Misc. 486, London, Library of Political and Economic Science

Gertrude Tuckwell Collection, 405a–d

National Society of Amalgamated Brassworkers and Metal Mechanics, Brass and Metalworkers Crusade against Sweating, London, Bishopsgate Institute Reference Library Collection, ref. no. 3318

Webb Trade Union Collection, section A, vols. 19–21, 30, 37, 47; section B, vols. 30, 53, 112; section C, vol. 52, London, Library of Political and Economic Science

White Slavery Collection, Goldsmiths' Collection, London, University of London Library

Reports

Amalgamated Society of Brassworkers, *Annual Reports*, 1874–1912

Birmingham Trades Council, *Annual Reports*, 1911–12

Trades Union Congress, "Parliamentary Reports"

Trades Union Congress Reports, 1874–1912

Women's Protective and Provident League, *Annual Reports*, 1883–90

Women's Trade Union League, *Annual Reports*, 1891–1913

British Parliamentary Papers

Report of the Select Committee on the State of the Children Employed in the Manufactories of the United Kingdom, 1816, iii.

Report from the Select Committee on the Bill to Regulate the Labour of Children in the Mills and Factories of the United Kingdom with Minutes of Evidence, Appendix and Index, 1831–2, xv.

First Report of the Factories Inquiry Commission with Minutes of Evidence, 1833, xx.

First Report from the Select Committee on the Act for the Regulation of Mills and Factories, 1840, x.

Reports of Leonard Horner and Robert Baker, Factory Inspectors, 1841–75.

1841 Census of Great Britain: Age Abstract with Appendices, 1843, xxii.

1841 Census of Great Britain: Occupation Abstract with Preface, 1844, xxvii.

1851 Census of Great Britain: Ages, Civil Condition, Occupations, and Birthplaces, 1852–3, part 2, xxv.

1871 Census of England and Wales: Ages, Civil Condition, Occupations, and Birthplaces, part 1, 1873, lxxi.

Returns of the Number of Cotton, Woollen, Worsted, Flax and Silk Factories Subject to the Factories Acts, 1850, xlii.

Returns of the Number of Cotton, Woollen, Worsted, Flax and Silk Factories, 1857, xiv.

Returns of the Number of Cotton, Woollen, Worsted, Flax, Hemp, Jute, Hosiery, and Silk Factories Subject to the Factories Act, 1862, lv.

Report of the Commissioners Appointed to Inquire into the Working of the Factory and Workshops Acts, with Minutes of Evidence, 1876, xxx.

Report as to the Condition of Nail Makers and Small Chain Makers in South Staffordshire and East Worcestershire, by the Labour Correspondent of the Board of Trade, 1888, xci.

Third Committee from the House of Lords on the Sweating System, 1889, xiii.

Second Report of the Royal Commission on Labour, with Minutes of Evidence, 1893–4, xxxii.

Report from the Departmental Committee on the Conditions of Labour in the Manufacture of Brass and of Kindred Amalgams, 1896, xxv.

Books and articles

Abram, William Alexander, *Blackburn Characters of Past Generation*, Blackburn, 1894.

Allen, G. C., *The Industrial Development of Birmingham and the Black Country 1860–1927*, London, George Allen and Unwin, 1929.

Anderson, Michael, *Family Structure in Nineteenth Century Lancashire*, Cambridge, Cambridge University Press, 1971.

Baines, Edward, Jr., *History of the Cotton Manufacture in Great Britain,* London, H. Fisher, R. Fisher, and P. Jackson, 1835.

Baker, J. A. C., "Richard Juggins and Black Country unionism in the late nineteenth century," *Transactions of the Lichfield and South Staffordshire Archaeological and Historical Society*, 1968, vol. 9, pp. 67–72.

Bakhtin, M. M., "Discourse in the novel," in Michael Holquist (ed.) and Caryl Emerson and Michael Holquist (trans.) *The Dialogic Imagination: Four Essays by M. M. Bakhtin*, Austin and London, University of Texas Press, 1981, pp. 259–341.

Bamford, Samuel, *Passages in the Life of a Radical*, 2 vols., London, Simpkin, Marshall, and Co., 1844.

Barnsby, George, *The Working Class Movement in the Black Country, 1750 to 1867*, Wolverhampton, Integrated Publishing Services, 1977.

—— *Birmingham Working People*, Wolverhampton, Integrated Publishing Services, 1989.

Baron, Ava, "Gender and labor history: learning from the past, looking to the future," in Ava Baron (ed.) *Work Engendered: Toward a New History of American Labor*, Ithaca and London, Cornell University Press, 1991, pp. 1–46.

Behagg, Clive, *Politics and Production in the Early Nineteenth Century*, London and New York, Routledge, 1990.

Benenson, Harold, "The 'family wage' and working women's consciousness in Britain, 1880–1914," *Politics and Society*, 1991, vol. 19, pp. 71–108.

Bennett, Judith M., "Feminism and history," *Gender and History*, Autumn 1989, vol. 1, pp. 251–72.

Berg, Maxine, *The Age of Manufactures: Industry, Innovation and Work in Britain 1700–1820*, Totowa, NJ, Barnes and Noble, 1985.

Berg, Maxine, and Pat Hudson, "Rehabilitating the Industrial Revolution," *Economic History Review*, February 1992, vol. 45, pp. 24–50.

Bigg, Ada Heather, "Female labour in the nail trade," *Fortnightly Review*, 1886, vol. 45, pp. 24–50, 829–38.

Blackburn, Sheila, "Employers and social policy: Black Country chain-masters, the minimum wage campaign and the Cradley Heath strike of 1910," *Midland History*, 1987, vol. 12, pp. 85–102.

—— "Working-class attitudes to social reform: Black Country chainmakers and anti-sweating legislation, 1880–1930," *International Review of Social History*, 1988, vol. 33, pp. 42–69.

—— "'No necessary connection with homework': gender and sweated labour, 1840–1909," *Social History*, October 1997, vol. 22, pp. 269–85.

Bourke, Joanna, "Housewifery in working-class England 1860–1914," *Past and Present*, no. 143, May 1994, pp. 167–97.

Bradley, Harriet, "Frames of reference: skill, gender and new technology in the hosiery industry," in Gertjan de Groot and Marlou Schrover (eds.) *Women Workers and Technological Change in Europe in the Nineteenth and Twentieth Centuries*, London, Taylor and Francis, 1995, pp. 17–34.

Buhle, Mari Jo, "Gender and labor history," in J. Carroll Moody and Alice Kessler-Harris (eds.) *Perspectives on American Labor History: The Problems of Synthesis*, DeKalb, Northern Illinois University Press, 1989, pp. 55–79.

Bythell, Duncan, *The Handloom Weavers: A Study in the English Cotton Industry during the Industrial Revolution*, Cambridge, Cambridge University Press, 1969.

Cadbury, Edward, M. Cecile Matheson and George Shann, *Women's Work and Wages*, London, T. Fisher Unwin, 1906.

Canning, Kathleen, "Feminist history after the linguistic turn: historicizing discourse and experience," in Barbara Laslett, Ruth-Ellen B. Joeres, Mary Jo Maynes, Evelyn Brooks Higginbotham, and Jeanne Barker-Nunn (eds.) *History and Theory: Feminist Research, Debates, Contestations*, Chicago, University of Chicago Press, 1997, pp. 416–52.

Chadwick, David, "On the rate of wages in Manchester and Salford, and the manufacturing districts of Lancashire, 1839–1859, *Journal of the Royal Statistical Society*, series A, March 1860.

Chinn, Carl, *They Worked All Their Lives: Women of the Urban Poor in England, 1880–1939*, Manchester, Manchester University Press, 1988.

Clark, Anna, "The rhetoric of Chartist domesticity: gender, language, and class in the 1830s and 1840s," *Journal of British Studies*, 1992, vol. 31, pp. 62–88.

—— *The Struggle for the Breeches: Gender and the Making of the British Working Class*, Berkeley, University of California Press, 1995.

—— "Manhood, womanhood, and the politics of class in Britain, 1790–1845," in Laura Frader and Sonya Rose (eds.) *Gender and Class in Modern Europe*, Ithaca and London, Cornell University Press, 1996, pp. 263–79.

—— "The New Poor Law and the breadwinner wage: contrasting assumptions," *Journal of Social History*, December 2000.

Cole, G. D. H., *Attempts at General Union: A Study in British Trade Union History, 1818–1834*, London, Macmillan and Co., 1953.

Collier, Frances, "An early factory community," *Economic History*, 1930, vol. 2, Supplement, pp. 117–24.

—— *The Family Economy of the Working Classes in the Cotton Industry, 1784–1833*, R. S. Fitton (ed.) Manchester, The Chetham Society, 1965.

Connell, R. W., *Gender and Power: Society, the Person and Sexual Politics*, Stanford, Calif., Stanford University Press, 1987.

Copies of the True Bills Found Against the Rev. J. R. Stephens, at Liverpool and Chester, with Comments Thereon, published with Joseph Rayner Stephens, *The Political Pulpit*, no place or date.

Corbett, John, *The Birmingham Trades Council, 1866–1966*, with Foreword by George Woodcock, London, Lawrence and Wishart, 1966.

Cott, Nancy, "Feminist theory and feminist movements: the past before us," in

Juliet Mitchell and Ann Oakley (eds.) *What is Feminism?* New York, Pantheon Books, 1986, pp. 49–62.

Dalley, William A., *The Life Story of W. J. Davis, J.P.*, Birmingham, Birmingham Printers Limited, 1914.

Davidoff, Leonore and Catherine Hall, *Family Fortunes: Men and Women of the English Middle Class, 1780–1850*, Chicago, University of Chicago Press, 1987.

Davis, W. J., *A Short History of the Brass Trade*, Birmingham, Hudson and Son, 1892.

De Groot, Gertjan and Marlou Schrover (eds.) *Women Workers and Technological Change in Europe in the Nineteenth and Twentieth Centuries*, London, Taylor and Francis, 1995.

Downs, Laura Lee, "If 'woman' is just an empty category, then why am I afraid to walk alone at night? Identity politics meets the postmodern subject," *Comparative Studies in Society and History*, April 1993, vol. 35, pp. 414–37.

Driver, Cecil, *Tory Radical: The Life of Richard Oastler*, New York, Oxford University Press, 1946.

Dutton, H. I. and J. E. King, "The limits of paternalism: the cotton tyrants of North Lancashire, 1836–54," *Social History*, January 1982, vol. 7, pp. 59–74.

Edsall, Nicholas C., *The Anti-Poor Law Movement, 1834–44*, Manchester, Manchester University Press, 1971.

Ellison, Thomas, *The Cotton Trade of Great Britain*, London, E. Wilson, 1886; reprint edn., New York, Augustus M. Kelley, 1968.

Engels, Friedrich, *The Condition of the Working Class in England*, W. O. Henderson and W. H. Chaloner (eds. and trans.) Stanford, Calif., Stanford University Press, 1968.

English, W., *The Textile Industry*, London, Longmans, Green, and Co., 1969.

Epstein, James, "Rethinking the categories of working-class history," *Labour/Le Travail*, 1986, vol. 18, pp. 195–208.

Evans, Clare, "Unemployment and the making of the feminine during the Lancashire cotton famine," in Pat Hudson and W. R. Lee (eds.) *Women's Work and the Family Economy in Historical Perspective*, Manchester, Manchester University Press, 1990, pp. 248–70.

Famie, D. A., *The English Cotton Industry and the World Market, 1815–1896*, Oxford, Oxford University Press, 1970.

Feurer, Rosemary, "The meaning of 'sisterhood': the British women's movement and protective labor legislation, 1870–1900," *Victorian Studies*, Winter 1988, vol. 31, pp. 233–60.

Forrest, Noah, "The chain and tracemakers of cradley heath and its vicinity and their employers; or union and disunion, and their consequences," *Transactions of the National Association for the Promotion of Social Science*, 1859, pp. 654–6.

Frader, Laura, "Bringing political economy back in: gender, culture, race, and class in labor history," *Social Science History*, Spring 1998, vol. 22, pp. 7–18.

Frader, Laura L. and Sonya O. Rose (eds.) *Gender and Class in Modern Europe*, Ithaca and London, Cornell University Press, 1996.

Fraser, Derek (ed.) *The New Poor Law in the Nineteenth Century*, New York, 1976.

Fraser, Nancy, "The uses and abuses of French discourse theories for feminist politics," in Nancy Fraser and Sandra Lee Bartky (eds.) *Revaluing French Feminism: Critical Essays on Difference, Agency, and Culture*, Bloomington, Indiana University Press, 1992, pp. 177–94.

Fraser, Nancy and Linda J. Nicholson, "Social criticism without philosophy: an encounter between feminism and postmodernism," in Linda J. Nicholson (ed.) *Feminism/Postmodernism*, New York and London, Routledge, 1990, pp. 19–38.

Freifeld, Mary, "Technological change and the 'self-acting mule': a study of skill and the sexual division of labour," *Social History*, 1986, vol. 11, pp. 319–43.

Frow, Emund and Ruth, "Women in the early radical and labour movement," *Marxism Today*, April 1968, vol. 12, pp. 105–12.

Gaskell, Peter, *Artisans and Machinery*, London, John W. Parker, 1836.

Gittins, Diana, *Fair Sex: Family Size and Structure in Britain, 1900–39*, New York, St. Martin's Press, 1982.

Glucksmann, Miriam, *Women Assemble: Women Workers and the New Industries in Interwar Britain*, London and New York, Routledge, 1990.

Gordon, Ann D., Mari Jo Buhle, and Nancy Schrom Dye, "The problem of women's history," in Berenice A. Carroll (ed.) *Liberating Women's History: Theoretical and Critical Essays*, Urbana, University of Illinois Press, 1976, pp. 75–92.

Gordon, Eleanor, *Women and the Labour Movement in Scotland, 1850–1914*, Oxford, Clarendon Press, 1991.

Grant, Philip, *The Ten Hours Bill: The History of Factory Legislation*, Manchester, John Heywood, 1866.

Gray, Robert, *The Factory Question and Industrial England 1830–1860*, Cambridge, Cambridge University Press, 1996.

Greg, William Rathbone, *An Enquiry into the State of the Manufacturing Population and the Causes and Cures of the Evils Therein Existing*, London, 1831.

Hall, Catherine, "The tale of Samuel and Jemima: gender and working-class culture in nineteenth-century England," in Harvey J. Kaye and Keith McClelland (eds.) *E. P. Thompson: Critical Perspectives*, Philadelphia, Temple University Press, 1990, pp. 78–102.

Hammond, J. L. and Barbara, *The Town Labourer, 1760–1832*, London, Longmans, Green, and Co., 1920.

Hartmann, Heidi I. and Ann R. Markusen, "Contemporary Marxist theory and practice: a feminist critique," *Review of Radical Political Economics*, Summer 1980, vol. 12, pp. 87–94.

Hobsbawm, E. J., "The British standard of living, 1790–1850," in *Labouring Men: Studies in the History of Labour*, E. J. Hobsbawm (ed.) New York, Basic Books, 1964, pp. 64–104.

Holyoake, George Jacob, *Life of Joseph Rayner Stephens, Preacher and Political Orator*, with an introductory chapter by John Stephens, Storr, London, 1881.

Honeyman, Katrina and Jordan Goodman, "Women's work, gender conflict, and labour markets in Europe, 1500–1900," *Economic History Review*, 1991, vol. 44, pp. 608–28.

Hopkins, Eric, "Working conditions in Victorian Stourbridge," *International Review of Social History*, 1974, vol. 19, pp. 401–25.

Horrell, Sara and Jane Humphries, "Women's labour force participation and the transition to the male-breadwinner family, 1790–1865," *Economic History Review*, February 1995, vol. 48, pp. 89–117.

Huberman, Michael, "The economic origins of paternalism: Lancashire cotton spinning in the first half of the nineteenth century," *Social History*, May 1987, vol. 12, pp. 177–92.

Hudson, Pat and W. R. Lee, "Women's work and the family economy in historical perspective," in Pat Hudson and W. R. Lee (eds.) *Women's Work and the Family Economy in Historical Perspective,* Manchester, Manchester University Press, 1990, pp. 2–47.

Humphries, Jane, "Class struggle and the persistence of the working-class family," *Cambridge Journal of Economics,* 1977, vol. 1, pp. 241–58.

—— "'. . . The most free from objection . . .' the sexual division of labor and women's work in nineteenth-century England," *Journal of Economic History,* December 1987, vol. 47, pp. 929–49.

Hutchins, B. L. and B. Harrison, *A History of Factory Legislation,* 2nd edn., rev., London, P. S. King and Son, 1911.

Jenkins, Mick, *The General Strike of 1842,* Introduction by John Foster, London, Lawrence and Wishart, 1980.

John, Angela, *By the Sweat of their Brow: Women Workers at Victorian Coal Mines,* London, Routledge & Kegan Paul, 1984.

Jones, Gareth Stedman, "Rethinking Chartism," in his *Languages of Class: Studies in English Working Class History, 1832–1982,* Cambridge, Cambridge University Press, 1983, pp. 90–178.

Joyce, Patrick, *Work, Society, and Politics: The Culture of the Factory in Later Victorian England,* New Brunswick, Rutgers University Press, 1980.

—— *Visions of the People: Industrial England and the Question of Class, 1848–1914,* Cambridge, Cambridge University Press, 1991.

Kay, James Phillips, *The Moral and Physical Condition of the Working Classes Employed in the Cotton Manufacture in Manchester,* London, James Ridgeway, 1832.

Kelly, Joan, *Women, History and Theory: The Essays of Joan Kelly,* Chicago, University of Chicago Press, 1984.

Kessler-Harris, Alice, "A new agenda for American labor history: a gendered analysis and the question of class," in J. Carroll Moody and Alice Kessler-Harris (eds.) *Perspectives on American Labor History: The Problems of Synthesis,* DeKalb, Northern Illinois University Press, 1989, pp. 217–34.

Kings, Bill and Margaret Cooper, *Glory Gone: The Story of Nailing in Bromsgrove,* Bromsgrove, Halfshire Books, 1989.

Kirby, R. G. and A. E. Musson, *The Voice of the People: John Doherty, 1798–1854, Trade Unionist Radical, and Factory, Reformer,* Manchester, Manchester University Press, 1975.

Kirk, Neville, *The Growth of Working Class Reformism in Mid-Victorian England,* Urbana and Chicago, University of Illinois Press, 1985.

—— "In defence of class: a critique of recent revisionist writing upon the nineteenth-century English working class," *International Review of Social History,* 1987, no. 32, pp. 2–47.

—— "History, language, ideas and post-modernism: a materialist view," *Social History,* 1994, vol. 19, pp. 221–40.

—— "Class and the 'linguistic turn' in Chartist and post-Chartist historiography," in Neville Kirk (ed.) *Social Class and Marxism: Defences and Challenges,* Aldershot, Scolar Press, 1996, pp. 87–134.

—— *Change, Continuity and Class: Labour in British Society, 1850–1920,* Manchester, Manchester University Press, 1998.

Kuhn, Annette and AnnMarie Wolpe, "Feminism and materialism," in Annette Kuhn and AnnMarie Wolpe (eds.) *Feminism and Materialism: Women and Modes of Production,* London, Routledge and Kegan Paul, 1978, pp. 1–10.

Kydd [Alfred], Samuel, *The History of the Factory Movement*, 2 vols., London, Sirap-kin, Marshall, and Co., 1857, vol. 2.

Laqueur, Thomas Walter, *Religion and Respectability: Sunday Schools and Working Class Culture, 1780–1850*, New Haven, Yale University Press, 1976.

Lee, C. H., *A Cotton Enterprise, 1795–1840: A History of M'Connel and Kennedy, Fine Cotton Spinners*, Manchester, Manchester University Press, 1972.

Lerner, Gerda, "New approaches to the study of women in American history," *Journal of Social History*, Fall 1969, vol. 3, pp. 53–62.

—— "Placing women in history: definitions and challenges," *Feminist Studies*, Fall 1975, vol. 3, pp. 5–14.

Lewis, Jane "The working-class wife and mother and state intervention, 1870–1918," in Jane Lewis (ed.) *Labour and Love: Women's Experience of Home and Family, 1850–1940*, Oxford, Basil Blackwell, 1985, pp. 96–110.

—— "Feminism and welfare," in Juliet Mitchell and Ann Oakley (eds.) *What is Feminism?* New York, Pantheon Books, 1986, pp. 85–100.

Liddington, Jill and Jill Norris, *One Hand Tied Behind Us: The Rise of the Women's Suffrage Movement*, London, Virago, 1978.

Long, Jane, *Conversations in Cold Rooms: Women, Work and Poverty in Nineteenth-century Northumberland*, Rochester, NY, Boydell Press, 1999.

Lown, Judy, *Women and Industrialization: Gender at Work in Nineteenth-century England*, Minneapolis, University of Minnesota Press, 1990.

McClelland, Keith, "Some thoughts on masculinity, and the 'representative artisan' in Britain, 1850–1880," *Gender and History*, Summer 1989, vol. 1, pp. 164–77.

—— "Rational and respectable men: gender, the working class, and citizenship in Britain, 1850–1867," in Laura L. Frader and Sonya O. Rose (eds.) *Gender and Class in Modern Europe*, Ithaca, Cornell University Press, 1996, pp. 280–93.

McDonough, Roisin and Rachel Harrison, "Patriarchy and relations of production," in Annette Kuhn and AnnMarie Wolpe (eds.) *Feminism and Materialism: Women and Modes of Production*, London, Routledge and Kegan Paul, 1978, pp. 11–41.

Marsden, Richard, *Cotton Weaving: Its Development, Principles, and Practice*, London, 1895.

Mitchell, Juliet, *Woman's Estate*, Baltimore, Penguin Books, 1971.

Mitchell, Juliet and Ann Oakley (eds.) *What is Feminism?* New York, Pantheon Books, 1986.

Moody, J. Carroll and Alice Kessler-Harris (eds.) *Perspectives on American Labor History: The Problems of Synthesis*, DeKalb, Northern Illinois University Press, 1989.

Morgan, Carol E., "Industrialization and women's labor," *Nature, Society, and Thought*, 1989, vol. 2, pp. 252–7.

—— "Women, work and consciousness in the mid-nineteenth-century English cotton industry," *Social History*, January 1992, vol. 17, pp. 23–41.

—— "The domestic image and factory culture: the cotton district in mid-nine-teenth-century England," *International Labor and Working-Class History*, Spring 1996, no. 49, pp. 26–46.

—— "Gender constructions and gender relations in cotton and chain-making in England: a contested and varied terrain," *Women's History Review*, 1997, vol. 6, pp. 367–89.

Mudie-Smith, Richard (comp.) *Handbook of the 'Daily News' Sweated Industries' Exhi-bition*, London, Burt and Sons, 1906.

Murgatroyd, Linda, Mike Savage, Dan Shapiro, John Urry, Sylvia Walby, Alan Warde, with Jane Mark-Lawson (eds.) *Localities, Class, and Gender*, London, Pion Press, 1985.

Murray, Janet Horowitz, "Class vs. gender identification in the Englishwoman's Review of the 1880s," *Victorian Periodicals Review*, Winter 1985, vol. 18, pp. 138–42.

Nicholson, Linda J. (ed.) *Feminism/Postmodernism*, New York and London, Routledge, 1990.

Palmer, Bryan D., "Response to Joan Scott," *International Labor and Working-Class History*, Spring 1987, no. 31, pp. 14–23.

Pedersen, Susan, *Family, Dependence, and the Origins of the Welfare State: Britain and France, 1914–1945*, Cambridge, Cambridge University Press, 1993.

Philips, David, *Crime and Authority in Victorian England: The Black Country, 1835–1860*, London, Croom Helm, 1977.

Phillips, Anne and Barbara Taylor, "Sex and skill: notes towards a feminist economics," *Feminist Review*, 1980, vol. 6, pp. 79–88.

Pinchbeck, Ivy, *Women Workers and the Industrial Revolution, 1750–1850*, London, George Routledge and Sons, 1930.

Postgate, Raymond and G. D. H. Cole, *The Common People, 1746–1946*, 2nd edn., London, Methuen and Co., 1946.

Pratt, E. A., *Trade Unionism and British Industry*, London, John Murray, 1904.

Prentice, Archibald, *Historical Sketches and Personal Recollections of Manchester*, 3rd edn, with Introduction by Donald Read, London, Frank Cass and Co., 1970.

Price, Richard, "Conflict and co-operation: a reply to Patrick Joyce," *Social History*, May 1984, vol. 9, pp. 217–24.

Purvis, June, *Hard Lessons: The Lives and Education of Working-class Women in Nineteenth-century England*, Minneapolis, University of Minnesota Press, 1989.

Radcliffe, William, *Origin of the New System of Manufacture*, Stockport, James Lomax, 1828.

Ramelson, Marian, *The Petticoat Rebellion: A Century of Struggle for Women's Rights*, London, Lawrence and Wishart, 1967.

Razzell, P. E., and R. W. Wainwright, (eds.) *The Victorian Working Class: Selections from Letters to the Morning Chronicle*, London, Frank Cass, 1973.

Reach, Angus Bethune, *Manchester and the Textile Districts in 1849*, C. Aspin (ed.) Helmshore, 1972.

Read, Donald, *Peterloo: 'The Massacre' and its Back-ground*, Manchester, Manchester University Press, 1958.

Redford, Arthur, *Labour Migration in England, 1800–1850,* 2nd edn., W. H. Chaloner (ed.) Manchester, Manchester University Press, 1964.

Riley, Denise, *Am I That Name? Feminism and the Category of 'Women' in History*, London, Macmillan, 1988.

Roberts, Elizabeth, *A Woman's Place*, Oxford, Basil Blackwell, 1984.

Roper, Michael and John Tosh, *Manful Assertions: Masculinities in Britain since 1800*, London and New York, Routledge, 1991.

Rose, Sonya O., *Limited Livelihoods: Gender and Class in Nineteenth-century England*, Berkeley, University of California Press, 1992.

—— "Respectable men, disorderly others: the language of gender and the Lancashire weavers' strike of 1878 in Britain," *Gender and History*, Autumn 1993, vol. 5, pp. 382–97.

—— "Gender and labor history: the nineteenth-century legacy," *International Review of Social History*, 1993, no. 38, Supplement, pp. 145–62.

—— "Protective labor legislation in nineteenth-century Britain: gender, class, and the liberal state," in Laura L. Frader and Sonya O. Rose (eds.) *Gender and Class in Modern Europe*, Ithaca and London, Cornell University Press, 1996, pp. 193–210.

—— "Resuscitating class," *Social Science History*, Spring 1998, vol. 22, pp. 19–27.

Rostgard, Marianne, "The creation of a gendered division of labour in the Danish textile industry," in Gertjan de Groot and Marlou Schrover (eds.) *Women Workers and Technological Change in Europe in the Nineteenth and Twentieth Centuries*, London, Taylor and Francis, 1995, pp. 35–51.

Rowbotham, Sheila, "The trouble with 'patriarchy,'" in Raphael Samuel (ed.) *People's History and Socialist Theory*, London, Routledge and Kegan Paul, 1981, pp. 364–9.

Rowlands, Marie B., *Masters and Men in the West Midland Metalware Trades before the Industrial Revolution*, Manchester, Manchester University Press, 1975.

—— "Continuity and change in industrialising society: the case of the West Midlands industries," in Pat Hudson (ed.) *Regions and Industries: A Perspective on the Industrial Revolution in Britain*, Cambridge, Cambridge University Press, 1989, pp. 103–31.

Rule, John, "The property of skill in the period of manufacture," in Patrick Joyce (ed.) *The Historical Meanings of Work*, Cambridge, Cambridge University Press, 1987, pp. 99–118.

Rules of Chain and Trace Makers Anti-Truck and Price Protective Association, 1860.

Rylett, Rev. Harold, "Nails and Chains," *The English Illustrated Magazine*, 1890, pp. 163–75.

Sarsby, Jacqueline, "Gender and technological change in the North Staffordshire pottery industry," in Gertjan de Groot and Marlou Schrover (eds.) *Women Workers and Technological Change in Europe in the Nineteenth and Twentieth Centuries*, London, Taylor and Francis, 1995, pp. 119–34.

Savage, Michael, "Capitalist and patriarchal relations at work: Preston cotton weaving, 1890–1914," in Linda Murgatroyd, Michael Savage, Don Shapiro, John Urry, Sylvia Walby, Alan Warde, with Jane Mark-Lawson (eds.) *Localities, Class, and Gender*, London, Pion Ltd., 1985, pp. 177–94.

—— *The Dynamics of Working-class Politics: The Labour Movement in Preston, 1880–1940*, Cambridge, Cambridge University Press, 1987.

—— "Space, networks and class formation," in Neville Kirk (ed.) *Social Class and Marxism: Defences and Challenges*, Aldershot, Scolar Press, 1996, pp. 58–86.

Scott, Joan W., "On language, gender, and working-class history," *International Labor and Working-Class History*, Spring 1987, no. 31, pp. 1–13.

—— *Gender and the Politics of History*, New York, Columbia University Press, 1988.

—— "The evidence of experience," *Critical Inquiry*, Summer 1991, no. 17, pp. 773–97.

—— "The woman worker," in Genevieve Fraisse and Michelle Perrot (eds.) *A History of Women in the West: Emerging Feminism from Revolution to World War*, vol. 4, Cambridge, Mass., Harvard University Press, 1993, pp. 399–426.

Sewell, Jr., William H., "A theory of structure: duality, agency, and transformation," *American Journal of Sociology*, July 1992, vol. 98, pp. 1–29.

Sharpe, Pamela, *Adapting to Capitalism: Working Women in the English Economy, 1700–1850*, New York, St. Martin's Press, 1996.

Simonton, Deborah, *A History of European Women's Work, 1750 to the Present*, London and New York, Routledge, 1998.

Smelser, Neil J., *Social Change in the Industrial Revolution: An Application of Theory to the British Cotton Industry*, Chicago, University of Chicago Press, 1959.

Smith, Dennis, *Conflict and Compromise: Class Formation in English Society 1830–1914: A Comparative Study of Birmingham and Sheffield*, London, Routledge and Kegan Paul, 1982.

Smith, Ruth L. and Deborah M. Valenze, "Mutuality and marginality: liberal moral theory and working-class women in nineteenth-century England," *Signs*, Winter 1988, vol. 13, pp. 277–98.

Sommestad, Lena, "Creating gender: technology and femininity in the Swedish dairy industry," in Gertjan de Groot and Marlou Schrover (eds.) *Women Workers and Technological Change in Europe in the Nineteenth and Twentieth Centuries*, London, Taylor and Francis, 1995, pp. 151–69.

Stansell, Christine, "A response to Joan Scott," *International Labor and Working-Class History*, Spring 1987, no. 31, pp. 24–9.

Steinberg, Marc W., "Culturally speaking: finding a commons between post-structuralism and the Thompsonian perspective," *Social History*, May 1996, vol. 21, pp. 193–214.

Stephens, Joseph Rayner, *The Political Pulpit*, 1839.

Tawney, R. H., *The Establishment of Minimum Rates in the Chainmaking Industry under the Trade Boards Act of 1909*, London, G. Bell & Sons Ltd., 1914.

Taylor, Barbara, *Eve and the New Jerusalem. Socialism and Feminism in the Nineteenth Century*, London, Virago, 1983.

Taylor, Carole Anne, "Positioning subjects and objects: agency, narration, relationality," *Hypatia*, Winter 1993, vol. 8, pp. 55–80.

Taylor, Eric, "The Midland Counties Trades Federation 1886–1914," *Midland History*, Spring 1972, vol. 1, pp. 26–40.

—— "Richard Juggins," in Joyce M. Bellamy and John Saville (eds.) *Dictionary of Labour Biography*, vol. 1, London, Macmillan, 1972.

Thompson, Dorothy, *The Chartists: Popular Politics in the Industrial Revolution*, New York, Pantheon Books, 1984.

—— "Women, work and politics in nineteenth-century England: the problem of authority," in Jane Rendall (ed.) *Equal or Different: Women's Politics 1800–1914*, Oxford, Basil Blackwell, 1987.

Thompson, E. P., *The Making of the English Working Class*, New York, Random House, 1963.

Tilly, Louise A. and Joan W. Scott, *Women, Work, and Family*, New York, Holt, Rinehart and Winston, 1978.

Timmins, Samuel (ed.) *Birmingham and the Midland Hardware District*, London, Robert Hardwicke, 1866.

The Trial of Feargus O'Connor and 58 Others, London, 1843.

Turner, H. A., *Trade Union Growth, Structure, and Policy: A Comparative Study of the Cotton Unions in England*, Toronto, University of Toronto Press, 1962.

Turner, Ralph, "The cultural significance of the early English industrial town," *Studies in British History*, 1941, vol. 11, pp. 359–75.

Valenze, Deborah, *The First Industrial Woman*, New York and Oxford, Oxford University Press, 1995.

Von Plener, Ernst, *The English Factory Legislation, from 1802 till the Present Time*, Frederick L. Weinmann (trans.) London, Chapman and Hall, 1873.

Walby, Sylvia, *Patriarchy at Work: Patriarchal and Capitalist Relations in Employment*, Minneapolis, University of Minnesota Press, 1986.

Walton, John K., *Lancashire: A Social History, 1558–1939*, Manchester, Manchester University Press, 1987.

Ward, J. T., *The Factory Movement, 1830–1850*, London, Macmillan and Co., 1962.

—— "The factory movement," in J. T. Ward (ed.) *Popular Movements, c. 1830–1850*, London, Macmillan and Co., 1970. pp. 54–77.

Wearmouth, Robert F., *Some Working-class Movements of the Nineteenth Century*, London, The Epworth Press, 1948.

Whittle, P. A., *Blackburn As It Is: A Topographical, Statistical, and Historical Account*, Preston, 1852.

Wiener, Martin J., "The sad story of George Hall: adultery, murder and the politics of mercy in mid-Victorian England," *Social History*, May 1999, vol. 24, pp. 174–95.

Wikander, Ulla, "Periodization and the engendering of technology: the pottery of Gustavsberg, Sweden, 1880–1980," in Gertjan de Groot and Marlou Schrover (eds.) *Women Workers and Technological Change in Europe in the Nineteenth and Twentieth Centuries*, London, Taylor and Francis, 1995, pp. 135–50.

Women at Work: Chainmaking in the Black Country, Gateshead, H. Kelly, 1877.

Wood, George Henry, *The History of Wages in the Cotton Trade during the Past Hundred Years*, London, 1910.

Wright, J. S., "On the employment of women in factories in Birmingham," *Transactions of the National Association for the Promotion of Social Science*, 1857, pp. 538–44.

Yeo, Eileen, "Chartist religious belief and the theology of liberation," in Jim Obelkevich, Lyndal Roper, and Raphael Samuel (eds.). *Disciplines of Faith: Studies in Religion, Politics and Patriarchy*, London, 1987, pp. 410–21.

Zimmeck, Meta, "'The mysteries of the typewriter': technology and gender in the British civil service, 1870–1914," in Gertjan de Groot and Marlou Schrover (eds.) *Women Workers and Technological Change in Europe in the Nineteenth and Twentieth Centuries*, London, Taylor and Francis, 1995, pp. 67–96.

Unpublished theses

Coates, Christine, "The Cradley Heath Chainmakers' Strike 1910," unpublished MA Dissertation, Birkbeck College, 1987.

Woods, David Charles, "Crime and Society in the Black Country 1860–1900," Ph.D. dissertation, University of Aston, 1979.

Index